ASIA BOND MONITOR
SEPTEMBER 2020

ASIAN DEVELOPMENT BANK

Contents

Emerging East Asian Local Currency Bond Markets: A Regional Update

Highlights

Key Trends

- From 15 June to 11 September, 2-year and 10-year bond yields fell in nearly all emerging East Asian markets due to monetary easing by the region's central banks and slowing economic growth.[1]
- Global investment sentiment recovered and financial conditions in emerging East Asia improved, resulting from accommodative monetary stances and relatively better coronavirus disease (COVID-19) containment efforts in the region. During the review period, most emerging East Asian equity markets rallied, most bond yield spreads and credit default swaps narrowed, and most emerging East Asian currencies strengthened against the United States dollar.
- Although the shares of foreign holdings in regional bond markets fell in the first quarter, they stabilized in some markets toward the end of the second quarter of 2020. Other markets saw continued declines in their government bond foreign holdings share.
- Emerging East Asia's local currency bond market expanded to USD17.2 trillion at the end of the second quarter of 2020, rising 5.0% quarter-on-quarter and 15.5% year-on-year, up from 4.2% quarter-on-quarter and 14.0% year-on-year in the prior quarter. The growth was largely driven by the increased financing needs of both the public and private sectors as they sought to mitigate the impact of the COVID-19 pandemic. Government bonds comprised 60.8% of the region's total local currency bonds outstanding at the end of June.

Risks to Financial Stability

- Risks remain tilted to the downside. The overriding risk is a possible worsening of the COVID-19 pandemic and/or it lasting longer than expected.
- Other risks include ongoing trade tensions between the People's Republic of China and the United States, as well as heightened social unrest due to the economic impact of COVID-19.

---

[1] Emerging East Asia comprises the People's Republic of China; Hong Kong, China; Indonesia; the Republic of Korea; Malaysia; the Philippines; Singapore; Thailand; and Viet Nam.

Executive Summary

Global investment sentiment recovered and financial conditions in emerging East Asia improved amid monetary easing and fiscal stimulus that softened the impact of the coronavirus disease (COVID-19) pandemic.

From 15 June to 11 September, 2-year and 10-year local currency (LCY) government bond yields in most emerging East Asian markets declined on the back of accommodative monetary policies and weakening economic growth across the region.[1]

The improved sentiment led to gains in equity markets and narrowed credit spreads in most emerging East Asian economies during the review period. Most regional currencies also strengthened against the United States (US) dollar. However, trends in foreign investor holdings were mixed.

Despite improved sentiment, risk appetite has not fully recovered to pre-pandemic levels. Regional equity indexes were 11.0% lower on 11 September compared with 2 January, on average, while credit spreads were up an average of 16 basis points. Risks remain tilted to the downside. The economic impact of the pandemic may be deeper and more persistent than initially expected. The worsening of the COVID-19 outbreak and/or it lasting longer than expected is the biggest risk factor to the projections. Other risks include heightened social unrest due to the economic impact of the pandemic, as well as ongoing trade tensions between the People's Republic of China (PRC) and the US.

The size of emerging East Asia's local currency bond market reached USD17.2 trillion at the end of June.

LCY bonds in emerging East Asia reached USD17.2 trillion at the end of June. The market expanded by 5.0% quarter-on-quarter (q-o-q) and 15.5% year-on-year (y-o-y) in the second quarter (Q2) of 2020, accelerating from growth of 4.2% q-o-q and 14.0% y-o-y in the first quarter of 2020.

Government bonds stood at USD10.5 trillion and accounted for 60.8% of the region's aggregate bond stock at the end of June, while corporate bonds reached USD6.7 trillion, or 39.2% of the total.

The PRC remained home to the region's largest bond market at the end of June, accounting for 76.6% of emerging East Asia's total bond stock. The PRC was followed by the Republic of Korea with 12.3%. Members of the Association of Southeast Asian Nations (ASEAN) had a collective share of 9.3%.[2]

The size of emerging East Asia's LCY bonds as a share of regional gross domestic product climbed to 91.6% at the end of June from 87.8% at the end of March and 81.5% at the end of June 2019. The uptick was due to the large amount of funding needed to fight the pandemic and mitigate its impact.

LCY bond issuance in the region climbed to USD2.0 trillion in Q2 2020, growing by 21.3% q-o-q and 32.0% y-o-y. Issuance of government bonds grew 29.1% q-o-q and 27.8% y-o-y in Q2 2020, and issuance of corporate bonds rose 11.7% q-o-q and 38.5% y-o-y.

The September issue of the *Asia Bond Monitor* includes four special discussion boxes. One box reviews recent trends and changes in the investor profile in LCY bond markets in Asia. Another box discusses the increased use of digital payment amid the COVID-19 pandemic. Two boxes examine environmental, social, and governance (ESG) investments and their resilience during the COVID-19 era.

Box 1: Asian Bond Markets— Recent Trends and Developments

This box analyzes trends and changes in the investor profile in emerging East Asian bond markets since January 2020. The bond spreads of select emerging East Asian markets widened amid March market turmoil,

---

[1] Emerging East Asia comprises the People's Republic of China; Hong Kong, China; Indonesia; the Republic of Korea; Malaysia; the Philippines; Singapore; Thailand; and Viet Nam.
[2] LCY bond statistics for the Association of Southeast Asian Nations include the markets of Indonesia, Malaysia, the Philippines, Singapore, Thailand, and Viet Nam.

which saw large outflows of portfolio investments and rapid declines in foreign holdings in LCY bond markets. Domestic institutions such as banks increased their holdings of LCY bonds as foreign investors retreated in the first quarter of 2020. To maintain financial stability and mitigate the impact of COVID-19, the region's central banks cut interest rates, which contributed to the improved financial conditions beginning in April. Regional bond markets recovered in Q2 2020. Portfolio investment flows stabilized, bond spreads narrowed, equity markets rose, and currencies appreciated. The box also notes that bond markets in emerging East Asia continue to expand to help meet the funding needs of both the public and private sectors as they try to contain the epidemic and mitigate its impact.

Box 2: Contactless Payment in Post-COVID Asia

This box discusses the increasing use and development of contactless payment technology in Asia as a result of the COVID-19 pandemic. While Asia still lags behind the global average, the use of digital payment is growing rapidly across the region. The box highlights the role of economic and health shocks in triggering the development of digital payment. The region's economies must build the necessary infrastructure to further advance contactless payment technologies, including robust identification systems, reliable internet networks, secure financial services, and strong regulatory frameworks.

Box 3: Environmental, Social, and Governance Investment Growth amid the COVID-19 Crisis

This box examines the growth of ESG investment in Asia since the onset of COVID-19. Data show that cumulative ESG investment in mutual funds expanded between December 2019 and May 2020. Using stock market data from Q1 2020 for the top 100 Japanese-listed companies, the study found that firms with the highest ESG ratings had the smallest average decline and the most stable stock prices. This finding points to the resilience of ESG investment amid COVID-19. The box concludes with a discussion of the remaining challenges in promoting ESG investment in Asia.

Box 4: Is Green the New Gold? ESG Resilience during the COVID-19 Crisis

This box discusses the resilience of ESG funds during the COVID-19 crisis, which have thus far outperformed equity markets and exchange-traded funds globally. The superior performance of ESG funds can be partly attributed to their exposure to sectors that are less impacted by containment and social distancing measures. Amid the crisis, investment has continued to flow to ESG funds, possibly due to (i) investors perceiving that ESG funds are "pandemic-proof"; (ii) investors tending to hold their ESG investments even during a crisis, as they potentially derive utility from the act of investing responsibly; and (iii) ESG funds benefiting from investor preference for a safe-haven investment.

Global and Regional Market Developments

Financial conditions improve in emerging East Asia.

From 15 June to 11 September 2020, financial conditions in emerging East Asia improved and global investor sentiment gradually recovered.[1] The yields on 2-year and 10-year local currency (LCY) government bonds fell in most emerging East Asian economies amid lower interest rates and slowing economic growth. Despite a dim global economic outlook that is being weighed down by the coronavirus disease (COVID-19), a combination of easing global monetary stances, relatively better containment of COVID-19 in the region, and higher returns on emerging market assets buoyed the recovery in emerging East Asia's financial conditions (**Table A**).

In emerging East Asia, the overall decline in 2-year government bond yields was driven by expectations that most central banks in the region would maintain accommodative monetary policy stances to support economic recovery. During the review period, regional central banks collectively maintained easy monetary policies, with a few central banks further lowering policy rates. The Bangko Sentral ng Pilipinas and Bank Indonesia lowered their respective policy rates by 50 basis points (bps) each, while Bank Negara Malaysia reduced its policy rate by 25 bps (**Table B**). Four regional central banks have lowered rates by at least 100 bps since the beginning of 2020. The largest decline in the 2-year bond yield occurred in Indonesia, which shed 134 bps, driven by a cumulative 50-bps policy rate cut during the review period that brought its 7-day reverse repurchase rate to a 4-year low of 4.00%.

Partly driven by weak economic performances that were weighed down by the COVID-19 pandemic, 10-year government bond yields also fell in most emerging East Asian markets. Except for the People's Republic of China (PRC) and Viet Nam, all emerging East Asian markets reported contractions in gross

Table A: Changes in Global Financial Conditions

	2-Year Government Bond (bps)	10-Year Government Bond (bps)	5-Year Credit Default Swap Spread (bps)	Equity Index (%)	FX Rate (%)
Major Advanced Economies					
United States	(6)	(6)	–	8.9	–
United Kingdom	(9)	(2)	(11)	(0.5)	1.5
Japan	4	2	(2)	6.9	1.1
Germany	(3)	(4)	(6)	10.8	4.6
Emerging East Asia					
China, People's Rep. of	31	34	(17)	12.8	3.7
Hong Kong, China	(9)	(4)	–	3.1	0.001
Indonesia	(134)	(28)	(46)	4.2	(5.2)
Korea, Rep. of	3	11	(6)	18.0	2.5
Malaysia	(35)	(29)	(34)	0.4	3.1
Philippines	(35)	(40)	(25)	(3.2)	3.7
Singapore	(11)	(0.1)	–	(4.7)	1.8
Thailand	0.6	16	(9)	(4.6)	(0.8)
Viet Nam	(46)	(16)	(70)	6.8	0.2

( ) = negative, – = not available, bps = basis points, FX = foreign exchange.
Notes:
1. Data reflect changes between 15 June and 11 September 2020.
2. A positive (negative) value for the FX rate indicates the appreciation (depreciation) of the local currency against the United States dollar.
Sources: Bloomberg LP and Institute of International Finance.

[1] Emerging East Asia comprises the People's Republic of China; Hong Kong, China; Indonesia; the Republic of Korea; Malaysia; the Philippines; Singapore; Thailand; and Viet Nam.

Table B: Policy Rate Changes

| Economies | Policy Rate 31-Dec-2019 (%) | Rate Changes (%) | | | | | | | | | Policy Rate 11-Sep-2020 (%) | Year-to-Date Change in Policy Rates (basis points) |
		Jan-2020	Feb-2020	Mar-2020	Apr-2020	May-2020	Jun-2020	Jul-2020	Aug-2020	Sep-2020		
United States	1.75			↓ 1.50							0.25	↓ 150
Euro Area	(0.50)										(0.50)	
Japan	(0.10)										(0.10)	
China, People's Rep. of	3.25		↓ 0.10		↓ 0.20						2.95	↓ 30
Indonesia	5.00		↓ 0.25	↓ 0.25			↓ 0.25	↓ 0.25			4.00	↓ 100
Korea, Rep. of	1.25			↓ 0.50		↓ 0.25					0.50	↓ 75
Malaysia	3.00	↓ 0.25		↓ 0.25		↓ 0.50		↓ 0.25			1.75	↓ 125
Philippines	4.00		↓ 0.25	↓ 0.50	↓ 0.50		↓ 0.50				2.25	↓ 175
Thailand	1.25		↓ 0.25	↓ 0.25		↓ 0.25					0.50	↓ 75
Viet Nam	6.00			↓ 1.00		↓ 0.50					4.50	↓ 150

( ) = negative.
Notes:
1. Data as of 11 September 2020.
2. For the People's Republic of China, data used in the chart are for the 1-year medium-term lending facility rate. While the 1-year benchmark lending rate is the official policy rate of the People's Bank of China, market players use the 1-year medium-term lending facility rate as a guide for the monetary policy direction of the People's Bank of China.
Sources: Various central bank websites.

domestic product (GDP) in the second quarter (Q2) of 2020. The Philippines posted the largest decline in 10-year yields at 40 bps amid a continued increase in confirmed COVID-19 cases and prolonged quarantine restrictions that significantly limited economic activities. The Philippine economy contracted 16.5% year-on-year (y-o-y) in Q2 2020 after a decline of 0.7% y-o-y in the first quarter (Q1), the worst performance since 1981 when such data became available.

The exceptions to the trend of declining yields were the PRC, the Republic of Korea, and Thailand, where the 2-year and 10-year yields picked up between 15 June and 11 September. In the PRC, the rise in yields was largely driven by hints of economic recovery. The PRC was one of two markets in the region that posted economic expansion in Q2 2020, recording GDP growth of 3.2% y-o-y in Q2 2020. Investor sentiment toward CNY-denominated bonds improved on the back of a low-interest-rate regime across the globe. In the case of the Republic of Korea, yields inched up on expectations the government will need to fund more fiscal spending to contain the COVID-19 outbreak and support recovery. On 3 July, the National Assembly approved a third supplementary budget worth KRW35.1 trillion, the largest ever in history in terms of amount. In Thailand, the rise in yields was driven by uncertainties relating to political issues and investors' rising concern that the government would hit the public debt to GDP ceiling of 60%.

In advanced economies, 10-year government bond yields fell in June and July before beginning to rise in August, then either stabilized or moved downward toward September (**Figure A**). In the United States (US), bond yields remained largely stable through July and spiked starting in the first week of August over signs of economic recovery. However, yields showed a slight downward trend on concerns that the economic downturn would be prolonged. The Federal Reserve left its monetary policy stance unchanged at its 9–10 June and 28–29 July meetings. The federal funds target range was kept at between zero and 0.25%, and asset purchases were continued given the ongoing economic impact of COVID-19. US GDP in Q2 2020 fell at an annual rate of 31.7% after a decline of 5.0% in Q1 2020. The Federal Reserve revised its previous GDP growth forecasts, made in December 2019, from 2.0% to –6.5% in 2020, from 1.9% to 5.0% in 2021, and from 1.8% to 3.5% in 2022. Forecasts also show that interest rates are expected to remain at current levels until 2022. Since May, the US labor market has shown some signs of recovery after bottoming out in April. Nonfarm payrolls declined by 20.8 million in April but have since posted gains, with July seeing an additional 1.7 million jobs and August an additional 1.4 million jobs. The unemployment rate peaked at 14.7% in April but has since declined. The unemployment rate slipped to 10.2% in July and to 8.4% in August. Inflation also improved slightly, with the Personal Consumption Expenditures inflation rate rising to 0.9% in June and 1.0% in July from

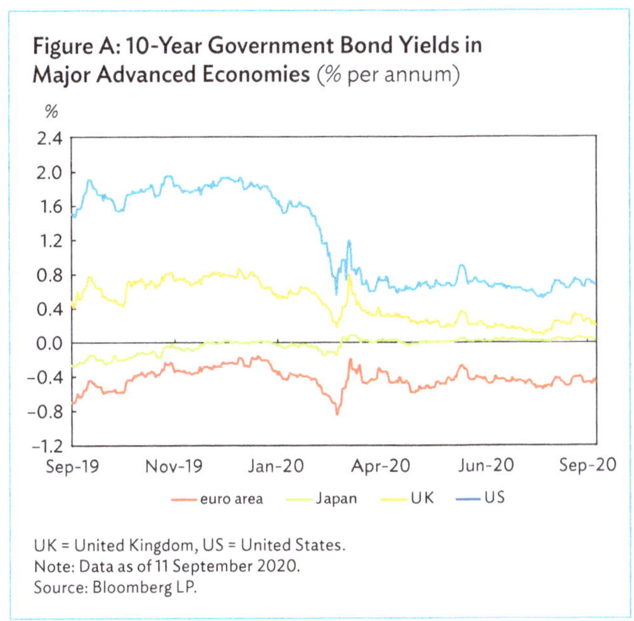

Figure A: 10-Year Government Bond Yields in Major Advanced Economies (% per annum)

UK = United Kingdom, US = United States.
Note: Data as of 11 September 2020.
Source: Bloomberg LP.

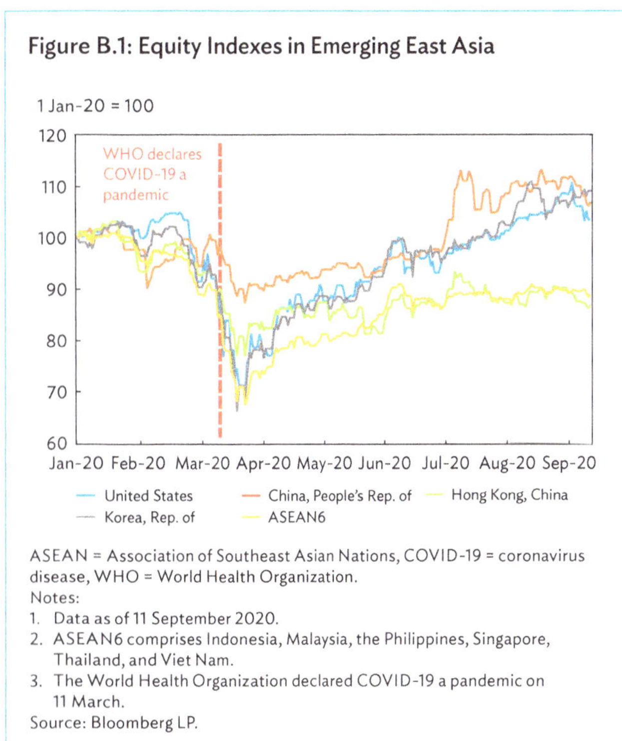

Figure B.1: Equity Indexes in Emerging East Asia

ASEAN = Association of Southeast Asian Nations, COVID-19 = coronavirus disease, WHO = World Health Organization.
Notes:
1. Data as of 11 September 2020.
2. ASEAN6 comprises Indonesia, Malaysia, the Philippines, Singapore, Thailand, and Viet Nam.
3. The World Health Organization declared COVID-19 a pandemic on 11 March.
Source: Bloomberg LP.

0.5% in May. While the US economy has shown signs of recovery, significant uncertainty remains stemming from the ongoing impact of the pandemic.

Similar to the Federal Reserve, the European Central Bank kept its monetary policy unchanged at its 16 July meeting, leaving key policy rates and existing asset purchases at the same levels. After the euro area's GDP contracted by 3.2% y-o-y in Q1 2020 and 14.7% y-o-y in Q2 2020, the European Central Bank noted signs of economic recovery beginning in May and expects a rebound in growth in the third quarter. Inflation inched up to 0.4% y-o-y in July from 0.3% y-o-y in June and 0.1% y-o-y in May. However, August inflation fell to –0.2% y-o-y. The euro area's industrial production also grew 4.1% month-on-month in July and 9.5% month-on-month in June. To further support economic recovery, the European Commission announced a fiscal stimulus program worth EUR750 billion on 20 July.

The Bank of Japan (BOJ) left its monetary policy unchanged at its meetings on 16 June and 15 July. The BOJ revised its GDP forecast for fiscal year 2020 in its July meeting to a contraction of between 5.7% and 4.5% from its previous forecast of a contraction of between 5.0% and 3.0% in April. While Japan's GDP contracted 28.1% y-o-y in Q2 2020 after a decline of 2.3% y-o-y in Q1 2020, the BOJ expects a moderate rebound in economic activity in the second half of 2020. It also slightly upgraded its GDP growth forecast for fiscal year 2021 to 3.0%–4.0% from 2.8%–3.9%.

Improved financial conditions were observed in different aspects of global financial markets. Most regional equity markets have picked up since April as investor sentiment improved (**Figure B.1**). At the height of market turmoil in March, which was driven by the oil price shock and the rapid spread of the pandemic, emerging East Asian markets had collectively fallen by 29.4% from 2 January to 23 March. Since April, equity markets in emerging East Asia have rallied. Between 15 June and 11 September, equity markets in the Republic of Korea and the PRC gained the most, posting increases of 18.0% and 12.8%, respectively (**Figure B.2**). Both markets have reached new high since January 2020, benefited from improved sentiment on the back of relatively good containment of, and recovery from, the pandemic. Nevertheless, equity markets in emerging East Asia posted an average loss of 11.0% from 2 January to 11 September weighed down by ASEAN markets, as investor sentiment failed to fully recover.

Foreign portfolio investment witnessed similar trends during the review period (**Figure C**). The largest monthly capital outflows from the region were observed in March before foreign portoflio investment stablized in April. The PRC was the only market in the region with stable foreign capital flows into equity market from April through July, benefiting from improved investor sentiment and growth recovery. Outflows were seen in most other emerging

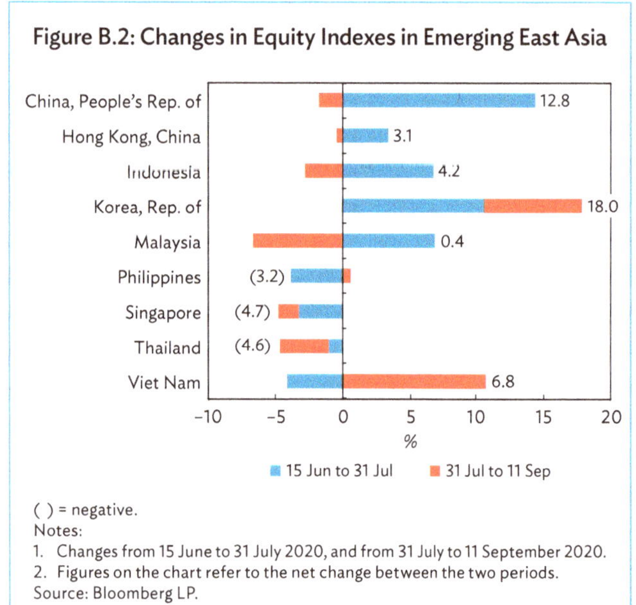

Figure B.2: Changes in Equity Indexes in Emerging East Asia

( ) = negative.
Notes:
1. Changes from 15 June to 31 July 2020, and from 31 July to 11 September 2020.
2. Figures on the chart refer to the net change between the two periods.
Source: Bloomberg LP.

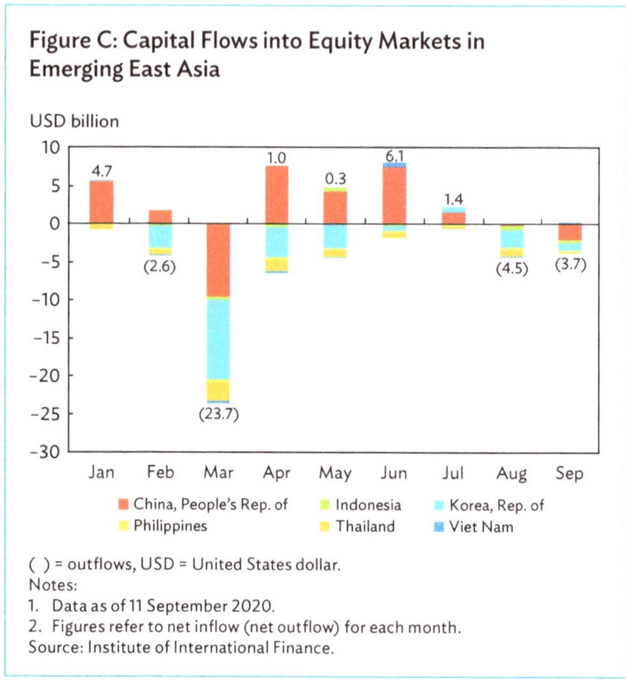

Figure C: Capital Flows into Equity Markets in Emerging East Asia

( ) = outflows, USD = United States dollar.
Notes:
1. Data as of 11 September 2020.
2. Figures refer to net inflow (net outflow) for each month.
Source: Institute of International Finance.

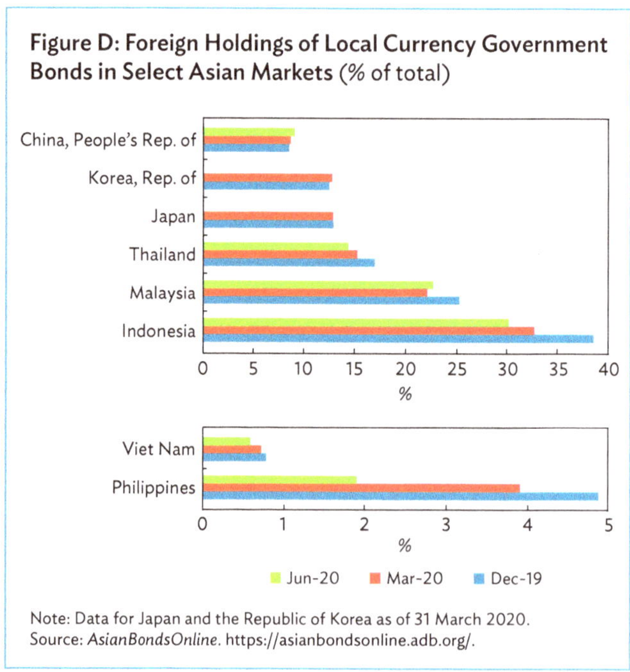

Figure D: Foreign Holdings of Local Currency Government Bonds in Select Asian Markets (% of total)

Note: Data for Japan and the Republic of Korea as of 31 March 2020.
Source: *AsianBondsOnline*. https://asianbondsonline.adb.org/.

East Asian markets during the same period, albeit to a much less degree compared with March. Outflows, however, were observed for all markets in August and for almost all markets in September.

Foreign holdings of LCY government bonds in emerging East Asia were mixed during the review period (**Figure D**). The foreign holdings share fell in Indonesia, declining from 32.7% at the end of March to 30.2% at the end of June, largely due to a more rapid increase in outstanding government bonds as the government sought to fund its stimulus packages. Similarly, the Philippines saw a decline in the foreign holdings share from 3.9% at the end of March to 1.9% at the end of June. Thailand and Viet Nam also experienced slight declines during the review period, while slight increases were observed in the PRC and Malaysia. **Box 1** reviews recent trends in LCY bond markets and changes in the investor profile in ASEAN+3 markets.

The weakness of the US dollar since 25 May resulted in the strengthening of most emerging East Asian currencies between 15 June and 11 September (**Figure E.1**). As of 11 September, most regional currencies had appreciated against the US dollar year-to-date (**Figure E.2**). The Chinese renminbi and the Philippine peso gained the most, strengthening by 3.7% each. The appreciation of the Chinese renminbi was driven by economic recovery while the Philippine peso strengthened on the back of a narrower trade deficit and lower demand for US dollars as quarantine restrictions limited economic activities. Bucking the trend were the Indonesian rupiah

and the Thai baht, which depreciated by 5.2% and 0.8%, respectively, between 15 June and 11 September. The weakness of the Indonesian rupiah was partly driven by a sluggish economic performance and concerns over debt monetization. Economic contraction and rising political risks drove the Thai baht's depreciation.

Key risk sentiment indicators have trended downward amid improved investor sentiment and easing liquidity

Box 1: Asian Bond Markets—Recent Trends and Developments

Market Review

Risk appetite in emerging East Asian bond markets soured in the first quarter (Q1) of 2020 before partially recovering in April.[a, b] The spread of the coronavirus disease (COVID-19) and the oil price shock rocked global financial markets in March. The JP Morgan Emerging Markets Bond Index Global (EMBIG) sovereign spreads of four Association of Southeast Asian Nations (ASEAN) markets and the People's Republic of China (PRC) widened amid the March turmoil, with average bond spreads in these markets jumping to 364 basis points (bps) on 23 March compared with 123 bps on 2 January (**Figure B1.1**). The Chicago Board Options Exchange Market Volatility Index also climbed from an average of 13.7 points in January to 57.2 points in March. Financial markets only began to stabilize in April, supported by the introduction of fiscal stimulus packages, accommodative monetary policies, and pandemic containment measures. By the end of August, average bond yield spreads narrowed to 171 bps and the Volatility Index had fallen to 26.4 points. However, risk sentiment has not yet recovered to pre-pandemic levels. On 31 August, the average bond yield spread remained 48 bps above where it stood on 2 January.

To maintain financial stability and mitigate the impact of COVID-19, most major central banks in emerging East Asia have cut interest rates at least once this year, releasing abundant liquidity into the financial sector and lowering borrowing costs (**Figure B1.2**). Lower interest rates across the region contributed to falling government bond yields in most emerging East Asian markets since the peak of the market turmoil in March. With the largest cumulative rate cut through the first 8 months of the year at 175 bps, the Philippines has witnessed the biggest drop in yields since March. By 31 August, government bond yields in most emerging East Asian economies had fallen below their December 2019 levels (**Figure B1.3**). At the end of Q1 2020, following the market sell-offs in March, government bond yields were higher than in December 2019 in a few relatively smaller bond markets in the region. Yields rose despite policy rate cuts, pointing to the importance of deeper financial markets in stabilizing asset prices.

Foreign Holdings in Emerging East Asian Markets

Foreign holdings in most emerging East Asian bond markets declined sharply in March and April before stabilizing in May.

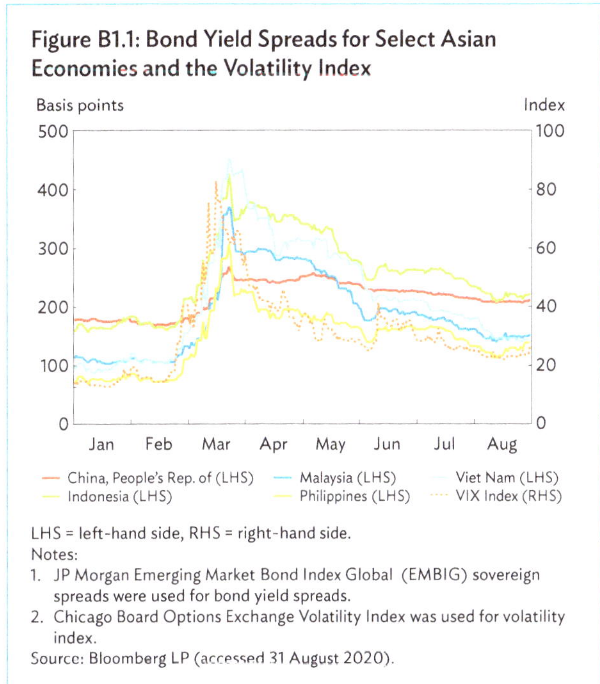

Figure B1.1: Bond Yield Spreads for Select Asian Economies and the Volatility Index

LHS = left-hand side, RHS = right-hand side.
Notes:
1. JP Morgan Emerging Market Bond Index Global (EMBIG) sovereign spreads were used for bond yield spreads.
2. Chicago Board Options Exchange Volatility Index was used for volatility index.
Source: Bloomberg LP (accessed 31 August 2020).

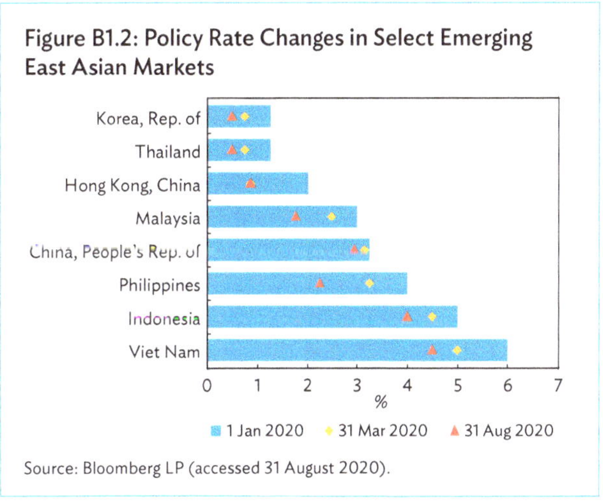

Figure B1.2: Policy Rate Changes in Select Emerging East Asian Markets

Source: Bloomberg LP (accessed 31 August 2020).

Heightened risk aversion during the peak of market turmoil in March led to a drop in foreign holdings of local currency (LCY) bonds for most emerging East Asian economies. The LCY government bond market in Indonesia witnessed the largest decline in foreign holdings, from a share of 38.6% at the end of December 2019 to 32.7% at the end of March. The corresponding figures for the Malaysian and Thai LCY government bond markets fell from 25.3% and 17.0% at the

---

^a This box was written by Donghyun Park (Principal Economist), Shu Tian (Economist), and Mai Lin Villaruel (Economics Officer) in the Economic Research and Regional Cooperation Department of the the Asian Development Bank.

^b Emerging East Asia comprises the People's Republic of China; Hong Kong, China; Indonesia; the Republic of Korea; Malaysia; the Philippines; Singapore; Thailand; and Viet Nam.

continued on next page

Box 1: Asian Bond Markets—Recent Trends and Developments   *continued*

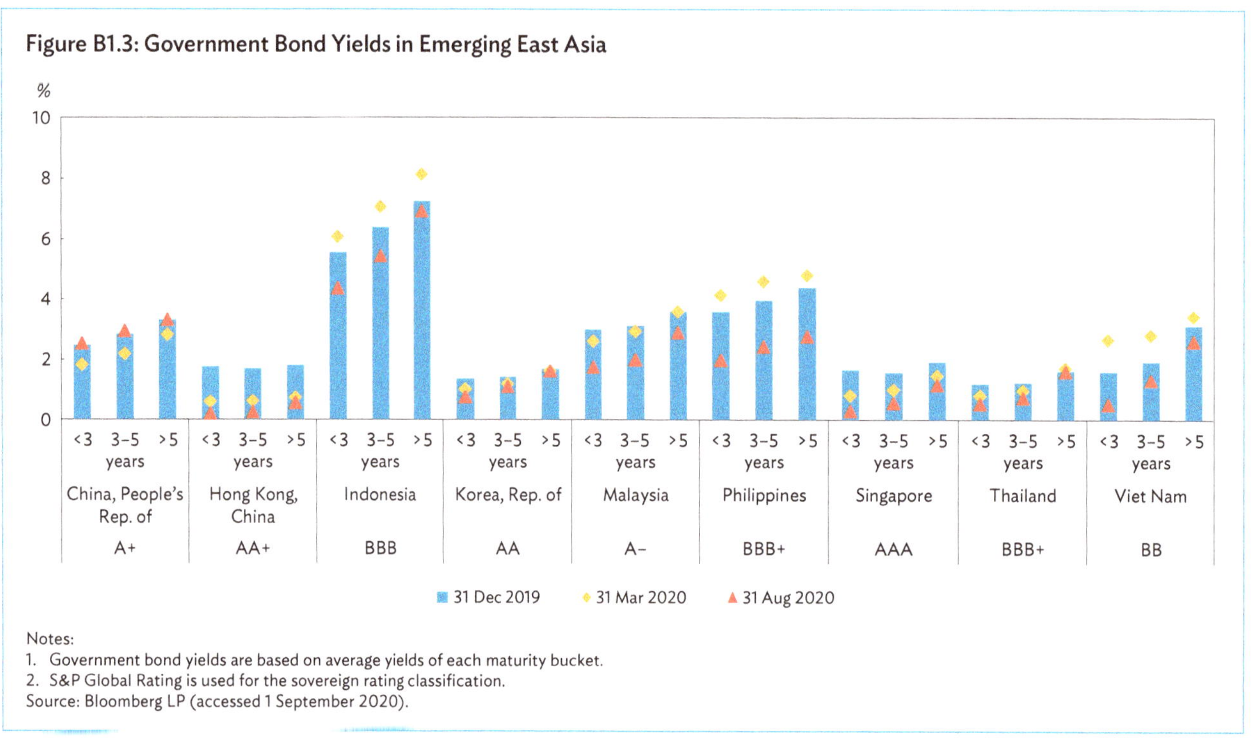

Figure B1.3: Government Bond Yields in Emerging East Asia

Notes:
1. Government bond yields are based on average yields of each maturity bucket.
2. S&P Global Rating is used for the sovereign rating classification.
Source: Bloomberg LP (accessed 1 September 2020).

end of December 2019 to 22.2% and 15.3%, respectively, at the end of March. Meanwhile, foreign holdings in the PRC market remained stable during the review period (**Figure B1.4**).

With reduced foreign holdings of Indonesian government bonds in Q1 2020, domestic institutions such as banks increased their holdings from 21.1% at the end of December to 33.3% at the end of June. Domestic institutions also increased their holdings in Thailand and Malaysia (**Figure B1.5**).

With improved sentiment, foreign portfolio investment in select emerging East Asian economies gradually stabilized after substantial outflows in March. Emerging East Asian currencies have also strengthened in recent months. Foreign portfolio investment in both equity and debt markets witnessed outflows starting in February, with outflows from equity markets peaking at USD11.2 billion in the week that ended 13 March. Outflows from debt markets peaked at USD4.1 billion in the week ending 20 March (**Figure B1.6**).

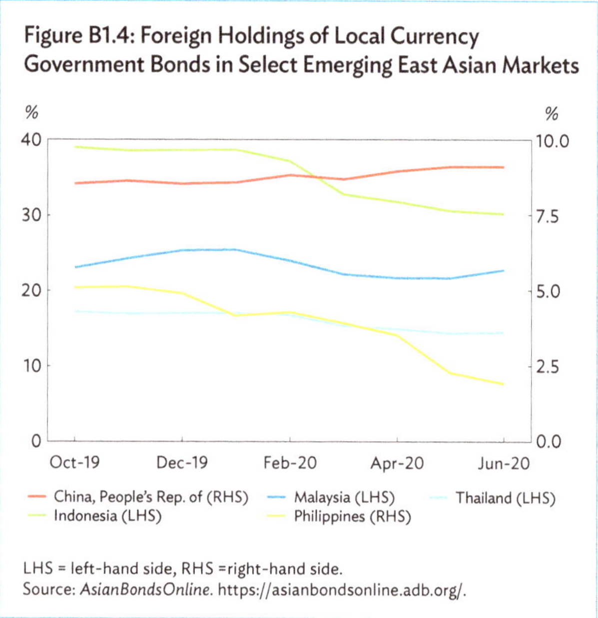

Figure B1.4: Foreign Holdings of Local Currency Government Bonds in Select Emerging East Asian Markets

LHS = left-hand side, RHS = right-hand side.
Source: *AsianBondsOnline*. https://asianbondsonline.adb.org/.

continued on next page

Box 1: Asian Bond Markets—Recent Trends and Developments *continued*

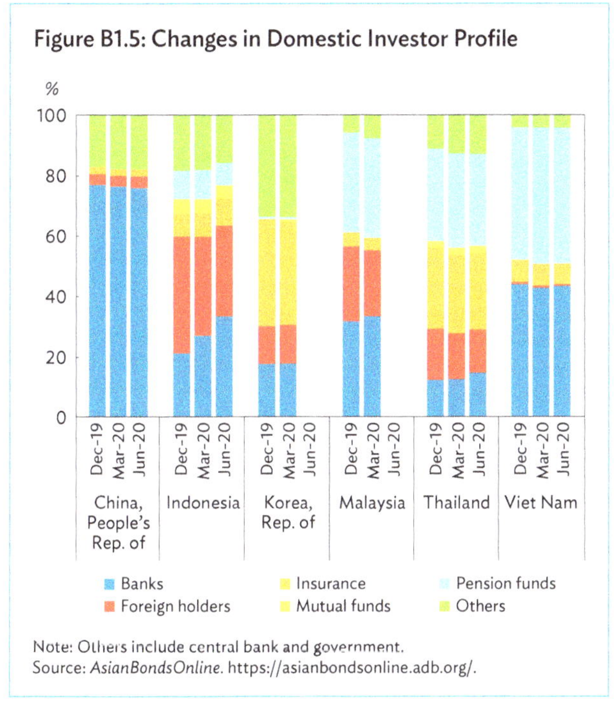

Figure B1.5: Changes in Domestic Investor Profile

Note: Others include central bank and government.
Source: *AsianBondsOnline*. https://asianbondsonline.adb.org/.

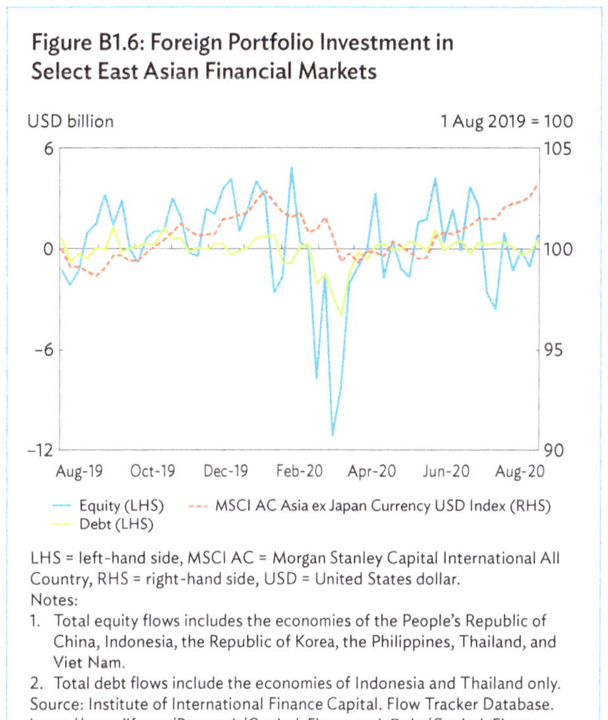

Figure B1.6: Foreign Portfolio Investment in Select East Asian Financial Markets

LHS = left-hand side, MSCI AC = Morgan Stanley Capital International All Country, RHS = right-hand side, USD = United States dollar.
Notes:
1. Total equity flows includes the economies of the People's Republic of China, Indonesia, the Republic of Korea, the Philippines, Thailand, and Viet Nam.
2. Total debt flows include the economies of Indonesia and Thailand only.
Source: Institute of International Finance Capital. Flow Tracker Database. https://www.iif.com/Research/Capital-Flows-and-Debt/Capital-Flows-Tracker (accessed 31 August 2020).

As financial markets stabilized in late March, portfolio outflows slowed, with inflows resuming in May. Between June and August, cumulative portfolio investment in select Asian equity and debt markets reached USD5.7 billion and USD2.4 billion, respectively. Meanwhile, emerging East Asian currencies depreciated versus the United States dollar in late March but have strengthened since June.

Bond Market Developments

Bond markets in emerging East Asia continued to expand to help meet the funding needs of both the public and private sectors in containing the COVID-19 pandemic and tackling its impact. The volume of bonds outstanding in the regional market rose in both Q1 and Q2 2020, with LCY bond financing playing a bigger role (**Figure B1.7**). At the end of June, LCY bonds outstanding in emerging East Asia reached

USD17.2 trillion on growth of 5.0% quarter-on-quarter (q-o-q) and 15.5% year-on-year (y-o-y). Foreign-currency-denominated bonds outstanding increased steadily as well, growing 0.7% q-o-q and 5.5% y-o-y to reach USD1.9 trillion at the end of June.

Government bonds still dominate the region's bond markets, accounting for almost 70% of total outstanding bonds at the end of Q2 2020. While LCY-denominated bonds already comprised more than 90% of the region's bonds outstanding, the share of LCY bonds inched higher in Q2 2020 relative to 2019, signaling the importance of LCY financing in supporting economic recovery from the COVID-19 pandemic (**Figure B1.8**).

continued on next page

Box 1: Asian Bond Markets—Recent Trends and Developments *continued*

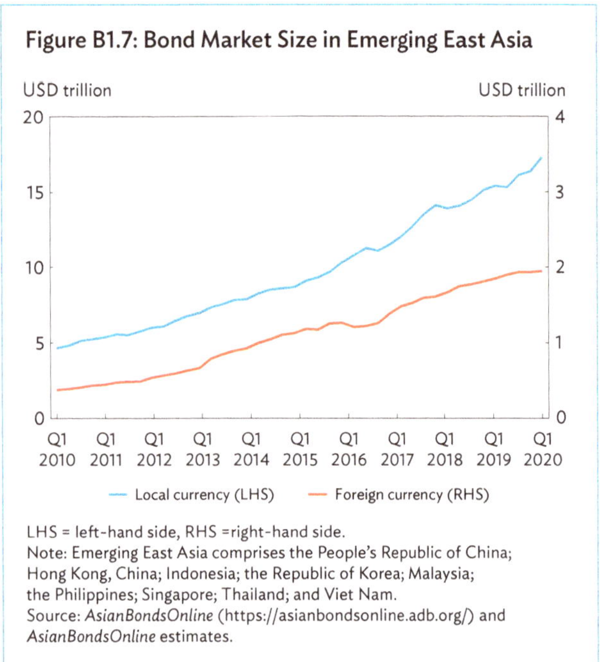

Figure B1.7: Bond Market Size in Emerging East Asia

LHS = left-hand side, RHS =right-hand side.
Note: Emerging East Asia comprises the People's Republic of China;
Hong Kong, China; Indonesia; the Republic of Korea; Malaysia;
the Philippines; Singapore; Thailand; and Viet Nam.
Source: *AsianBondsOnline* (https://asianbondsonline.adb.org/) and
AsianBondsOnline estimates.

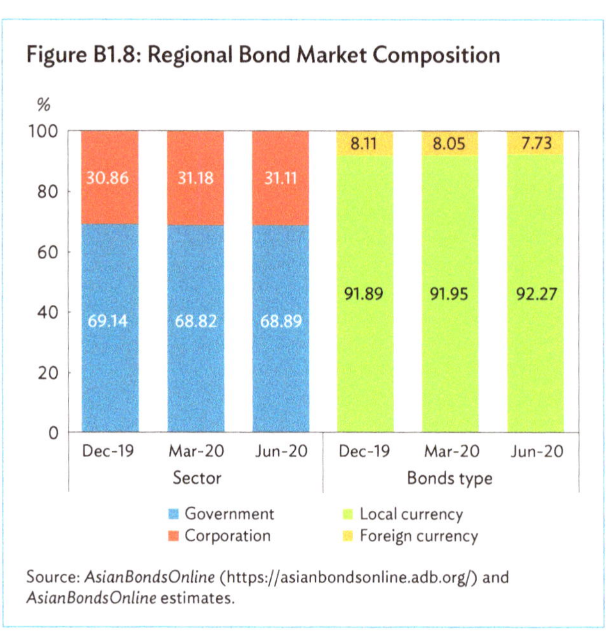

Figure B1.8: Regional Bond Market Composition

Source: *AsianBondsOnline* (https://asianbondsonline.adb.org/) and
AsianBondsOnline estimates.

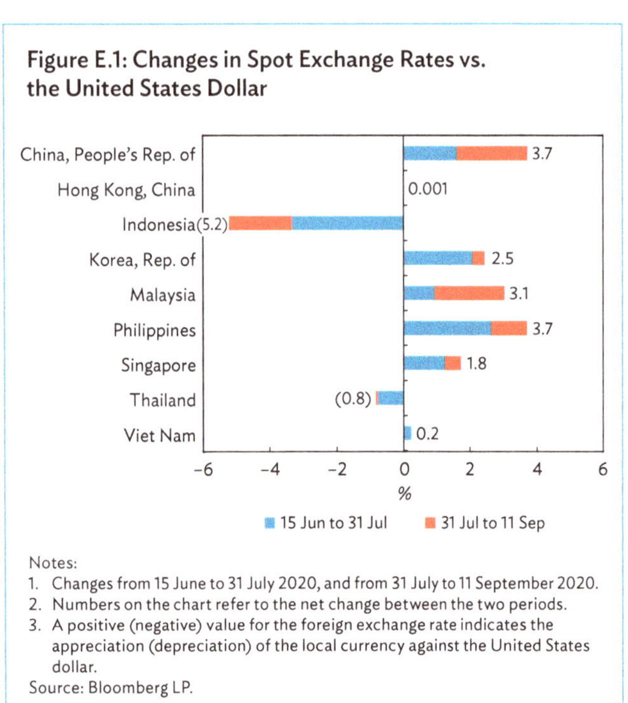

Figure E.1: Changes in Spot Exchange Rates vs.
the United States Dollar

Notes:
1. Changes from 15 June to 31 July 2020, and from 31 July to 11 September 2020.
2. Numbers on the chart refer to the net change between the two periods.
3. A positive (negative) value for the foreign exchange rate indicates the
   appreciation (depreciation) of the local currency against the United States
   dollar.
Source: Bloomberg LP.

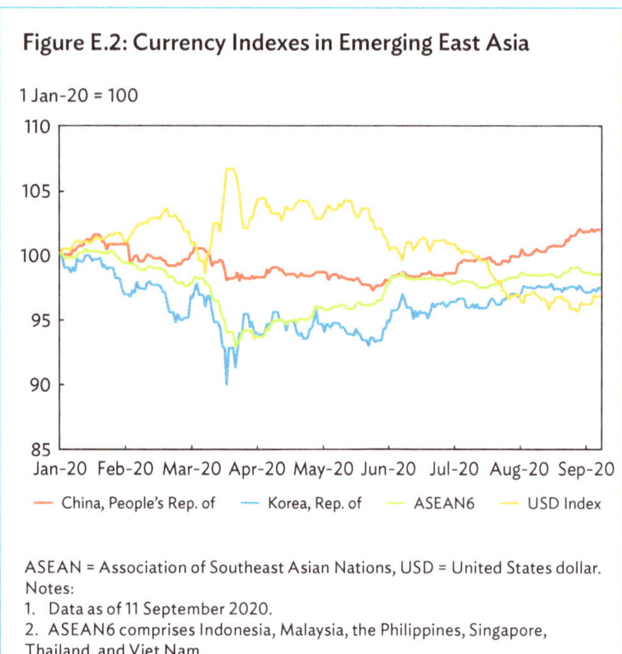

Figure E.2: Currency Indexes in Emerging East Asia

ASEAN = Association of Southeast Asian Nations, USD = United States dollar.
Notes:
1. Data as of 11 September 2020.
2. ASEAN6 comprises Indonesia, Malaysia, the Philippines, Singapore,
Thailand, and Viet Nam.
Source: Bloomberg LP.

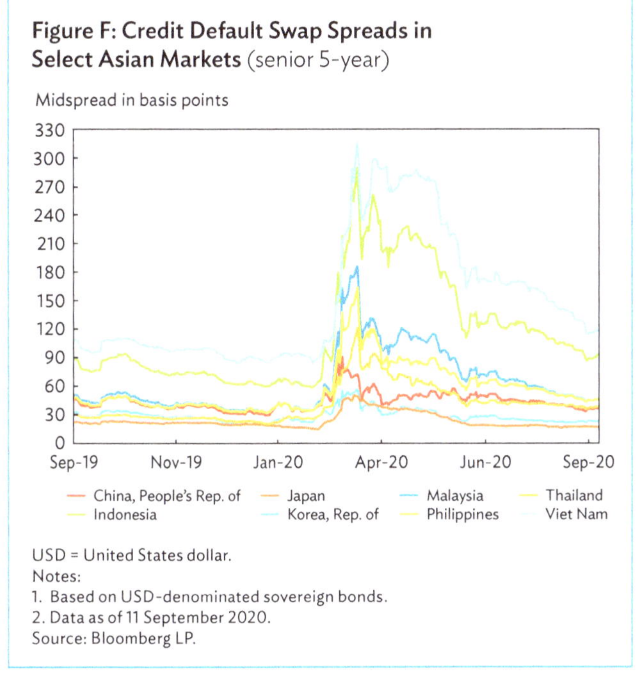

Figure F: Credit Default Swap Spreads in Select Asian Markets (senior 5-year)

USD = United States dollar.
Notes:
1. Based on USD-denominated sovereign bonds.
2. Data as of 11 September 2020.
Source: Bloomberg LP.

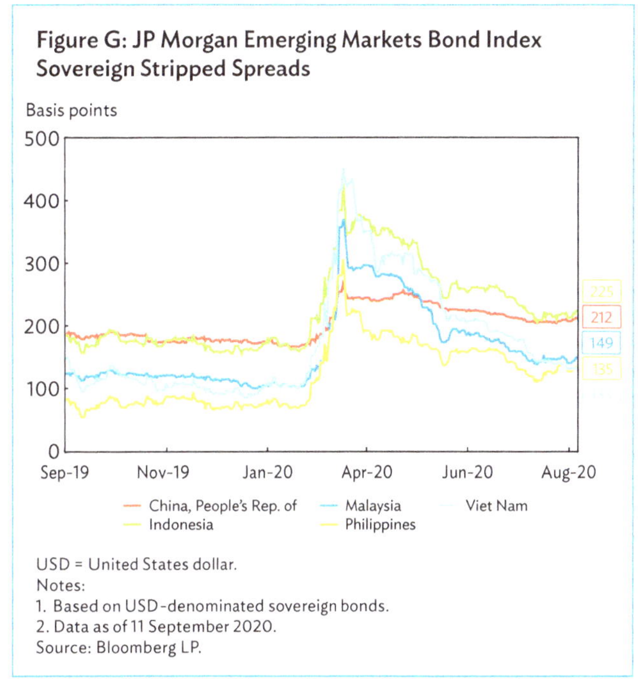

Figure G: JP Morgan Emerging Markets Bond Index Sovereign Stripped Spreads

USD = United States dollar.
Notes:
1. Based on USD-denominated sovereign bonds.
2. Data as of 11 September 2020.
Source: Bloomberg LP.

conditions. Credit default swap (CDS) spreads in emerging East Asia have declined since peaking in March. Between 15 June and 11 September, CDS spreads in regional markets narrowed by 29 bps on average (**Figure F**). Nevertheless, in most regional markets, CDS spreads remained higher than their levels in January, indicating that investment sentiment had not fully recovered. As of 11 September, the average CDS spread was 16 bps higher than on 2 January. JP Morgan Emerging Market Bond Index sovereign stripped spreads showed similar trends, rising to 171 bps on average by 11 September (**Figure G**). While the region's bond yield spreads have steadily declined since April, the average yield spread as of 11 September remained 48 bps higher than on 2 January.

While uncertainty associated with COVID-19 has hampered economic activities, it has also boosted the use of new technologies. **Box 2** describes the expanded opportunities for contactless payment in the COVID-19 era and beyond. Governments and markets continue to emphasize green and inclusive development as economies recover from the COVID-19 pandemic. **Box 3** and **Box 4** discuss how investments in environmental-, social-, and governance-themed assets have demonstrated resilience in 2020 amid the pandemic.

Overall, as improved liquidity conditions buoy financial conditions in the region, risks still tilt toward the downside. The largest risk remains the uncertain impact of COVID-19 globally. Aside from this, tension between the PRC and the US remains, casting a shadow on the post-COVID recovery. In addition, dim economic performances, abundant liquidity, and an uptick in nonperforming loans pose risks to financial soundness that may require more attention from policy makers.

Box 2: Contactless Payment in Post-COVID Asia

Cashless and contactless payments have increasingly become the preferred means of payment since the coronavirus disease (COVID-19) broke out.[a,b] The key driver of the shift to cashless and contactless payments, which do away with human contact including indirect human contact via surfaces, is the general public's desire to minimize the risk of infection. Specifically, the highly contagious nature of COVID-19 is encouraging businesses and customers to avoid banknotes, which can be a source of surface transmission since they typically change hands many times. The shift away from cash will encourage greater use of credit and debit cards. However, using a credit card at a restaurant, for example, does not eliminate the risk of surface transmission altogether since the server will touch your credit card. As such, it is not contactless payment.

Well before the COVID-19 pandemic, cashless payment technology was rapidly evolving toward contactless payment. Enabled by advances in financial technology, the "fintech boom" ushered in innovative payment solutions that complemented traditional financial services. It has generally made payments for goods and services faster, easier, and more convenient and cost-efficient for customers with payment methods ranging from digital cash to e-wallets and biometric payments. These innovations have spanned several companies and countries. For instance, Apple paired its wristwatch with an electronic app, Apple Pay, that allowed users to pay from their wrists. In Sweden, thousands have microchip implants in their hands to buy goods instead of using credit cards or cash.[c]

The development of contactless payment technology is being given a big push by the fear of COVID-19 infection through direct and indirect human contact. In particular, digital (or online) payment has gained a lot of traction since the outbreak. At a broader level, digital technology is redefining how we work, shop, play, learn, and live in the COVID-19 world. Work from home would not be possible without the internet. E-commerce and online shopping are a necessity during lockdowns and community quarantines when physical stores are shut down. Even after the restrictions are lifted, e-commerce is likely to grow in popularity as consumers prioritize health safety, which explains the soaring stock prices of e-commerce giants like Amazon and Alibaba. E-commerce requires e-payment, and the post-COVID growth of e-commerce will thus translate into the growth of digital payment.

What does the data say at a broader level about the current state of digital payment in Asia? The Global Findex database plotted in **Figure B2.1** suggests that a sample of 28 economies from developing Asia is still below the global average in its use of digital payments, which is led by member countries of the Organisation for Economic Co-operation and Development. While the use of digital payments varies across the region as illustrated in **Figure B2.2**, it is rapidly increasing. Consumers throughout Asia tend to use fintech products regularly.[d] Digital banking is also gaining ground in Southeast Asia, with most banks reducing the number of physical branches and improving the convenience and efficiency of online banking transactions.[e] In the Philippines, the Bangko Sentral ng Pilipinas aims to increase the use of electronic payments to 50% of the total volume of financial transactions by 2023. Digital payments have soared in the Philippines since quarantine restrictions were imposed in March 2020. The country's largest provider of mobile money services reported in May 2020 that the total amount of payments through its platform had increased eightfold from the previous year. The lender also announced plans to roll out electronic payments in transport, telemedicine, and government services by the end of 2020.[f] Other markets in the region are catching up quickly and launching various programs to tap into the potential of digital payments in the post-COVID world.

The experiences of two of Asia's largest economies, India and the People's Republic of China (PRC), provide valuable insights. The use of digital payments in India increased when the government demonetized its currency in 2016, forcing Indian consumers to shift to phone-based, cashless payment applications. Even when the availability of bank notes recovered, the use of electronic payments continued trending upward. Upgraded information and communication

---

[a] This box was written by Donghyun Park (Principal Economist) and Irfan Qureshi (Young Pofessional) in the Economic Research and Regional Cooperation Department of the Asian Development Bank.

[b] Cashless payments are made without using physical cash or money, offering a simple, efficient, and safe way to settle all point-of-sale and online purchases. Existing types of cashless payment systems include credit cards and debit cards, smart cards with radio frequency identification or near-field communications, and mobile payments using smartphones and other devices with QR codes.

[c] *NPR.* 2018. Thousands of Swedes Are Implanting Microchips under Their Skin. https://www.npr.org/2018/10/22/658808705/thousands-of-swedes-are-inserting-microchips-under-their-skin#:~:text=In%20Sweden%2C%20a%20country%20rich,their%20hands%20against%20digital%20readers.

[d] *Bloomberg.* 2019. Why Asia Is Leading the Fintech Revolution. https://www.bloomberg.com/professional/blog/asia-leading-fintech-revolution/.

[e] Asian Development Bank Institute. 2019. *The Digital Revolution in Asia and its Macroeconomic Effects.* https://www.adb.org/sites/default/files/publication/535846/adbi-wp1029.pdf.

[f] *Nikkei Asian Review.* 2020. Digital Payment Grows in Philippines Amid COVID-19 Fears. https://asia.nikkei.com/Business/Companies/Digital-payment-grows-in-Philippines-amid-COVID-19-fears.

continued on next page

Box 2: Contactless Payment in Post-COVID Asia   *continued*

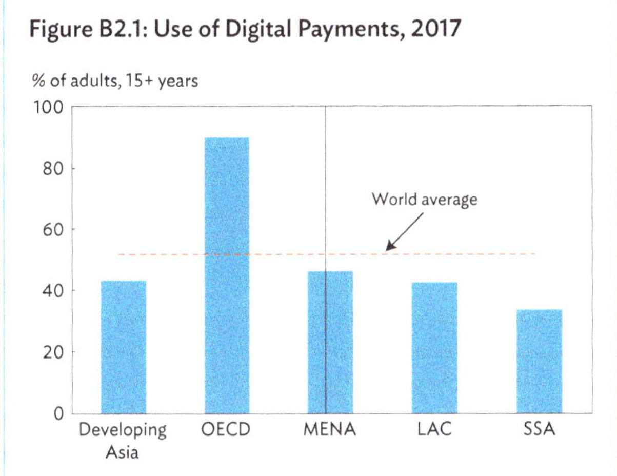

Figure B2.1: Use of Digital Payments, 2017

OECD = Organisation for Economic Co-operation and Development,
MENA = Middle East and North Africa, LAC = Latin America and the
Caribbean, SSA = Sub-Saharan Africa.
Notes:
1. Percentage of adults (15 years and above) who made and received digital
   payments in the past year.
2. Developing Asia comprises Afghanistan; Armenia; Azerbaijan; Bangladesh;
   the People's Republic of China; Georgia; Hong Kong, China; Indonesia;
   India; Kazakhstan; the Kyrgyz Republic; Cambodia; the Republic of Korea;
   the Lao People's Democratic Republic; Sri Lanka; Myanmar; Mongolia;
   Malaysia; Nepal; Pakistan; the Philippines; Singapore; Thailand; Tajikistan;
   Turkmenistan; Taipei,China; Uzbekistan; and Viet Nam.
Source: Global Findex Database.

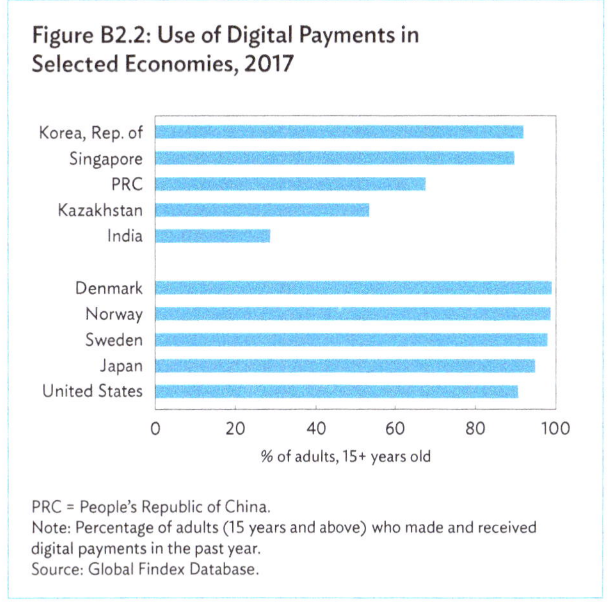

**Figure B2.2: Use of Digital Payments in
Selected Economies, 2017**

PRC = People's Republic of China.
Note: Percentage of adults (15 years and above) who made and received
digital payments in the past year.
Source: Global Findex Database.

technology infrastructure made this possible. The success of India's Unified Payments Interface and Aadhaar biometric identity systems shows that a government-backed utility for electronic payments can be quickly accessed by a large portion of the population. Mobile payments through the Unified Payments Interface, where people link their bank accounts with their phone numbers through payment apps, increased by 163% to USD287 billion in 2019.[8]

The transition to a cashless, contactless payment system began much earlier in the PRC. Digital payment and e-commerce took off in the aftermath of the 2003 severe acute respiratory syndrome (SARS) epidemic with the introduction of Alipay and similar payment systems.[h] The PRC's payment transition was based on a strong foundation. By 2003, the PRC had already established the critical networks and digital infrastructure needed to enable digital payments. Several projects were launched by the central government, including the Golden Bridge Project, which built extensive internet networks; the Golden Card Project,

which established the unified card system; and the Golden Customs Project, which provided a national system for cashless transactions. In fact, in terms of contactless payment, the PRC has become one of the most advanced economies in the world. In particular, QR code payment, a contactless method where payment is made by scanning a QR code from a mobile app, is now one of the leading means of payment throughout the PRC. There is no physical touch required at all, which makes QR code payment ideal for the COVID-19 environment. In the PRC, you can even give alms to street beggars via QR code!

Notwithstanding the rapid ascent of digital payment in Asia, several challenges remain. Digital payment transactions require increased accountability and tracking, which will reduce the risk of theft and breaches of security.[i] Data privacy presents another major challenge. Digitalization brings new threats such as cyberattacks, digital crimes, data breaches of payment systems, and online fraud. Thus, banks and fintech companies will need to invest heavily in advanced and reliable cybersecurity systems to protect consumer data and transactions. On the supply side, payment providers also expect some challenges ahead, such as increased oversight and regulation of the global payments industry, the impact of government-imposed restrictions

---

[8] S&P Global Market Intelligence. 2020. *2020 India Mobile Payments Market Report*. https://www.spglobal.com/marketintelligence/en/documents/indiamobilepayments_2020
finalreport.pdf.

[h] Y. Xiao and M. Chorzempa. 2020. *How Digital Payments Can Help Countries Cope with COVID-19 and Other Pandemics*. https://www.weforum.org/agenda/2020/05/digital-
payments-cash-and-covid-19-pandemics/.

[i] K. Muralidharan, P. Niehaus, and S. Sukhtankar. 2016. Building State Capacity: Evidence from Biometric Smartcards in India. *NBER Working Paper*. No. 199999. Cambridge, MA:
National Bureau of Economic Research.

continued on next page

Box 2: Contactless Payment in Post-COVID Asia *continued*

on international payment systems, and increasingly intense competition for clients and merchants in the payments industry.[j] Finally, digital payments, including QR code payments, require a stable internet connection, so a strong digital infrastructure is essential.

Market demand is driving the relentless growth of contactless payment. Economic and health shocks such as India's demonetization and the SARS crisis in the PRC catalyzed

contactless payment in these two markets. It is reasonable to expect that COVID-19 will lead to a large and lasting expansion of digital payments. To seamlessly transition to digital payments, which will be an integral part of the more digital post-COVID world, Asian economies must invest in digital networks and infrastructure, and strengthen their regulatory frameworks. Robust identification systems, reliable internet networks, and trustworthy financial services are prerequisites for contactless payment systems.

---

[j] Visa Inc. Q2 2020 *Financial Results*. https://s1.q4cdn.com/050606653/files/doc_financials/2020/q2/Visa-Inc.-Q2-2020-Financial-Results.pdf.

[k] *Fintech*. 2019. The Great Shift Towards a Cashless Society. https://www.fintechmagazine.com/mobile-payments/great-shift-towards-cashless-society.

Box 3: Environmental, Social, and Governance Investment Growth amid the COVID-19 Crisis

Environmental, social, and governance (ESG) investment is critical for achieving inclusive growth in Asia and can play a vital role in reducing the income inequality being exacerbated by the coronavirus disease (COVID-19).[a]

ESG investment is defined as a type of investment that factors corporates' extra-financial performance—such as environmental, social, and corporate governance factors—in decision-making. This concept has become increasingly popular since 2006, when major investors first announced their adherence to the United Nations Principles for Responsible Investment, and subsequently with the announcement of the United Nations Sustainable Development Goals in 2015. The 2008–2009 global financial crisis also spurred a widespread movement to reshape excess capitalism and an overemphasis on shareholder profits. Meanwhile, the younger generation, with activists such as Greta Thunberg, has further brought ESG issues into the public and media spotlight. In 2018, global ESG investment reached USD31 trillion, which was seven times its value in 2014.

Despite a slow start, Asia and the Pacific has witnessed a rapid uptake in ESG investment. Exchanges in some Asian economies—such as India, Singapore, and Thailand—have asked listed companies to disclose ESG-related information to stimulate ESG investment. Such investment can help boost Asian economies' potential growth by creating a virtuous cycle in which companies' increased environmental

protection, employee education, and women's participation will, in turn, raise corporate values and spur economic growth.

Companies with high ESG scores are less susceptible to market fluctuations.

Constraints to ESG investment can include declines in the value of investor assets, declines in profits, and shifts toward safe assets (e.g., cash and government bonds). Firms may also face difficulties in continuing ESG investing during periods of significant economic deterioration or crisis. In fact, achievement of the Millennium Development Goals, the predecessors to the Sustainable Development Goals, was delayed due to economic deterioration in developed countries in the aftermath of the 2008–2009 global financial crisis.

In recent years, however, ESG investment has expanded. According to a report by Sustainable Research and Analytics, the cumulative amount that mutual funds invested based on ESG factors increased to USD2.6 trillion in May 2020 from USD1.6 trillion in December 2019. ESG issues have become an extremely important consideration for medium- and long-term investors seeking to avoid long-term risks such as changes in consumer orientation and declines in corporate brands.

From a corporate perspective, ESG initiatives support resilience against market fluctuations. Recent leading studies found a strong correlation between ESG evaluation and stock prices during the 2008–2009 global financial crisis,

---

[a] This box was written by Naoko Nemoto (Financial Economist) and Lian Liu (Research Associate) of the Asian Development Bank Institute.

continued on next page

Box 3: Environmental, Social, and Governance Investment Growth amid the COVID-19 Crisis
continued

when corporate trust was questioned.[b] To see whether this hypothesis still holds during the COVID-19 crisis, we adopted a simple approach to divide the top 100 Japanese-listed companies into four groups based on their ESG ratings and compare their respective stock price performances in the first quarter of 2020. Although most firms faced a decline in equity prices during the review period, the group with the highest ESG ratings showed the smallest average decline and most stable stock prices among all groups (**Figure B3**).

Figure B3: Stock Price Changes in the First Quarter of 2020 among Top 100 Japanese Companies Grouped by Average ESG Rating

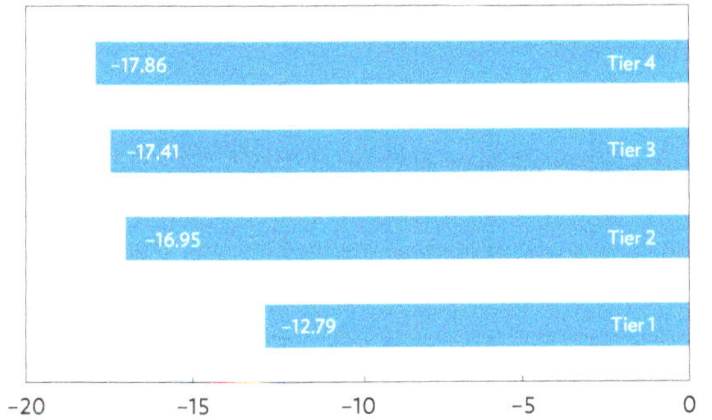

ESG = environmental, social, and governance.
Notes:
1. Tier 1 has the highest average corporate social responsibility (CSR) ranking, and Tier 4 group has the lowest.
2. The CSR ranking reflects employment, environment, society, and governance factors.
3. The sample comprises the top 100 listed Japanese firms by market capitalization.
Source: Authors' calculations based on 2020 CSR Enterprise Rankings by Toyo Keizai.

Social factors are attracting more attention.

Traditionally, social factors were considered to have a smaller impact on stock prices and corporate value than environmental and governance factors. Amid the COVID-19 crisis, society has started to focus more on the health and safety of its employees, as well as on the security of employment and maintenance of suppliers and customers. As such, social factors are attracting more investor attention.

Some companies have been severely criticized by investors for maintaining high compensation packages for management and offering high-dividend payouts while also reducing their workforces. The *Financial Times* has highlighted that companies are under increasing pressure from investors to not only focus on the interests of stockholders but also on the diverse interests of stakeholders.[c] Facing criticism for its working conditions, Amazon announced that it would reinvest second quarter profits to improve safety measures and add more than 170,000 jobs to improve working conditions.

To assess the importance of social factors, we further analyzed the relationship between capital costs and ESG factors for the top 100 Japanese companies based on the 2020 CSR Enterprise Rankings by Toyo Keizai, controlling for corporate size, revenue growth, industry, and leverage. Our results found a significant correlation between social factors and capital costs. Companies with better human resource utilization—such as promoting diversity, supporting human rights, and improving working conditions—tend to have lower capital costs and higher corporate values.

Asian economies should work collectively to create effective ESG standards.

ESG investment is crucial for supporting sustainable growth in Asia, but several challenges remain:

i.   **Mediocre quality and accuracy of ESG information.** The financial data of listed firms are audited by an independent external auditor, but nonfinancial data are not endorsed by third parties in many cases. In addition, available ESG information for Asian corporates is insufficient. The rules of disclosure vary by economy, and the conversion and standardization of disclosure guidelines still needs to be developed.

ii. **Difficulty in analyzing and evaluating the huge amount of necessary information.** Investors are increasingly referring to ESG indexes, but there are criticisms that these indexes have not fully incorporated the specific features of industries and companies.

iii. **Risk of resource misallocation.** ESG investing criteria and standards have been developed mainly in European countries. Applying uniform standards to countries in different stages of economic development could result in the misallocation of economic resources. The effectiveness of ESG investment has not been tested across countries.

---

[b] Sustainable Research and Analytics. 2020. Sustainable Funds Cashflows Summary. 24 May; and June Lins, K., and T. Ane. 2019. Social Capital, Trust, and Corporate Performance: How CSR Helped Companies During the Financial Crisis (and Why It Can Keep Helping Them). *Sustainable Finance Management*. 31 (2020). pp. IV-2.

[c] *Financial Times*. 2020. Proxy Battles Heat Up as Investors Target Climate and Social Issues. 24 April.

continued on next page

Box 3: Environmental, Social, and Governance Investment Growth amid the COVID-19 Crisis
continued

To overcome these obstacles, policy makers and companies in Asia need to be proactive in disclosing ESG information, encouraging ongoing dialogue with global investors, engaging in the creation of effective investment standards, and ensuring the outcome of investments. A full discussion of these challenges and the benefits of ESG investment is included in a new Asian Development Bank Institute book, *Environmental, Social, and Governance Investment: Opportunities and Risks for Asia.*[d] The book examines the current state of ESG investment in Asia and offers insights into leveraging the benefits of ESG investment for sound and sustainable development.

---

[d]   N. Nemoto and P. J. Morgan. 2020. *Environmental, Social, and Governance Investment: Opportunities and Risks for Asia.* Tokyo: Asian Development Bank Institute.

Box 4: Is Green the New Gold? ESG Resilience during the COVID-19 Crisis

Pandemic: A Neglected Risk

When the World Health Organization declared the coronavirus disease (COVID-19) a pandemic on 11 March 2020, it signaled that what had started as an emerging disease in the People's Republic of China in late 2019 had turned into one of the most serious health crises ever known.[a]

Evidence is mounting of the devastating economic impact of the pandemic. Equity markets in global financial centers plunged, and the International Monetary Fund is expecting growth in Asia to stall at zero in 2020, the worst economic performance in 60 years.

The world has been caught by surprise; a global pandemic was not included among the top risks for investors. Markets are not set up to anticipate the impact of a pandemic of this nature, and the impending risk of such events have traditionally been overlooked. For example, a pandemic did not make the list of the 10 most probable risks cited in the World Economic Forum's *Global Risks Report* published in January 2020, making way for other concerns such as climate and cyber risks.

For now, losses from the pandemic are difficult to estimate as the magnitude of the impact depends on the continued spread of the disease (i.e., sick people no longer contribute to gross domestic product) and political responses to limit the contagion. The only certainty is uncertainty as economies brace for impending recessions.

The Resilience of Environmental, Social, and Governance Investing

Amid the COVID-19 chaos, trends in sustainable and environmental, social, and governance (ESG) investing stand out. Before the pandemic, corporate social responsibility had already become a major investment criterion, significantly influencing the valuation of financial assets in both the equity and debt markets. The rise of ESG investing in recent years can be attributed to increased investor demand. During the COVID-19 market sell-off, ESG funds outperformed strikingly, proving their resilience amid the crisis. For example, when the MSCI World Index dipped in March, 62% of large-cap ESG funds outperformed the index. Furthermore, 42% of ESG open-ended funds and exchange-traded funds (ETFs) in the United States (US) were ranked in the first quartile of their Morningstar category.

This outperformance was partly due to the exposure of these funds to sectors less impacted by containment and social distancing measures, such as tech and telecoms.

Recent analysis by Amundi of 1,662 ETFs listed in the US shows that investment flows into ESG funds have also been much more resilient during the COVID-19 crisis. From 31 December 2019 to 14 April 2020, the daily growth rate for ESG funds was over four times higher than for conventional funds (1.3% vs 0.3%).

Cumulative flows continued to increase throughout the early crisis period even after the initial phase of the lockdown in

---

[a]   This box is a summary of an Amundi research paper written by Jean-Jacques Barbéris, Head of Institutional and Corporate Clients Coverage, and Marie Brière, Head of the Investor Research Center. The full paper is available at https://research-center.amundi.com/page/Article/2020/05/The-day-after-3-ESG-Resilience-During-the-Covid-Crisis-Is-Green-the-New-Gold.

continued on next page

Box 4: Is Green the New Gold? ESG Resilience during the COVID-19 Crisis   *continued*

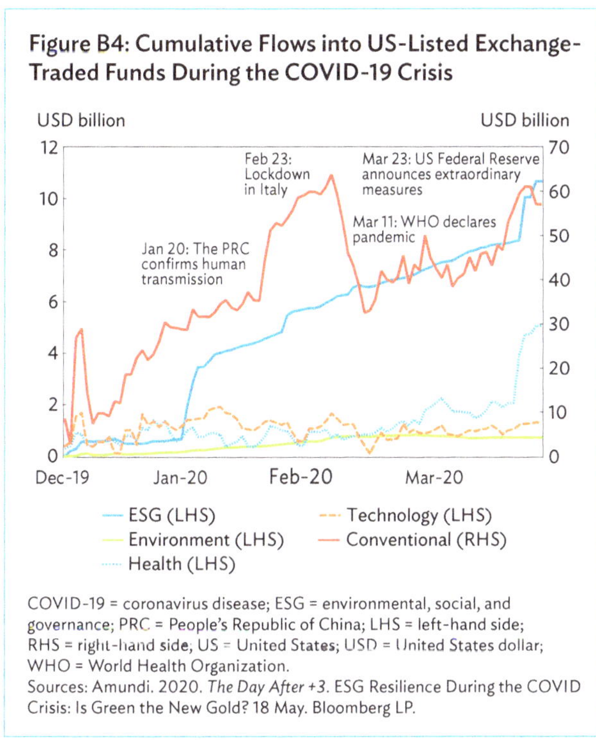

Figure B4: Cumulative Flows into US-Listed Exchange-Traded Funds During the COVID-19 Crisis

COVID-19 = coronavirus disease; ESG = environmental, social, and governance; PRC = People's Republic of China; LHS = left-hand side; RHS = right-hand side; US = United States; USD = United States dollar; WHO = World Health Organization.
Sources: Amundi. 2020. *The Day After +3*. ESG Resilience During the COVID Crisis: Is Green the New Gold? 18 May. Bloomberg LP.

Italy in February when massive sales of traditional equity ETFs occurred. ETFs that specialized in sectors with little exposure such as tech and, to a lesser extent, health care also sold off during this period (**Figure B4**).

Is Environmental, Social, and Governance Investing "Pandemic-Proof"?

There are several possible reasons for the resilience of investment flows into ESG funds. Investors may perceive that ESG funds are "pandemic-proof." By design, ESG funds tend to overweight sectors that have weathered the crisis better such as health care and tech. At the same time, ESG funds underweight those that have been most impacted such as transport, energy, and materials.

Another reason may be that investors have shown greater loyalty to their ESG investments. Past analysis has shown that compared to conventional funds, flows into ESG mutual funds are more sensitive to past positive returns and less sensitive to negative returns. Investors potentially derive positive utility from the simple act of investing responsibly, which can lead them to hold their investments during crises.

There may be one final reason. Even without loyalty, ESG funds may have benefited from investor preferences and played the role of safe havens within equity markets for the sole reason that investors anticipated others would do the same. Amid the COVID-19 crisis, which clearly has strong social and environmental implications, it seems that investors perceive a strong ESG fund performance as a defensive characteristic.

Outlook on Future ESG Trends

The COVID-19 crisis has moved social considerations to the forefront of ESG investing. Companies' decisions affecting workers have become increasingly important. This was seen in the reactions of Amazon's share price to the controversy over the working conditions of its employees during the crisis, as well as in the widespread publicity of COVID-related corporate social responsibility policies.

Companies' environmental and climate actions could also be better valued by market participants. It is becoming impossible to argue that investors do not have to worry about the environmental externalities generated by companies. The pandemic reminds us that unanticipated adverse events can happen suddenly and unexpectedly, and they can have long-term consequences. We are more vulnerable than we previously imagined.

It is difficult to predict if ESG issues will continue to be a priority for investors in the long-term, but investors' taste for ESG funds has not decreased during a pandemic like COVID-19. In fact, its impact has been quite the opposite.

Economic Outlook

The once-in-a-lifetime global public health crisis caused by COVID-19 is proving to be much deeper and more persistent than initially expected. The highly contagious nature of the virus means that it is a uniquely harmful pandemic. No other pandemic has shut down international travel and closed borders to the extent that COVID-19 has done. Based on the patterns of earlier pandemics, there were hopes during the early stages of the outbreak that COVID-19 would fade away as the weather turned warmer in the northern hemisphere during the summer months. For instance, the 1918 influenza pandemic broke out in the northern hemisphere in the spring but died down in the summer before returning from the southern hemisphere with a vengeance in the fall. However, the prevalence of COVID-19 seems unrelated to weather in either the northern or southern hemispheres. Hopes that warm weather would kill the virus have been dashed. Through the end of August, the pandemic had shown no signs of abating in either hemisphere.

To the contrary, the world remains mired knee-deep in a public health crisis without any clear signs of or pathways to containment. As of 30 August, the number of confirmed cases neared 25 million worldwide and the number of fatalities closed in on 800,000.[2] The US, the world's biggest and technologically most advanced economy, continued to hold the unenviable lead in confirmed cases and deaths, with around a quarter of the global total for both. A list of the 15 countries with the most infections—the US, Brazil, India, the Russian Federation, South Africa, Peru, Mexico, Colombia, Spain, Chile, Iran, the United Kingdom, Argentina, Saudi Arabia, and Pakistan—confirms that the pandemic is truly global, affecting all corners of the world. The best way to contain COVID-19 is likely to be the development and mass production of a safe and effective vaccine. While there has been progress on the vaccine front, it is unlikely that a working vaccine will emerge and be widely available by the end of this year. In short, COVID-19 still hangs over the world economy like a dark cloud.

As a result, the global economic outlook remains decidedly bleak. In its *World Economic Outlook Update* released in June 2020, the International Monetary Fund (IMF) forecast the world economy, which had grown by 3.6% in 2018 and 2.9% in 2019, would contract by 4.9% in 2020 before rebounding to growth of 5.4% in 2021. The forecast contraction in 2020 represents a downgrade of 1.9 percentage points since April, when the IMF forecast a contraction of 3.0%. In January, the IMF had predicted that the world economy would expand by 3.3% in 2020. As such, the IMF downgraded its global growth forecast by a jaw-dropping 8.2 percentage points between January and June. The IMF's consecutive downgrades mean that 2021 global output will be down 6.5 percentage points relative to its January projections. The title of its June report, *A Crisis Like No Other, An Uncertain Recovery*, captured the severity of the global downturn as well as the highly uncertain prospects for recovery. The pandemic has had a bigger impact on the world economy than expected, and the eventual recovery is projected to be more gradual. It is now clear that we are unlikely to see a quick and robust V-shaped recovery. It is also clear that the economic downturn due to COVID-19 will be much deeper and more persistent than the Great Recession triggered by the global financial crisis.

The IMF's assessments are as equally bleak for emerging markets and developing economies as they are for advanced economies. The IMF projects the GDP of emerging markets and developing countries to contract by 3.0% in 2020, a sizable downgrade from its forecast of a 1.0% contraction in April, before rebounding with an expansion of 5.9% in 2021. The corresponding forecasts for advanced economies are a contraction of 8.0% in 2020 and growth of 4.8% in 2021. The IMF has downgraded its growth forecasts for all regions of the world relative to its April projections, when it had already downgraded its forecasts for all regions relative to January. The truly global pandemic has led to a truly global economic downturn. The collapse of global demand, along with pandemic-related measures such as border closures and other restrictions, have had a significant impact on international trade, which is projected to decline by 11.9% in 2020 before bouncing back into positive territory with 8.0% growth in 2021.

Developing Asia's economies are being hit hard by the pandemic even though they will likely fare better than other parts of the world, largely on the back of the PRC's resilience. According to the *Asian Development*

---

[2] World Health Organization. Coronavirus Disease (COVID-19) Weekly Epidemiological Update. 2020. https://www.who.int/docs/default-source/coronaviruse/situation-reports/20200831-weekly-epi-update-3.pdf?sfvrsn=d7032a2a_4.

Outlook 2020 Update released in September by the Asian Development Bank (ADB) , the region's economy, which grew by 5.1% in 2019, is expected to contract 0.7% in 2020 before rebounding with growth of 6.8% in 2021. The PRC's economy, which grew by 6.1% in 2019, will expand by only 1.8% in 2020 but is forecast to bounce back with robust 7.7% growth in 2021. The corresponding figures for (i) the Association of Southeast Asian Nations are 4.4%, −3.8%, and 5.5%; (ii) the Republic of Korea are 2.0%, −1.0%, and 3.3%; and (3) Hong Kong, China are −1.2%, −6.5%, and 5.1%. The PRC's positive growth forecast in 2020, which is albeit much lower than usual, largely explains why ADB expects developing Asia to avoid a downright contraction. Still, the deterioration of the global outlook is bad news for many Asian economies that depend heavily on exports and trade.

Overall, the economic outlook remains grim for both the world and members of the Association of Southeast Asian Nations plus the People's Republic of China; Hong Kong, China; and the Republic of Korea. The primary reason for the consecutive downgrades of global and regional growth forecasts is that the world is still struggling against COVID-19. It is unclear when the pandemic will either be contained or at least brought under a measure of control. The high level of uncertainty over global and regional economic prospects is grounded in a high level of uncertainty over COVID-19. The pandemic seems to throw up breaking news, most of it had, with alarming frequency—for example, it may leave longer-lasting effects on infected persons than initially believed. In addition to persistent and elevated uncertainty, it is now clear that the global health impact of the pandemic will be larger and more persistent than expected. It is equally clear that the economic impact of the pandemic is likely to be much more pronounced than initially expected.

Risks to Economic Outlook and Financial Stability

The risks to the global and regional economic outlook remain decidedly tilted toward the downside. As noted earlier, the global health impact of the pandemic will be larger and more persistent than expected. As a result, the economic impact of the pandemic is likely to be much more pronounced than initially expected. The consecutive downgrades of global growth forecasts by the IMF and of developing Asia's growth forecasts

by ADB reflect an increasingly pessimistic assessment of the pandemic and its economic effects. But the downgrades may not be large enough if COVID-19 worsens further and precipitates a return to widespread lockdowns, community quarantines, and other measures that are needed to contain the disease but also severely disrupt the economy. As bleak as the current global and economic outlook is, it may get even worse unless and until the pandemic is brought under control, perhaps not completely but at least to the extent that some semblance of normalcy returns.

From an economic perspective, COVID-19 is both a supply and demand shock. That is, the pandemic-related health measures, such as travel restrictions and social distancing, adversely affect both the production of goods and services as well as the demand for and consumption of goods and services. Factories and shops that are closed during lockdowns and community quarantines cannot produce or sell. At the same time, consumers who cannot go to bars, restaurants, or shopping malls spend less. Furthermore, workers who are laid off or furloughed during lockdowns earn less income, so they cut back on their consumption. On the other hand, if the pandemic recedes much sooner than currently expected, perhaps due to the surprisingly quick development of a safe, affordable, and effective vaccine, the global and regional economy could stage a V-shaped recovery after all. The upshot is that the trajectory of economic recovery is tightly intertwined with the trajectory of the COVID-19 outbreak.

This is why the biggest risk to the region's economic outlook and financial stability is a major resurgence of COVID-19. As explained earlier, the pandemic has not yet been contained to a level that allows the world to carry on most of the activities that were part of the pre-pandemic normal. To name just one such activity, international air travel remains at a fraction of its pre-COVID-19 levels, and some aviation industry experts are predicting that it may not return to pre-pandemic levels until 2024. Some countries have done a solid job of containing the pandemic and managed to flatten the curve. But overall, the global picture is decidedly grim, and as bad as the current situation is, we cannot rule out further deterioration. In fact, some health experts are fearing the worst in the coming fall and winter in the northern hemisphere. In particular, they are expressing concerns about the potentially dangerous combination of the common flu, which tends to be prevalent during fall and winter, and COVID-19.

Alarmingly, even countries that had seemingly crushed the curve are witnessing second waves of new infections. For instance, New Zealand, which received global praise for its effective containment while remaining virus-free for 102 days, reported new cases in August. In response, the government reintroduced stay-at-home restrictions for Auckland, the country's largest city. Also in August, the Republic of Korea, another country that was admired around the world as a model for successfully tackling COVID-19, suffered a new outbreak. In late February, the Republic of Korea experienced the world's second major outbreak, following the initial outbreak centered in the city of Wuhan in the PRC. What is remarkable about the Republic of Korea's achievement is that the country managed to contain the pandemic without any strict lockdowns, as daily life went on as more or less normal. Instead, the Republic of Korea relied on smart digital technology for contact tracing and mass testing.

Germany, another containment success story, has also recently experienced new localized outbreaks. Its second wave is part of a broader European second wave. In March, Italy became the leading global hot spot of COVID-19, with the number of new infections and deaths growing so rapidly that the country's hospitals and morgues were barely able to cope. The pandemic quickly spread to other parts of Europe, with France, Germany, Spain, and the United Kingdom, in addition to smaller European countries, all hit hard. The US and Europe were in similar positions in March in terms of cases and fatalities. Their trajectories since then could not be more different. The US suffered a sharp escalation, bordering on an explosion, while Europe managed to flatten the curve. As a result, the European economy has been on the mend since June, with all indicators pointing to a recovery. But a resurgence of new confirmed cases in August, most notably in Spain but also across all of Europe, is making companies, consumers, and travelers nervous. The Purchasing Managers Index, a key leading indicator of economic activity, dropped in August after a strong burst in July. The decline in the Purchasing Managers Index in European countries in response to the spike in cases underscores the fragility of economic recovery in the age of COVID-19.

But not all is doom and gloom. One significant positive development has been the marked improvement in financial conditions in emerging East Asia since late March, in line with a broader improvement of global financial conditions. This marks a welcome turnaround from early March when the region showed signs of financial stress. For instance, the region's major equity markets have rallied since April, and risk premia have declined although they remain above pre-COVID-19 levels. Furthermore, capital flows have remained relatively resilient, and emerging East Asia's currencies have strengthened against the US dollar since May. As noted earlier, there have been some positive developments on the vaccine front too. A safe, affordable, and effective COVID-19 vaccine would be a game changer that would drastically lift business and consumer confidence, and put the world economy back on track. In fact, seven potential vaccines are already in Phase 3 clinical trials, which involve administering the vaccine to thousands of people to test for safety and effectiveness. Phase 3 is the phase immediately preceding regulatory approval. While these developments are clearly promising, given the lengthy process of vaccine development and the intractable nature of COVID-19, it is unlikely that we will see a working vaccine available for widespread distribution by the end of 2020.

While major new waves of COVID-19 and the uncertainty surrounding the pandemic is the overriding downside risk facing the world and emerging East Asia, there are a number of other risks as well. For example, the pandemic has hit the poor and vulnerable disproportionately hard. In the absence of adequate relief, their smoldering discontent may morph into widespread social unrest, as it has in the US. A more immediate concern to emerging East Asia is the widening and deepening conflict between the PRC and the US, as evidenced by US sanctions against Chinese tech companies TikTok; WeChat; and, most significantly, Huawei. Other economies in the region depend heavily on trade with the two economic giants, so the conflict places them in a difficult position. On the other hand, any improvement in PRC–US links would be welcome news for the rest of emerging East Asia. While these additional factors matter for the region's economic prospects, they pale in comparison to the impact of COVID-19's trajectory.

Bond Market Developments in the Second Quarter of 2020

Size and Composition

The outstanding amount of local currency bonds in emerging East Asia climbed to USD17.2 trillion at the end of June.

Emerging East Asia's local currency (LCY) bond market expanded in the second quarter (Q2) of 2020 to reach a size of USD17.2 trillion at the end of June.[3] The region's bond market growth quickened to 5.0% quarter-on-quarter (q-o-q) in Q2 2020 from 4.2% q-o-q in the first quarter (Q1) (**Figure 1a**). The expansion was bolstered primarily by increased issuance of government bonds as authorities raised funds to finance policies designed to combat the effects of the global economic contraction brought about by the coronavirus disease (COVID-19).

Except for Viet Nam, all of the region's bond markets posted positive q-o-q growth in Q2 2020. Indonesia, the People's Republic of China (PRC), and the Philippines posted the fastest growth rates. Compared with Q1 2020, the q-o-q growth rate accelerated in six of the region's nine bond markets: the PRC; Hong Kong, China; Indonesia; the Republic of Korea; Singapore; and Thailand.

On a year-on-year (y-o-y) basis, emerging East Asia's LCY bond market grew at a faster pace of 15.5% in Q2 2020 versus 14.0% in Q1 2020 (**Figure 1b**). Except for Hong Kong, China, all markets in the region registered positive y-o-y growth in Q2 2020, led by the PRC and Indonesia. The LCY bond markets of the PRC, Indonesia, the Republic of Korea, the Philippines, and Singapore

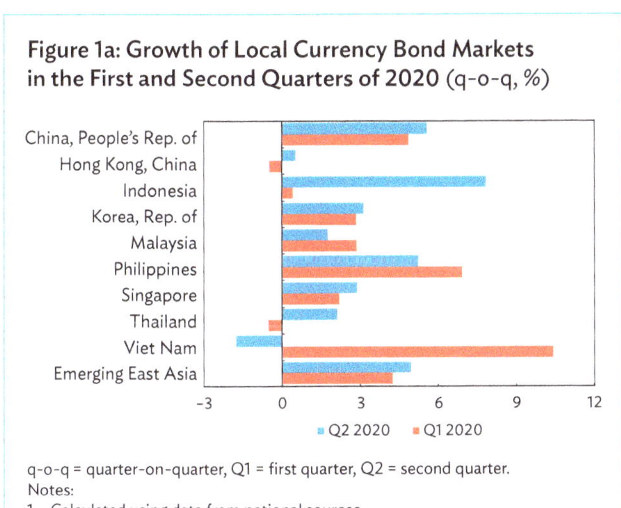

Figure 1a: Growth of Local Currency Bond Markets in the First and Second Quarters of 2020 (q-o-q, %)

q-o-q = quarter-on-quarter, Q1 = first quarter, Q2 = second quarter.
Notes:
1. Calculated using data from national sources.
2. Growth rates are calculated from local currency base and do not include currency effects.
3. Emerging East Asia growth figures are based on 30 June 2020 currency exchange rates and do not include currency effects.
4. For Singapore, corporate bonds outstanding are based on *AsianBondsOnline* estimates.
Sources: People's Republic of China (CEIC); Hong Kong, China (Hong Kong Monetary Authority); Indonesia (Bank Indonesia; Directorate General of Budget Financing and Risk Management, Ministry of Finance; and Indonesia Stock Exchange); Republic of Korea (*EDAILY BondWeb* and The Bank of Korea); Malaysia (Bank Negara Malaysia); Philippines (Bureau of the Treasury and Bloomberg LP); Singapore (Monetary Authority of Singapore, Singapore Government Securities, and Bloomberg LP); Thailand (Bank of Thailand); and Viet Nam (Bloomberg LP and Vietnam Bond Market Association).

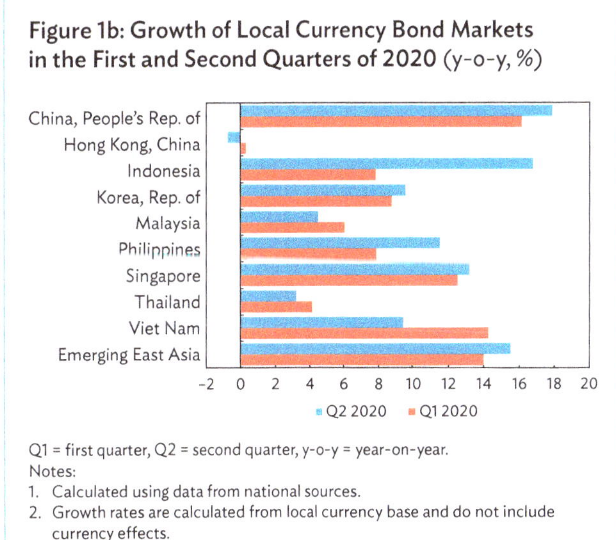

Figure 1b: Growth of Local Currency Bond Markets in the First and Second Quarters of 2020 (y-o-y, %)

Q1 = first quarter, Q2 = second quarter, y-o-y = year-on-year.
Notes:
1. Calculated using data from national sources.
2. Growth rates are calculated from local currency base and do not include currency effects.
3. Emerging East Asia growth figures are based on 30 June 2020 currency exchange rates and do not include currency effects.
4. For Singapore, corporate bonds outstanding are based on *AsianBondsOnline* estimates.
Sources: People's Republic of China (CEIC); Hong Kong, China (Hong Kong Monetary Authority); Indonesia (Bank Indonesia; Directorate General of Budget Financing and Risk Management, Ministry of Finance; and Indonesia Stock Exchange); Republic of Korea (*EDAILY BondWeb* and The Bank of Korea); Malaysia (Bank Negara Malaysia); Philippines (Bureau of the Treasury and Bloomberg LP); Singapore (Monetary Authority of Singapore, Singapore Government Securities, and Bloomberg LP); Thailand (Bank of Thailand); and Viet Nam (Bloomberg LP and Vietnam Bond Market Association).

---

[3] Emerging East Asia comprises the People's Republic of China; Hong Kong, China; Indonesia; the Republic of Korea; Malaysia; the Philippines; Singapore; Thailand; and Viet Nam.

posted higher y-o-y growth in Q2 2020 than in Q1 2020, while the region's remaining markets experienced a slowdown in y-o-y growth.

The PRC bond market remained the largest in the region with an outstanding bond stock of USD13.2 trillion at the end of June. The PRC's share of the regional bond market remained broadly stable at 76.6% in Q2 2020 compared with 76.2% in Q1 2020. Growth in the PRC's bond market accelerated to 5.6% q-o-q in Q2 2020 from 4.9% q-o-q in Q1 2020. The faster growth was primarily driven by strong issuance of Treasury and other government bonds, which rose 49.4% q-o-q in Q2 2020, as the PRC's central and local governments increased borrowing to support the economy amid the COVID-19 pandemic. Growth in the PRC's corporate bond stock eased to 5.9% q-o-q in Q2 2020 from 7.3% q-o-q in the previous quarter. On a y-o-y basis, the PRC's bond market expanded 17.9% y-o-y in Q2 2020, up from 16.1% y-o-y in Q1 2020.

The Republic of Korea remained home to the second-largest LCY bond market in the region, with its outstanding bonds reaching USD2.1 trillion at the end of June. Growth in the Republic of Korea's bond market rose to 3.1% q-o-q in Q2 2020 from 2.8% q-o-q in Q1 2020. Its share of the regional total slipped to 12.3% in Q2 2020 from 12.6% in the previous quarter. Government bonds outstanding increased 4.6% q-o-q in Q2 2020, up from 4.2% q-o-q growth in Q1 2020, due to strong issuance driven by the government's need to finance stimulus programs. The stock of corporate bonds rose 2.1% q-o-q in Q2 2020, up from 1.9% q-o-q growth in Q1 2020. On an annual basis, the Republic of Korea's bond market growth accelerated to 9.5% y-o-y in Q2 2020 from 8.7% y-o-y in Q1 2020.

The size of the LCY bond market in Hong Kong, China stood at USD292.6 billion at the end of June. The 0.5% q-o-q growth in Q2 2020 reversed the 0.5% q-o-q contraction in the previous quarter. The stock of government bonds dropped 1.1% q-o-q in Q2 2020, driven primarily by declines in Exchange Fund Bills and Exchange Fund Notes due to maturities and weaker issuance during the quarter. Growth in the corporate bond segment jumped to 2.3% q-o-q in Q2 2020 from 0.2% q-o-q in Q1 2020. Hong Kong, China's LCY bond market was the only market that posted

negative y-o-y growth in the region in Q2 2020, with the 0.8% contraction reversing the modest 0.3% gain posted in the previous quarter.

The aggregate amount of LCY bonds outstanding of the member economies of the Association of Southeast Asian Nations (ASEAN) was stable between Q1 2020 and Q2 2020 at USD1.6 trillion, even as growth accelerated to 3.2% q-o-q from 2.0% q-o-q.[4] The total government bond stock reached USD1.1 trillion at the end of June, while the corporate bond stock amounted to USD484.8 billion. Thailand, Malaysia, and Singapore remained the three largest bond markets in ASEAN.

Thailand's LCY bonds outstanding amounted to USD435.1 billion at the end of June on growth of 2.1% q-o-q and 3.2% y-o-y. The government bond stock rose 4.1% q-o-q in Q2 2020, reversing the 1.0% q-o-q contraction in Q1 2020. Growth stemmed mainly from the government's resumption of Treasury bill issuance, along with issuance of government savings bonds designed to finance programs to mitigate the negative economic impacts of COVID-19. The stock of corporate bonds contracted 2.6% q-o-q in Q2 2020, reversing the 0.8% q-o-q growth in the previous quarter. The decline was mainly driven by a 23.7% q-o-q drop in issuance, as weak investor confidence continued to curtail both the demand for and supply of corporate bonds.

The outstanding amount of Malaysia's LCY bonds totaled USD362.7 billion at the end of June, with growth slowing to 1.8% q-o-q in Q2 2020 from 2.9% q-o-q in Q1 2020. Growth in both the government and corporate bond segments slowed in Q2 2020 from the previous quarter. The stock of government bonds rose 3.2% q-o-q in Q2 2020, down from 3.9% q-o-q in Q1 2020. Growth in the corporate bond segment fell to 0.2% q-o-q from 1.7% q-o-q in Q1 2020. On a y-o-y basis, Malaysia's bond market growth also slowed to 4.5% in Q2 2020 from 6.0% in the previous quarter.

Malaysia is home to the largest *sukuk* (Islamic bond) market in emerging East Asia, with a total of USD227.5 billion of outstanding *sukuk* at the end of June. At the end of Q2 2020, about 47.5% of outstanding Malaysian government bonds were structured following Islamic principles, while 80.2% of corporate bonds were *sukuk*.

---

[4] LCY bond statistics for ASEAN include the markets of Indonesia, Malaysia, the Philippines, Singapore, Thailand, and Viet Nam.

Singapore's LCY bond market reached USD344.9 billion at the end of June on growth of 2.9% q-o-q and 13.2% y-o-y. The q-o-q growth in Q2 2020 was up from 2.2% q-o-q in the prior quarter due to increased government debt issuance to fund economic relief policies. Growth in the government bond segment rose to 4.4% q-o-q in Q2 2020 from 2.5% q-o-q in Q1 2020. In contrast, growth in the corporate bond segment weakened to 0.3% q-o-q in Q2 2020 from 1.7% q-o-q in the prior quarter.

The outstanding amount of Indonesia's LCY bonds reached USD251.3 billion at the end of June, with growth jumping to 7.8% q-o-q in Q2 2020 from 0.4% q-o-q in Q1 2020. The faster growth stemmed from the government bond segment, where growth quickened to 9.5% q-o-q in Q2 2020 from 0.6% q-o-q in Q1 2020, as the government accelerated issuance of debt to support economic relief efforts. Growth in the stock of outstanding corporate bonds continued to decline, with the contraction worsening to 3.0% q-o-q in Q2 2020 from 0.5% q-o-q in Q1 2020. Indonesia's bond market has been negatively affected by risk-off sentiment brought about by uncertainties related to COVID-19.

The Philippine LCY bond market reached a size of USD150.1 billion at the end of June, with overall growth easing to 5.2% q-o-q in Q2 2020 from 6.9% q-o-q in Q1 2020. Growth in the government bond segment slipped to 6.8% q-o-q in Q2 2020 from 7.5% q-o-q in the previous quarter. The corporate bond segment contracted 0.4% q-o-q in Q2 2020, reversing the 5.0% q-o-q gain posted in Q1 2020. On an annual basis, growth in the Philippine LCY bond market accelerated to 11.5% y-o-y in Q2 2020 from 7.9% y-o-y in Q1 2020.

Viet Nam's LCY bonds outstanding fell to USD58.2 billion at the end of June on a contraction of 1.7% q-o-q in Q2 2020, reversing the 10.4% q-o-q gain in Q1 2020. The decline stemmed from the government bond segment, which contracted 7.8% q-o-q in Q2 2020 following rapid growth of 10.5% in the prior quarter. In contrast, growth in the corporate bond segment jumped to 65.6% q-o-q in Q2 2020 from 10.2% q-o-q in Q1 2020, bolstered by strong issuance. On an annual basis, Viet Nam's LCY bond market expanded 9.4% y-o-y in Q2 2020, down from 14.2% y-o-y growth in Q1 2020.

At the end of June, government bonds continued to account for the majority of emerging East Asia's LCY bond stock, representing a 60.8% share. In nominal terms, the outstanding stock of government bonds in the region reached USD10.5 trillion at the end of Q2 2020 on growth of 5.2% q-o-q and 13.9% y-o-y (**Table 1**). The PRC and the Republic of Korea remained home to the two largest government bond markets in the region, accounting for a combined share of 87.9% of the regional total at the end of June.

ASEAN economies accounted for 10.7% of government bonds in emerging East Asia at the end of Q2 2020. Among ASEAN economies, Thailand had the most outstanding LCY government bonds at the end of June at USD314.8 billion. The next largest LCY government bond markets were those of Indonesia and Singapore with outstanding bonds totaling USD221.2 billion and USD219.4 billion, respectively. Malaysia followed with an LCY government bond stock of USD193.4 billion. The Philippines and Viet Nam continued to have the smallest LCY government bond markets in the region with bonds outstanding of USD118.5 billion and USD50.1 billion, respectively.

LCY corporate bonds outstanding in emerging East Asia amounted to USD6.7 trillion at the end of June. Growth in the region's aggregate corporate bonds outstanding moderated to 4.6% q-o-q in Q2 2020 from 5.7% q-o-q in Q1 2020. The slower growth was driven mostly by the PRC's weakening corporate bond segment. In addition, Indonesia, the Philippines, and Thailand posted negative q-o-q growth rates in their corporate bond segments in Q2 2020, while growth slowed considerably in Malaysia and Singapore. Overall, growth in the region's corporate bond segment during the review period was negatively affected by uncertainties surrounding the COVID-19 outbreak and investors' risk-off sentiment.

ASEAN economies accounted for 7.2% of emerging East Asia's LCY corporate bond market at the end of June. Within ASEAN, Malaysia had the largest LCY corporate bond market, followed by Singapore.

Emerging East Asia's total LCY bond market as a percentage of the region's gross domestic product (GDP) expanded to 91.6% at the end of June from 87.8% at the end of March and 81.5% at the end of June 2019 (**Table 2**). The GDP shares of both government and corporate bonds rose in Q2 2020 from the previous quarter. The government bonds-to-GDP share climbed to 55.7% from 53.2% during the review period, while

Table 1: Size and Composition of Local Currency Bond Markets

| | Q2 2019 | | Q1 2020 | | Q2 2020 | | Growth Rate (LCY-base %) | | | | Growth Rate (USD-base %) | | | |
| | Amount (USD billion) | % share | Amount (USD billion) | % share | Amount (USD billion) | % share | Q2 2019 | | Q2 2020 | | Q2 2019 | | Q2 2020 | |
							q-o-q	y-o-y	q-o-q	y-o-y	q-o-q	y-o-y	q-o-q	y-o-y
China, People's Rep. of														
Total	11,512	100.0	12,464	100.0	13,189	100.0	4.0	16.7	5.6	17.9	1.7	12.6	5.8	14.6
Government	7,447	64.7	7,886	63.3	8,332	63.2	4.2	15.9	5.4	15.1	1.9	11.8	5.6	11.9
Corporate	4,065	35.3	4,577	36.7	4,857	36.8	3.6	18.3	5.9	22.9	1.2	14.0	6.1	19.5
Hong Kong, China														
Total	293	100.0	291	100.0	293	100.0	1.6	5.1	0.5	(0.8)	2.1	5.5	0.5	(0.002)
Government	149	50.9	151	51.9	149	51.0	0.2	0.5	(1.1)	(0.7)	0.7	0.9	(1.1)	0.1
Corporate	144	49.1	140	48.1	143	49.0	3.1	10.3	2.3	(0.9)	3.6	10.8	2.3	(0.1)
Indonesia														
Total	217	100.0	204	100.0	251	100.0	(0.5)	17.6	7.8	16.8	0.4	19.3	23.3	15.6
Government	188	86.4	177	86.7	221	88.0	(0.3)	20.1	9.5	19.0	0.6	21.8	25.2	17.8
Corporate	30	13.6	27	13.3	30	12.0	(1.6)	3.7	(3.0)	3.0	(0.8)	5.2	10.9	2.0
Korea, Rep. of														
Total	2,019	100.0	2,032	100.0	2,123	100.0	2.4	5.0	3.1	9.5	0.6	1.3	4.5	5.2
Government	820	40.6	814	40.1	863	40.7	1.7	1.0	4.6	9.7	(0.1)	(2.5)	6.0	5.3
Corporate	1,200	59.4	1,218	59.9	1,260	59.3	2.9	7.9	2.1	9.4	1.1	4.2	3.5	5.0
Malaysia														
Total	360	100.0	354	100.0	363	100.0	3.3	8.7	1.8	4.5	2.0	6.2	2.6	0.7
Government	189	52.4	186	52.6	193	53.3	1.8	7.8	3.2	6.4	0.5	5.4	4.0	2.6
Corporate	172	47.6	168	47.4	169	46.7	5.0	9.7	0.2	2.4	3.7	7.2	1.0	(1.3)
Philippines														
Total	131	100.0	140	100.0	150	100.0	1.8	16.8	5.2	11.5	4.3	21.6	7.1	14.8
Government	103	78.9	109	77.8	119	79.0	1.7	15.2	6.8	11.6	4.2	19.9	8.7	14.9
Corporate	28	21.1	31	22.2	32	21.0	2.3	23.3	(0.4)	11.0	4.8	28.3	1.4	14.3
Singapore														
Total	314	100.0	329	100.0	345	100.0	2.3	8.8	2.9	13.2	2.5	9.5	5.0	9.9
Government	194	61.8	206	62.7	219	63.6	2.7	10.7	4.4	16.5	2.9	11.4	6.5	13.2
Corporate	120	38.2	123	37.3	126	36.4	1.7	5.8	0.3	7.7	1.9	6.6	2.4	4.6
Thailand														
Total	425	100.0	402	100.0	435	100.0	3.1	9.4	2.1	3.2	38.8	52.9	8.2	2.4
Government	304	71.5	286	71.0	315	72.4	2.3	7.9	4.1	4.4	34.4	46.0	10.2	3.6
Corporate	121	28.5	117	29.0	120	27.6	5.1	13.2	(2.6)	(0.03)	51.1	73.4	3.2	(0.8)
Viet Nam														
Total	53	100.0	58	100.0	58	100.0	2.6	4.1	(1.7)	9.4	2.1	2.5	0.1	9.9
Government	48	91.4	53	91.8	50	86.2	3.2	2.9	(7.8)	3.1	2.7	1.3	(6.0)	3.6
Corporate	5	8.6	5	8.2	8	13.8	(3.4)	18.7	65.6	76.0	(3.9)	16.8	68.8	76.8
Emerging East Asia														
Total	15,323	100.0	16,273	100.0	17,207	100.0	3.6	14.2	5.0	15.5	2.3	11.5	5.7	12.3
Government	9,441	61.6	9,868	60.6	10,462	60.8	3.7	13.6	5.2	13.9	2.5	11.1	6.0	10.8
Corporate	5,883	38.4	6,405	39.4	6,746	39.2	3.4	15.1	4.6	18.1	2.1	12.2	5.3	14.7
Japan														
Total	10,948	100.0	11,079	100.0	11,082	100.0	0.5	2.1	0.4	1.3	3.3	4.8	0.02	1.2
Government	10,191	93.1	10,282	92.8	10,288	92.8	0.3	1.8	0.4	1.0	3.1	4.5	0.1	0.9
Corporate	757	6.9	797	7.2	794	7.2	2.8	6.7	(0.1)	4.9	5.6	9.6	(0.4)	4.9

( ) = negative, LCY = local currency, q-o-q = quarter-on-quarter, Q1 = first quarter, Q2 = second quarter, USD = United States dollar, y-o-y = year-on-year.
Notes:
1. For Singapore, corporate bonds outstanding are based on *AsianBondsOnline* estimates.
2. Corporate bonds include issues by financial institutions.
3. Bloomberg LP end-of-period LCY–USD rates are used.
4. For LCY base, emerging East Asia growth figures are based on 30 June 2020 currency exchange rates and do not include currency effects.
5. Emerging East Asia comprises the People's Republic of China; Hong Kong, China; Indonesia; the Republic of Korea; Malaysia; the Philippines; Singapore; Thailand; and Viet Nam.
Sources: People's Republic of China (CEIC); Hong Kong, China (Hong Kong Monetary Authority); Indonesia (Bank Indonesia; Directorate General of Budget Financing and Risk Management, Ministry of Finance; and Indonesia Stock Exchange); Republic of Korea (*EDAILY BondWeb* and The Bank of Korea); Malaysia (Bank Negara Malaysia); Philippines (Bureau of the Treasury and Bloomberg LP); Singapore (Monetary Authority of Singapore, Singapore Government Securities, and Bloomberg LP); Thailand (Bank of Thailand); Viet Nam (Bloomberg LP and Vietnam Bond Market Association); and Japan (Japan Securities Dealers Association).

the corporate bonds-to-GDP share increased to 35.9% from 34.6%. The higher shares were due to accelerated increases in LCY bonds outstanding in Q2 2020, while at the same time the region's GDP growth moderated as most economies contracted. The expansion in the region's bond market during the quarter can be traced to the higher issuance volumes needed to fund government stimulus measures, and also to governments and corporates taking advantage of the high level of global liquidity and the region's low interest rates.

As a share of GDP, the bond markets of the Republic of Korea and Malaysia were the largest at the end of Q2 2020, with both exceeding 100%. Singapore nearly breached this level with a bonds-to-GDP share of 99.7%. Indonesia's bonds-to-GDP share, which in Q1 2020 was the region's smallest, inched up to 22.8% at the end of June, leaving Viet Nam with the region's smallest share at 22.0%. All emerging East Asian economies saw increases in their share of bonds-to-GDP between Q1 2020 and Q2 2020 except for Viet Nam.

By segment, Singapore had the largest government bonds-to-GDP share in the region at the end of June at 63.4%, while Viet Nam had the smallest at 19.0%. The Republic of Korea and Indonesia continued to have the largest and smallest corporate bonds-to-GDP shares at 82.3% and 2.7%, respectively.

Foreign Investor Holdings

The foreign holdings share in local currency government bonds continued to decline in most emerging East Asian economies in Q2 2020.

Foreign holdings of LCY government bonds in emerging East Asia posted quarterly declines in Q2 2020 in all economies except for the PRC and Malaysia (**Figure 2**). Weak economic performances, protracted recoveries, and uncertainty caused by the COVID-19 pandemic were the key factors that drove risk aversion among foreign investors, as evidenced by foreign ownership remaining at low levels or declining in most economies in the region.

The PRC's foreign holdings share for government bonds increased to 9.1% at the end of June from 8.7% at the end of March. The growth in foreign ownership in Q2 2020 is associated with relatively higher returns in the PRC bond market compared with large economies that are

Table 2: Size and Composition of Local Currency Bond Markets (% of GDP)

	Q2 2019	Q1 2020	Q2 2020
China, People's Rep. of			
Total	82.9	90.1	94.4
Government	53.6	57.0	59.7
Corporate	29.3	33.1	34.8
Hong Kong, China			
Total	79.4	80.0	82.1
Government	40.4	41.5	41.8
Corporate	38.9	38.5	40.2
Indonesia			
Total	19.9	20.8	22.8
Government	17.2	18.0	20.1
Corporate	2.7	2.8	2.7
Korea, Rep. of			
Total	127.5	133.5	138.6
Government	51.7	53.5	56.3
Corporate	75.7	80.0	82.3
Malaysia			
Total	106.8	107.3	114.0
Government	55.9	56.4	60.8
Corporate	50.9	50.9	53.2
Philippines			
Total	35.5	36.4	39.7
Government	28.0	28.3	31.3
Corporate	7.5	8.1	8.4
Singapore			
Total	83.3	92.6	99.7
Government	51.4	58.0	63.4
Corporate	31.8	34.5	36.3
Thailand			
Total	78.1	78.3	82.9
Government	55.9	55.6	60.0
Corporate	22.3	22.7	22.9
Viet Nam			
Total	21.4	22.5	22.0
Government	19.6	20.6	19.0
Corporate	1.8	1.8	3.0
Emerging East Asia			
Total	81.5	87.8	91.6
Government	50.2	53.2	55.7
Corporate	31.3	34.6	35.9
Japan			
Total	214.7	215.7	221.3
Government	199.9	200.1	205.4
Corporate	14.8	15.5	15.9

GDP = gross domestic product, Q1 = first quarter, Q2 = second quarter.
Notes:
1. Data for GDP are from CEIC.
2. For Singapore, corporate bonds outstanding are based on *AsianBondsOnline* estimates.
Sources: People's Republic of China (CEIC); Hong Kong, China (Hong Kong Monetary Authority); Indonesia (Bank Indonesia; Directorate General of Budget Financing and Risk Management, Ministry of Finance; and Indonesia Stock Exchange); Republic of Korea (*EDAILY BondWeb* and The Bank of Korea); Malaysia (Bank Negara Malaysia); Philippines (Bureau of the Treasury and Bloomberg LP); Singapore (Monetary Authority of Singapore, Singapore Government Securities, and Bloomberg LP); Thailand (Bank of Thailand); Viet Nam (Bloomberg LP and Vietnam Bond Market Association); and Japan (Japan Securities Dealers Association).

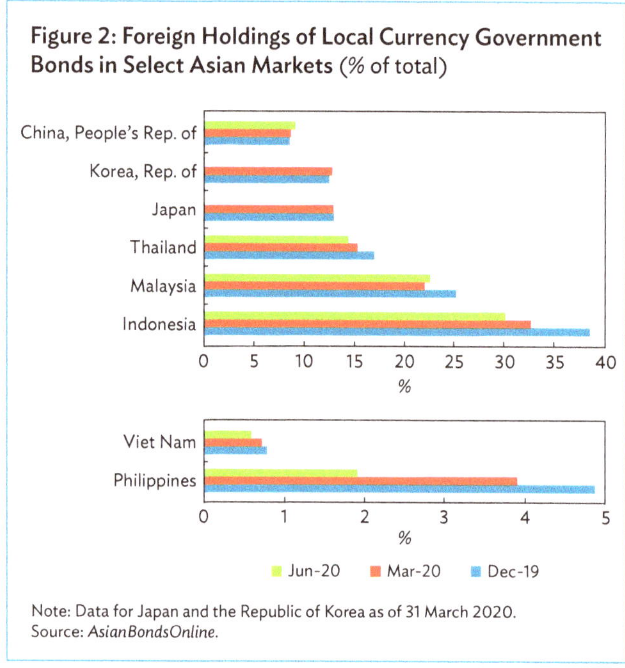

Figure 2: Foreign Holdings of Local Currency Government Bonds in Select Asian Markets (% of total)

Note: Data for Japan and the Republic of Korea as of 31 March 2020.
Source: *AsianBondsOnline*.

considered safe havens like the United States (US) and European markets. The attractiveness of the PRC's bond market was also due to the economy's quick recovery from the adverse impact of COVID-19, as evidenced by its GDP growth of 3.2% q-o-q growth in Q2 2020 while most economies in the region were contracting. Furthermore, the continuation of policies to open up the PRC's bond market to overseas investors have made it easier to attract foreign funds.

In Malaysia, the share of government bonds held by foreign investors rebounded in Q2 2020, albeit marginally, rising to 22.7% at the end of June from 22.2% at the end of March. Ample global liquidity accompanied by Malaysia's subdued inflation and the resumption of economic activities amid an easing of the lockdown may have encouraged inflows of foreign funds into the LCY government bond market. Expectations that FTSE Russell would retain Malaysia in the World Government Bond Index, resulting from Bank Negara Malaysia's effort to improve onshore bond liquidity, may have also fueled buying interest in Malaysian government bonds.

Risk-off sentiment among foreign investors was apparent in the Indonesian and Philippine markets in Q2 2020. Indonesia's foreign holdings remained on a downtrend, with the share falling to 30.2% at the end of June, the lowest level in 8 years. Deterred by pandemic risk, foreign investors appeared wary of

holding Indonesian government bonds as evidenced by relatively small foreign fund inflows amid an expansion of the LCY government bond market. This resulted in Indonesia posting the largest drop in its foreign holdings share in the region in Q2 2020 with a decline of 2.5 percentage points. However, Indonesia still retained the highest foreign holdings share in the region at the end of June.

Foreign ownership of government bonds in the Philippines dropped to its lowest level since such data have been available, falling to 1.9% at the end of June. The share of foreign holdings in the Philippine bond market posted a quarterly decline of 2.0 percentage points, making it the largest drop in the region in Q2 2020 next to Indonesia. Investors reduced their risk exposure during the quarter, leading to continued fund outflows against the backdrop of rising uncertainty from the pandemic and a low-interest-rate environment as the Bangko Sentral ng Pilipinas unexpectedly cut the policy rate in June by 50 basis points (bps).

Thailand and Viet Nam also saw declining foreign holdings shares in their respective government bond markets, albeit to a lesser extent than Indonesia and the Philippines. The foreign holdings share in Thailand fell to 14.4% at the end of June from 15.3% at the end of March on the back of a frail economic outlook and continued monetary policy easing. In May, the Bank of Thailand reduced its benchmark policy rate by 25 bps to a record low of 0.75%.

In Viet Nam, despite being successful in containing the spread of COVID-19, the foreign ownership share declined marginally to 0.6% at the end of June from 0.7% in the previous quarter. Viet Nam has the smallest foreign holdings share in the region.

The Republic of Korea saw its share of foreign holdings increase for the fourth consecutive quarter in Q1 2020. At the end of March, the foreign holdings share reached 12.8%, up from 12.5% at the end of December. One of the factors driving foreign investor interest in the Republic of Korea's LCY bond market is the successful preemptive measures taken by the government to contain COVID-19, which lessened the adverse impact on the economy. Better yields, fiscal soundness, and proceeds from currency hedges are also underlying factors that make the Republics of Korea's government bond market attractive to foreign investors.

Foreign Bond Flows

Foreign funds returned to emerging East Asian bond markets as most economies in the region posted net inflows from April to July.

The inflow of offshore funds to emerging East Asia's government bond markets signaled the return of confidence in the region, albeit in calculated manner (**Figure 3**). The positive flows were spurred by relatively higher yields in the region and abundant global liquidity as major central banks deployed stimulus measures. The economies that experienced outflows early in the review period mostly saw a recovery starting in May. In June, all emerging East Asian economies posted net inflows except for the Philippines, with the region's net inflows amounting to USD12.8 billion, the highest level of monthly foreign buying in 2020 through the first 7 months of the year. However, even with the return of foreign funds, the shares of foreign holdings remain low. Concerns of a possible

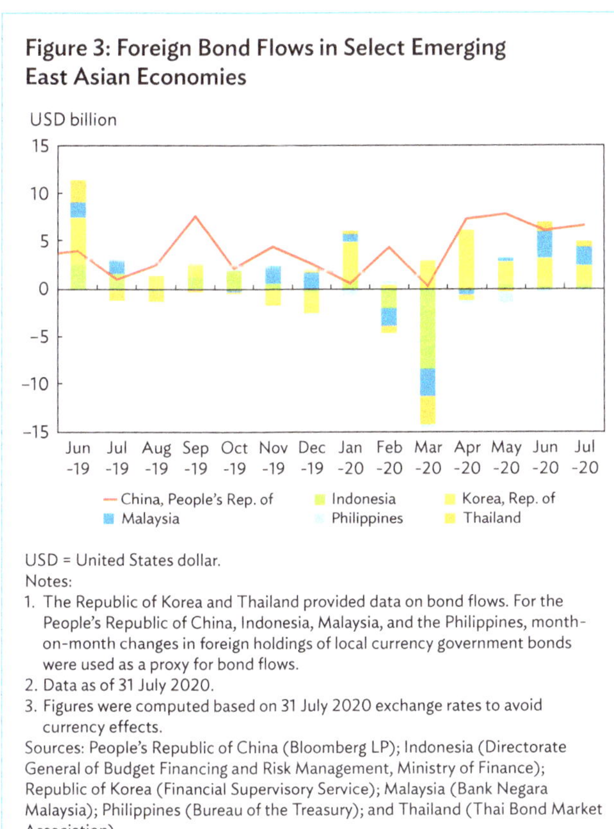

Figure 3: Foreign Bond Flows in Select Emerging East Asian Economies

USD = United States dollar.
Notes:
1. The Republic of Korea and Thailand provided data on bond flows. For the People's Republic of China, Indonesia, Malaysia, and the Philippines, month-on-month changes in foreign holdings of local currency government bonds were used as a proxy for bond flows.
2. Data as of 31 July 2020.
3. Figures were computed based on 31 July 2020 exchange rates to avoid currency effects.
Sources: People's Republic of China (Bloomberg LP); Indonesia (Directorate General of Budget Financing and Risk Management, Ministry of Finance); Republic of Korea (Financial Supervisory Service); Malaysia (Bank Negara Malaysia); Philippines (Bureau of the Treasury); and Thailand (Thai Bond Market Association).

COVID-19 recurrence and a gloomy economic outlook may have capped foreign fund flows into the region.

The PRC and the Republic of Korea have experienced positive monthly net inflows since the start of the year. From April to July, the PRC had total net inflows of USD28.0 billion, with the highest monthly total posted in May amounting to USD7.9 billion. In the same period, the Republic of Korea posted a total of USD13.3 billion of net inflows, with the highest monthly total in April at USD6.2 billion. The attractiveness of Chinese and Korean bonds is underpinned by sound economic fundamentals and the success of preemptive measures to avert the negative impact of COVID-19.

Malaysia experienced net foreign buying of government bonds amounting to USD4.6 billion in the April–July period. While net outflows of USD0.5 billion were recorded in April, foreign bond buying rebounded in May and has been positive since then, with net inflows peaking in June. Malaysia's low inflation attracted foreign interest despite the downgrade in its economic and sovereign rating outlooks.

Net inflows to Indonesia totaled USD1.3 billion in the April–July period, partially dragged down by the USD0.1 billion of net outflows in April. Monthly net inflows during the review period peaked at USD0.6 billion in July. While foreign funds returned to the Indonesian bond market during the review period, this came with investor cautiousness, resulting in smaller inflows that failed to offset the large outflows earlier in the year. Thus, the foreign holdings share remained below pre-COVID-19 levels.

In Thailand, foreign funds returned to the bond market in June after 4 months of sell-offs, with net inflows of USD1.0 billion, the highest monthly inflow through the first 7 months of the year. From April to July, Thailand recorded net inflows of USD0.8 billion.

In contrast to the trend in the region, the Philippines incurred net outflows in the April–July period totaling USD2.3 billion. The retreat of foreign funds was due to heightened risk aversion caused by a weak economic performance and slow progress in the containment of COVID-19.

LCY Bond Issuance

LCY bond issuance in emerging East Asia reached USD2 trillion in Q2 2020, driven by government efforts to fund stimulus programs.

LCY bond markets in emerging East Asia saw a surge in issuance in Q2 2020, driven mostly by the government bond segment. The region's aggregate issuance volume reached USD2.0 trillion in Q2 2020, with growth accelerating to 21.3% q-o-q from 19.5% q-o-q in the preceding quarter (**Table 3**). Driving much of the growth were Treasury instruments and other government bonds, given the active issuance by governments seeking to fund large-scale stimulus programs and recovery efforts amid the economic fallout from the COVID-19 outbreak. The corporate bond segment also witnessed increased issuance during the quarter, albeit to a lesser extent. In contrast, issuance by central banks declined compared with the previous quarter. All emerging East Asian markets posted higher bond sales in Q2 2020 compared with Q1 2020 except for the Philippines and Viet Nam, both of which recorded contractions in overall issuance volumes.

On a y-o-y basis, emerging East Asia's issuance growth accelerated to 32.0% in Q2 2020 from 21.9% in Q1 2020, with six out of nine markets in the region posting y-o-y increases in bond issuance in Q2 2020. The markets of Malaysia, Thailand, and Viet Nam recorded declines in their respective Q2 2020 issuance compared with Q2 2019.

Of the region's aggregate issuance volume during Q2 2020, 58.7% was accounted for by government bonds, comprising both Treasury and other government bonds and central bank instruments. Government bond issuance in Q2 2020 tallied USD1,199.4 billion, up 29.1% q-o-q and 27.8% y-o-y. Nearly three-quarters of this amount was accounted for by Treasuries and other government bonds. The bond markets of Indonesia, Singapore, and Thailand saw faster q-o-q increases in government bond issuance in Q2 2020 compared with Q1 2020. Indonesia and Thailand accelerated their issuance programs to fund higher fiscal spending. The q-o-q government bond issuance growth in the PRC, the Republic of Korea, and Malaysia moderated from Q1 2020 but remained positive. A q-o-q decline in government bond issuance was noted in Hong Kong, China; the Philippines; and Viet Nam.

Central bank issuance in the region slipped to USD310.1 billion in Q2 2020, down 2.3% q-o-q and 6.4% y-o-y. Most central banks had less issuance during the quarter, particularly Hong Kong, China; Indonesia; Malaysia; and Thailand. Singapore maintained its issuance pace for Monetary Authority of Singapore bills, while Viet Nam halted its central bank issuance during the quarter.

Corporate bond issuance from emerging East Asia tallied USD845.2 billion in Q2 2020, with growth picking up to 11.7% q-o-q and 38.5% y-o-y from 6.8% q-o-q and 36.1% y-o-y, respectively, in the preceding quarter. While corporate bond issuance in five markets in the region slowed, overall growth was buoyed by a higher volume of corporate debt from the PRC.

Nearly 70% of emerging East Asia's LCY bond issuance in Q2 2020 was accounted for by the PRC. New bond sales during the quarter totaled USD1,414.2 billion for a 31.2% q-o-q hike. Growth expanded at the same pace as in the prior quarter. Both government and corporate bonds contributed to the overall growth in LCY bond issuance during the quarter. While growth in government bond issuance moderated from 68.2% q-o-q in Q1 2020 to 49.4% q-o-q in Q2 2020, issuance was still substantial at USD736.1 billion. During the quarter, Treasury bond issuance more than doubled in Q2 2020 as the government had to fund a wider fiscal deficit. Issuance of local government bonds also grew but at a slower pace as the original quota for issuance of such bonds had largely been met by April. While an additional CNY1.0 trillion was added to the special local government bond quota by the State Council in May, it had to be tapped by the end of the same month. Corporate bond issuance during the quarter was quite active due to an easing of regulations that allowed firms to issue bonds for debt repayment in February. Total corporate bond issuance reached USD678.1 billion, with growth rising to 15.9% in Q2 2020 from 10.7% q-o-q in the preceding quarter. On an annual basis, LCY bond issuance surged to 48.2% y-o-y in Q2 2020 from 30.6% y-o-y in the prior quarter.

LCY bond issuance in the Republic of Korea totaled USD208.0 billion in Q2 2020, with q-o-q growth moderating to 4.0% from 6.1% in the prior quarter. Government bond issuance grew 15.4% q-o-q, decelerating from a 45.4% q-o-q hike in Q1 2020, due largely to the government's frontloading policy.

Table 3: Local-Currency–Denominated Bond Issuance (gross)

| | Q2 2019 | | Q1 2020 | | Q2 2020 | | Growth Rate (LCY-base %) | | Growth Rate (USD-base %) | |
| | | | | | | | Q2 2020 | | Q2 2020 | |
	Amount (USD billion)	% share	Amount (USD billion)	% share	Amount (USD billion)	% share	q-o-q	y-o-y	q-o-q	y-o-y
China, People's Rep. of										
Total	982	100.0	1,075	100.0	1,414	100.0	31.2	48.2	31.5	44.0
Government	540	54.9	491	45.7	736	52.1	49.4	40.3	49.8	36.4
Central Bank	0	0.0	0	0.0	0	0.0	–	–	–	–
Treasury and Other Govt.	540	54.9	491	45.7	736	52.1	49.4	40.3	49.8	36.4
Corporate	442	45.1	584	54.3	678	47.9	15.9	57.7	16.2	53.3
Hong Kong, China										
Total	133	100.0	136	100.0	137	100.0	1.4	2.2	1.4	3.0
Government	107	80.1	108	79.7	107	78.0	(0.8)	(0.4)	(0.8)	0.3
Central Bank	106	79.3	108	79.4	106	77.2	(1.5)	(0.5)	(1.4)	0.3
Treasury and Other Govt.	1	0.8	0.3	0.2	1	0.8	228.0	2.5	228.0	3.3
Corporate	27	19.9	28	20.3	30	22.0	9.8	13.0	9.8	13.9
Indonesia										
Total	17	100.0	19	100.0	31	100.0	44.1	88.0	64.8	86.2
Government	15	87.9	18	93.9	31	98.1	50.5	109.8	72.1	107.7
Central Bank	4	24.8	7	37.0	8	25.2	(1.8)	91.6	12.3	89.7
Treasury and Other Govt.	11	63.2	11	56.9	23	72.9	84.5	116.9	111.0	114.8
Corporate	2	12.1	1	6.1	1	1.9	(54.6)	(70.2)	(48.1)	(70.5)
Korea, Rep. of										
Total	187	100.0	197	100.0	208	100.0	4.0	16.2	5.4	11.5
Government	70	37.7	82	41.8	96	46.4	15.4	42.7	16.9	37.0
Central Bank	32	17.1	30	15.2	33	16.0	9.4	8.8	10.8	4.4
Treasury and Other Govt.	38	20.6	52	26.6	63	30.3	18.9	70.9	20.4	64.1
Corporate	116	62.3	115	58.2	112	53.6	(4.1)	0.1	(2.9)	(3.9)
Malaysia										
Total	27	100.0	21	100.0	22	100.0	1.7	(16.7)	2.6	(19.7)
Government	10	36.4	12	56.2	14	63.7	15.4	45.6	16.3	40.4
Central Bank	2	7.2	2	11.0	0.2	1.1	(90.2)	(87.8)	(90.1)	(88.2)
Treasury and Other Govt.	8	29.2	10	45.1	14	62.6	41.1	78.8	42.3	72.4
Corporate	17	63.6	9	43.8	8	36.3	(15.7)	(52.4)	(15.0)	(54.1)
Philippines										
Total	9	100.0	17	100.0	14	100.0	(19.6)	58.6	(18.2)	63.3
Government	6	71.2	14	83.0	13	96.0	(6.9)	114.0	(5.3)	120.3
Central Bank	0	0.0	0	0.0	0	0.0	–	–	–	–
Treasury and Other Govt.	6	71.2	14	83.0	13	96.0	(6.9)	114.0	(5.3)	120.3
Corporate	2	28.8	3	17.0	1	4.0	(81.3)	(78.2)	(81.0)	(77.6)
Singapore										
Total	116	100.0	125	100.0	133	100.0	4.1	17.5	6.2	14.1
Government	113	96.7	122	97.7	128	96.7	3.0	17.5	5.1	14.1
Central Bank	104	89.7	101	80.9	103	77.7	0.0	1.8	2.0	(1.2)
Treasury and Other Govt.	8	7.0	21	16.9	25	19.0	17.3	220.0	19.7	210.7
Corporate	4	3.3	3	2.3	4	3.3	50.8	17.0	53.8	13.5
Thailand										
Total	93	100.0	72	100.0	79	100.0	3.1	(14.1)	9.2	(14.8)
Government	76	81.7	62	85.9	71	89.6	7.5	(5.8)	13.9	(6.5)
Central Bank	65	70.4	56	77.8	59	75.2	(0.4)	(8.3)	5.5	(9.0)
Treasury and Other Govt.	10	11.3	6	8.1	11	14.4	83.8	9.6	94.8	8.8
Corporate	17	18.3	10	14.1	8	10.4	(23.7)	(51.1)	(19.1)	(51.5)

continued on next page

Table 3 *continued*

| | Q2 2019 | | Q1 2020 | | Q2 2020 | | Growth Rate (LCY-base %) | | Growth Rate (USD-base %) | |
| | | | | | | | Q2 2020 | | Q2 2020 | |
	Amount (USD billion)	% share	Amount (USD billion)	% share	Amount (USD billion)	% share	q-o-q	y-o-y	q-o-q	y-o-y
Viet Nam										
Total	23	100.0	8	100.0	6	100.0	(25.2)	(75.0)	(23.8)	(74.9)
Government	23	100.0	7	93.3	2	39.6	(68.3)	(90.1)	(67.7)	(90.1)
Central Bank	22	93.0	6	75.0	0	0.0	(100.0)	(100.0)	(100.0)	(100.0)
Treasury and Other Govt.	2	7.0	1	18.3	2	39.6	61.5	40.6	64.5	41.2
Corporate	0	0.0	1	6.7	4	60.4	578.2	–	591.1	–
Emerging East Asia										
Total	1,587	100.0	1,671	100.0	2,045	100.0	21.3	32.0	22.4	28.8
Government	959	60.4	918	54.9	1,199	58.7	29.1	27.8	30.7	25.0
Central Bank	335	21.1	310	18.6	310	15.2	(2.3)	(6.4)	(0.1)	(7.5)
Treasury and Other Govt.	624	39.3	607	36.3	889	43.5	45.3	46.5	46.4	42.5
Corporate	628	39.6	753	45.1	845	41.3	11.7	38.5	12.2	34.6
Japan										
Total	398	100.0	383	100.0	406	100.0	6.4	2.0	6.0	1.9
Government	355	89.2	356	92.9	370	91.1	4.3	4.2	4.0	4.1
Central Bank	0	0.0	0	0.0	20	5.0	–	–	–	–
Treasury and Other Govt.	355	89.2	356	92.9	350	86.1	(1.4)	(1.6)	(1.7)	(1.7)
Corporate	43	10.8	27	7.1	36	8.9	33.0	(16.1)	32.5	(16.1)

( ) = negative, – = not applicable, LCY = local currency, q-o-q = quarter-on-quarter, Q1 = first quarter, Q2 = second quarter, USD = United States dollar, y-o-y = year-on-year.
Notes:
1. Corporate bonds include issues by financial institutions.
2. Bloomberg LP end-of-period LCY–USD rates are used.
3. For LCY base, emerging East Asia growth figures are based on 30 June 2020 currency exchange rates and do not include currency effects.
Sources: People's Republic of China (CEIC); Hong Kong, China (Hong Kong Monetary Authority); Indonesia (Bank Indonesia; Directorate General of Budget Financing and Risk Management, Ministry of Finance; and Indonesia Stock Exchange); Republic of Korea (*EDAILY BondWeb* and The Bank of Korea); Malaysia (Bank Negara Malaysia); Philippines (Bureau of the Treasury and Bloomberg LP); Singapore (Singapore Government Securities and Bloomberg LP); Thailand (Bank of Thailand and ThaiBMA); Viet Nam (Bloomberg LP and Vietnam Bond Market Association); and Japan (Japan Securities Dealers Association).

In addition, increased borrowing by the government was necessitated to fund the supplemental budgets designed to support the economy amid the outbreak of COVID-19. Central bank issuance also grew at a slower pace, rising 9.4% q-o-q in Q2 2020 versus 10.7% q-o-q in Q1 2020. Corporate bond issuance contracted for the second consecutive quarter in Q2 2020, falling 4.1% q-o-q after declining 11.1% q-o-q in the previous quarter. On a y-o-y basis, bond issuance grew 16.2% in Q2 2020, down from 30.0% in Q1 2020.

Total bonds sales in Hong Kong, China hit USD137.5 billion in Q2 2020, with overall growth easing to 1.4% q-o-q from 5.0% q-o-q in the prior quarter. Government bond issuance dragged down overall growth as it fell 0.8% in Q2 2020. Central bank issuance declined 1.5% q-o-q as the drop in the issuance of Exchange Fund Bills exceeded the marginal increase in the issuance of Exchange Fund Notes during the quarter. Meanwhile, issuance of Hong Kong Special Administrative Region bonds more than tripled on a q-o-q basis during the quarter. Corporate bond issuance grew a modest 9.8% q-o-q in Q2 2020. On an annual basis, LCY bond sales climbed 2.2% y-o-y in Q2 2020 following a 1.4% y-o-y contraction in the previous quarter.

LCY bond issuance among ASEAN members summed to USD284.9 billion in Q2 2020, accounting for a 13.9% share of emerging East Asia's aggregate bond issuance for the quarter. This was lower compared with its issuance share in Q1 2020, which accounted for 16.2% of the regional total. Issuance growth among ASEAN members rose to 4.5% q-o-q and 1.6% y-o-y in Q2 2020 from modest expansions of 0.5% q-o-q and 2.3% y-o-y, respectively, in Q1 2020. A q-o-q increase in bond issuance was observed in the markets of Indonesia, Malaysia, Singapore, and Thailand in Q2 2020, while declines were recorded in the Philippines and Viet Nam. The most active issuers of LCY bonds in ASEAN in Q2 2020 were Singapore, Thailand, and Indonesia.

Singapore's LCY bond issuance totaled USD132.8 billion in Q2 2020, gaining 4.1% q-o-q after a rise of 1.3% q-o-q in the previous quarter. The rise was due to an increase in issuance of both government and corporate bonds. Government bond issuance was boosted by a 17.3% q-o-q rise in the issuance of Singapore Government Securities bonds in Q2 2020, while the issuance of Monetary Authority of Singapore bills was unchanged from the previous quarter. In Q2 2020, corporate bond issuance significantly increased by 50.8% q-o-q. On a y-o-y basis, Singapore's bond issuance grew 17.5% y-o-y, the same pace as in the prior quarter.

In Thailand, bond issuance summed to USD78.9 billion, with growth accelerating 3.1% q-o-q in Q2 2020 from 1.1% q-o-q in Q1 2020. The uptick was due to an increase in government bond issuance, which grew 7.5% q-o-q. While central bank bond issuance declined 0.4% q-o-q in Q2 2020, Treasury bond issuance was up 83.8% q-o-q as the government sought to fund fiscal stimulus measures. Corporate bond issuance remained weak, falling 23.7% q-o-q in Q2 2020 after declining 12.4% q-o-q in the previous quarter. On a y-o-y basis, bond issuance in Thailand contracted 14.1%, following a decline of 12.2% in Q1 2020.

Aggregate LCY bond sales in Indonesia soared to USD31.4 billion in Q2 2020, with growth accelerating to 44.1% q-o-q from 6.1% q-o-q in Q1 2020. Government bond issuance drove much of the growth, particularly Treasury instruments, as the government raised its issuance target to fund a wider budget deficit to finance stimulus and recovery measures to mitigate the economic fallout from the COVID-19 outbreak. The 2020 budget deficit ceiling was raised to 6.34% of GDP. In contrast, new issuance of central bank bills dipped 1.8% q-o-q in Q2 2020. Corporate bond issuance during the quarter fell 54.6% q-o-q as companies reconsidered their issuance plan due to the economic slowdown. On an annual basis, bond issuance rebounded to growth of 88.0% y-o-y in Q2 2020 from a 17.5% contraction in the prior quarter.

In Malaysia, bond issuance of USD22.0 billion in Q2 2020 reflected growth slowing to 1.7% q-o-q from 10.7% q-o-q in Q1 2020. The slower growth rate stemmed largely from declining issuance of both central banks bonds and corporate bonds. Government bond issuance grew 15.4% q-o-q, driven by a 41.1% q-o-q surge in the issuance of Treasury bonds during the quarter. The overall growth in government bond issuance was pulled down by a

90.2% q-o-q decline in central bank bond issuance as Bank Negara Malaysia reduced issuance to help boost liquidity. Corporate bond issuance continued its decline, falling 15.7% q-o-q in Q2 2020 after a 14.1% q-o-q drop in Q1 2020. On an annual basis, Malaysia's bond issuance fell 16.7% y-o-y in Q2 2020 after dipping 10.1% y-o-y in Q1 2020.

LCY bond issuance in the Philippines fell 19.6% q-o-q to USD14.0 billion in Q2 2020, as both government and corporate bond issuance declined during the quarter. Government bond issuance fell 6.9% q-o-q after a huge volume of retail Treasury bonds was issued in Q1 2020. Corporate bond issuance dramatically fell 81.3% q-o-q in Q2 2020, as slowing economic growth and quarantine restrictions made corporates reluctant to issue more debt. On a y-o-y basis, bond issuance grew 58.6% in Q2 2020, driven solely by a 114.0% increase in government bonds. In contrast, corporate bonds fell 78.2% y-o-y.

In Viet Nam, LCY bond issuance fell 25.2% q-o-q to USD5.9 billion in Q2 2020. The decline was driven solely by a fall in government bond issuance, which dropped 68.3% q-o-q. The State Bank of Vietnam did not issue any central bank bills during the quarter. Treasury bonds, on the other hand, grew 61.5% q-o-q. Issuance of corporate bonds grew 578.2% q-o-q in Q2 2020 due to increased private placement issues by corporates taking advantage of lower rates. On a y-o-y basis, LCY bond issuance in Viet Nam contracted 75.0% after rising 36.8% in Q1 2020.

Cross-Border Bond Issuance

Emerging East Asia's cross-border bond issuance reached USD3 billion in Q2 2020.

Emerging East Asia's total intra-regional bond issuance amounted to USD3.0 billion in Q2 2020, a 20.9% q-o-q increase from USD2.5 billion in the previous quarter. However, this was down 19.4% from the USD3.7 billion raised in the same period in 2019. Institutions from only four economies raised funds via cross-border bond issuance in Q2 2020 compared to six economies in Q1 2020. The start of the quarter saw tepid issuance in the region, with a total of only USD0.5 billion issued in April as economic activity slowed due to the COVID-19 pandemic. However, a surge in issuance to USD1.8 billion was recorded in May, mostly by firms from the PRC. The region's cross-border bond issuance then tapered again to USD0.6 billion in June.

The PRC continued to dominate in terms of intra-regional bond issuance, with an aggregate USD1.7 billion issued in Q2 2020, which comprised over half of the region's quarterly total (**Figure 4**). This was up 15.1% q-o-q from the USD1.5 billion raised in the previous quarter, but down 11.5% y-o-y from Q2 2019. Five out of the seventeen firms in emerging East Asia that issued intra-regional bonds in Q2 2020 were from the PRC; all of their bonds were all denominated in Hong Kong dollars. Zhongsheng Group Holdings, an automobile retail and services company, was the largest issuer overall and had the largest single issuance for the quarter in May with a zero-coupon, convertible 5-year bond worth USD588.3 million. Best Path Global raised USD500 million with a 1-year bond. Kingsoft Corporation, a software and internet services company, issued a 5-year bond worth USD400 million. Other PRC-based companies that issued HKD-denominated bonds were CBDL Funding 2 (USD210.3 million) and Petro-king Oilfield Services (USD3.4 million).

Almost half of the institutions that issued cross-border bonds in Q2 2020 were from Hong Kong, China. Their aggregate issuance volume reached the equivalent of USD735.9 million, accounting for about a quarter of the regional total, which was 59.2% q-o-q higher than the USD462.2 million raised in the previous quarter. The bulk of the issuances were denominated in Chinese renminbi, led by a 3-year bond worth USD212.3 million issued by

the Bank of China Group. The second-largest issuance was a short-term bond worth USD141.5 million issued by China Travel Services Group. State-owned railway company, MTR Corporation, raised the equivalent of USD101.9 million with two issuances of 1-year bonds in June. AMTD International was the only firm from Hong Kong, China that issued in Singapore dollars, raising USD35.9 million worth of perpetual bonds.

In Q2 2020, only three institutions from the Republic of Korea issued intra-regional bonds worth a total of USD501.9 million, which comprised 16.8% of the regional total. Cross-border bonds issued in the Republic of Korea were denominated in Chinese renminbi, Hong Kong dollars, and Thai baht. State-owned Korea Development Bank issued USD257 million worth of HKD-denominated bonds and CNY-denominated bonds. The other banks that issued intra-regional bonds in Q2 2020 were the Export–Import Bank of Korea (USD195 million) and Woori Bank (USD50 million).

In Singapore, only two institutions issued cross-border bonds in Q2 2020, both of which were denominated in Hong Kong dollars. These were Korea Development Bank Singapore (USD32.3 million) and DBS Bank (USD0.3 million).

The top 10 issuers of cross-border bonds in Q2 2020 had an aggregate issuance volume of USD2.7 billion and accounted for 90.7% of the regional total. The list mostly comprised firms from the PRC and Hong Kong, China. Two banks from the Republic of Korea made up the remainder of the list. The top three issuers were from the PRC, and they each issued HKD-denominated bonds.

The Hong Kong dollar continued to be the predominant currency of intra-regional bonds issued in Q2 2020 with a total volume equivalent to USD2.0 billion and accounting for 66.2% of the regional total (**Figure 5**). Institutions from the three economies issued bonds in this currency. The second most widely used currency was the Chinese renminbi with a share of 30.9% and total issuance equivalent to USD918.3 million from firms in Hong Kong, China and the Republic of Korea. Other currencies used in cross-border issuances included the Thai baht (1.7%, USD51.1 million) and the Singapore dollar (1.2%, USD35.9 million).

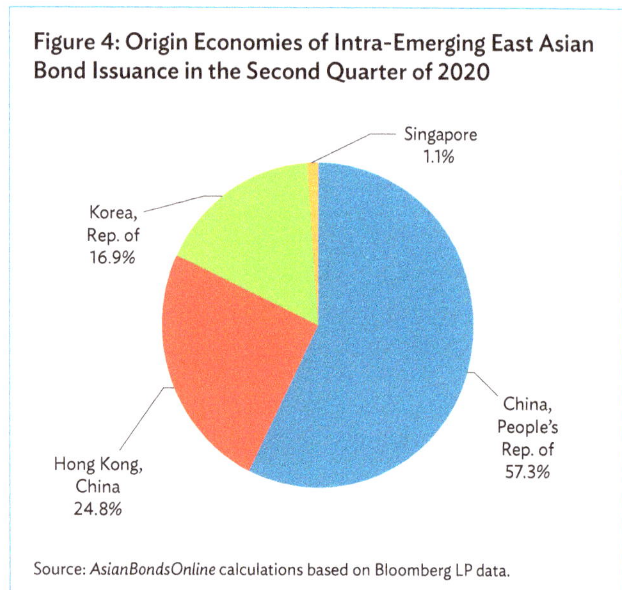

Figure 4: Origin Economies of Intra-Emerging East Asian Bond Issuance in the Second Quarter of 2020

Source: *AsianBondsOnline* calculations based on Bloomberg LP data.

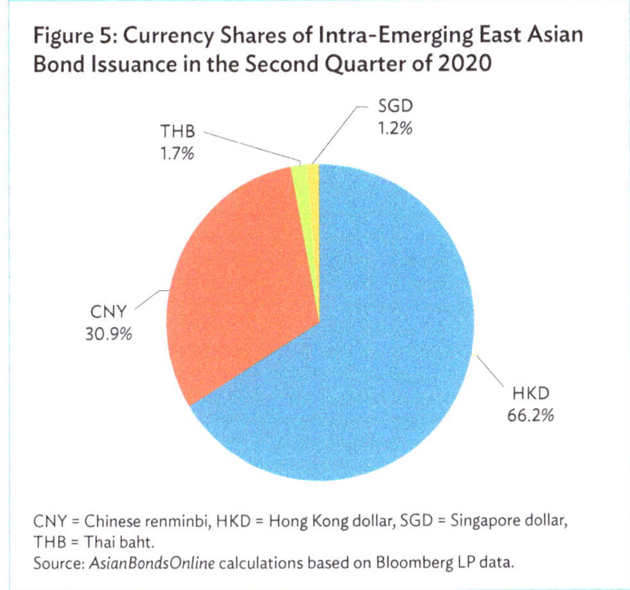

Figure 5: Currency Shares of Intra-Emerging East Asian Bond Issuance in the Second Quarter of 2020

CNY = Chinese renminbi, HKD = Hong Kong dollar, SGD = Singapore dollar, THB = Thai baht.
Source: *AsianBondsOnline* calculations based on Bloomberg LP data.

G3 Currency Issuance

Total G3 currency bond issuance in emerging East Asia amounted to USD217 billion in January–July.

The value of G3 currency bonds issued in emerging East Asia from January to July totaled USD217.0 billion, an increase of 3.0% y-o-y from USD210.7 billion in the same period in 2019 (**Table 4**).[5] The expansion was driven by higher G3 issuance volume in most of the region's economies with similar issuances in 2019.

Of all G3 currency bonds issued during the review period, 93.5% was denominated in US dollars, 5.6% was in euros, and 0.9% was in Japanese yen. In January–July, a total of USD202.9 billion worth of bonds denominated in US dollars was issued in emerging East Asia, representing a jump of 4.3% y-o-y. The equivalent of USD12.2 billion of EUR-denominated bonds was issued during the review period, an increase of 22.3% y-o-y, as more economies issued such bonds. Bonds issued in Japanese yen totaled USD2.0 billion, a decline of 68.2% y-o-y from a high base that was largely driven by Malaysia's samurai bond issuance in March 2019.

The PRC continued to dominate the issuance of G3 currency bonds, totaling USD122.9 billion during the January–July period, mainly supported by issuances

in US dollars. This was followed by Indonesia with USD23.7 billion and the Republic of Korea with USD18.5 billion, both issuing mainly in US dollars as well.

In the first 7 months of 2020, G3 currency bond issuance increased on a y-o-y basis in the Philippines (180.4%), Thailand (173.7%), Indonesia (57.7%), Malaysia (43.3%), and Singapore (34.0%). Issuance of G3 currency bonds from January to July declined on a y-o-y basis in Hong Kong, China (–13.0%); the PRC (–10.2%); and the Republic of Korea (–2.5%). Cambodia issued G3 currency bonds during the January–July period after not issuing any during the same period in 2019. On the other hand, Viet Nam chose not to issue any G3 currency bonds in January–July 2020 after issuing in January–July 2019.

The PRC accounted for 56.6% of all G3 currency issuance in emerging East Asia in January–July, issuing USD118.8 billion in US dollars and the equivalent of USD4.2 billion in euros. In May, state-owned oil and gas enterprise Sinopec Group issued a total of USD3.0 billion of USD-denominated callable bonds in three tranches with tenors of 5 years, 10 years, and 30 years. The bond offering benefited from an optimistic outlook that oil prices would rebound as global economies exited from lockdowns caused by the COVID-19 pandemic. Multinational conglomerate Tencent Holdings extended its yield curve with the issuance of a 40-year callable bond denominated in US dollars. The bond was part of a four-tranche issuance totaling USD6.0 billion, with the three other tranches having tenors of 6 years, 10 years, and 30 years. The issuance was the largest from an issuer in the PRC in 2020. Proceeds from the issuance of Sinopec Group and Tencent Holdings will be used to refinance existing obligations and for general corporate purposes.

The Republic of Korea accounted for an 8.5% share of all G3 currency bonds issued during the review period: USD14.6 billion in US dollars and the equivalent of USD3.9 billion in euros. From May to July, Korea Development Bank issued 11 USD-denominated bonds totaling USD1.6 billion with tenors ranging from 1 year to 5 years and carrying various coupon rates. The Export–Import Bank of Korea issued five USD-denominated bonds totaling USD0.4 billion with tenors of 2–5 years and carrying varying coupon rates ranging from 0.645% to 1.3265%.

---

[5] G3 currency bonds are denominated in either euros, Japanese yen, or US dollars.

Table 4: G3 Currency Bond Issuance

2019			January–July 2020		
Issuer	Amount (USD billion)	Issue Date	Issuer	Amount (USD billion)	Issue Date
Cambodia	**0.0**		**Cambodia**	**0.4**	
China, People's Rep. of	**225.2**		**China, People's Rep. of**	**122.9**	
Tencent Holdings 3.975% 2029	3.0	11-Apr-19	Bank of China 3.60% Perpetual	2.8	4-Mar-20
People's Republic of China (Sovereign) 0.125% 2026	2.2	12-Nov-19	Tencent Holdings 2.39% 2030	2.3	3-Jun-20
People's Republic of China (Sovereign) 1.950% 2024	2.0	3-Dec-19	Scenery Journey 11.50% 2022	2.0	24-Jan-20
Others	218.0		Others	115.9	
Hong Kong, China	**31.9**		**Hong Kong, China**	**18.0**	
Celestial Miles 5.75% Perpetual	1.0	31-Jan-19	AIA Group 3.375% 2030	1.0	7-Apr-20
Hong Kong, China (Sovereign) 2.50% 2024	1.0	28-May-19	Sino Biopharmaceutical 0.000% 2025	0.9	17-Feb-20
AIA Group 3.60% 2029	1.0	9-Apr-19	NWD Finance BVI 5.250% Perpetual	0.9	22-Jun-20
Others	28.9		Others	15.3	
Indonesia	**22.4**		**Indonesia**	**23.7**	
Perusahaan Penerbit SBSN *Sukuk* 4.45% 2029	1.3	20-Feb-19	Indonesia (Sovereign) 3.85% 2030	1.7	15-Apr-20
Indonesia (Sovereign) 1.40% 2031	1.1	30-Oct-19	Indonesia (Sovereign) 4.20% 2050	1.7	15-Apr-20
Indonesia (Sovereign) 3.70% 2049	1.0	30-Oct-19	Indonesia (Sovereign) 2.85% 2030	1.2	14-Jan-20
Others	19.0		Others	19.2	
Korea, Rep. of	**29.4**		**Korea, Rep. of**	**18.5**	
Republic of Korea (Sovereign) 2.500% 2029	1.0	19-Jun-19	Korea Housing Finance Corporation 0.010% 2025	1.2	5-Feb-20
Export–Import Bank of Korea 0.375% 2024	0.8	26-Mar-19	Korea Development Bank 1.250% 2025	1.0	3-Jun-20
LG Display 1.500% 2024	0.7	22-Aug-19	Export–Import Bank of Korea 0.829% 2025	0.8	27-Apr-20
Others	26.8		Others	15.5	
Lao People's Democratic Republic	**0.2**		**Lao People's Democratic Republic**	**0.0**	
Malaysia	**13.7**		**Malaysia**	**11.7**	
Malaysia (Sovereign) 0.530% 2029	1.8	15-Mar-19	Petronas Capital 4.55% 2050	2.8	21-Apr-20
Resorts World Las Vegas 4.625% 2029	1.0	16-Apr-19	Petronas Capital 3.50% 2030	2.3	21-Apr-20
Others	10.9		Others	6.7	
Philippines	**6.7**		**Philippines**	**11.2**	
Philippines (Sovereign) 3.750% 2029	1.5	14-Jan-19	Philippines (Sovereign) 2.950% 2045	1.4	5-May-20
Philippines (Sovereign) 0.875% 2027	0.8	17-May-19	Philippines (Sovereign) 2.457% 2030	1.0	5-May-20
Others	4.4		Others	8.8	
Singapore	**9.7**		**Singapore**	**7.0**	
DBS Group 2.85% 2022	0.8	16-Apr-19	BOC Aviation 3.25% 2025	1.0	29-Apr-20
BOC Aviation 3.50% 2024	0.8	10-Apr-19	DBS Group Holdings 3.30% Perpetual	1.0	27-Feb-20
Others	8.2		Others	5.0	
Thailand	**6.4**		**Thailand**	**3.6**	
Bangkok Bank/Hong Kong 3.733% 2034	1.2	25-Sep-19	PTT Treasury 3.70% 2070	0.7	16-Jul-20
Kasikornbank 3.343% 2031	0.8	2-Oct-19	Thaioil Treasury 3.75% 2050	0.6	18-Jun-20
Others	4.4		Others	2.3	
Viet Nam	**1.0**		**Viet Nam**	**0.0**	
Emerging East Asia Total	**346.6**		**Emerging East Asia Total**	**217.0**	
Memo Items:			**Memo Items:**		
India	**21.9**		**India**	**9.4**	
Indian Oil Corporation 4.75% 2024	0.9	16-Jan-19	Bharti Airtel 1.5% 2025	1.0	17-Jan-20
Others	21.0		Others	8.4	
Sri Lanka	**4.9**		**Sri Lanka**	**0.4**	
Sri Lanka (Sovereign) 7.55% 2030	1.5	28-Jun-19	Sri Lanka (Sovereign) 6.57% 2021	0.1	30-Jul-20
Others	3.4		Others	0.3	

USD = United States dollar.
Notes:
1. Data exclude certificates of deposits.
2. G3 currency bonds are bonds denominated in either euros, Japanese yen, or US dollars.
3. Bloomberg LP end-of-period rates are used.
4. Emerging East Asia comprises Cambodia; the People's Republic of China; Hong Kong, China; Indonesia; the Republic of Korea; the Lao People's Democratic Republic; Malaysia; the Philippines; Singapore; Thailand; and Viet Nam.
5. Figures after the issuer name reflect the coupon rate and year of maturity of the bond.
Source: *AsianBondsOnline* calculations based on Bloomberg LP data.

Hong Kong, China accounted for an 8.3% share of G3 currency bond issuance in January–July. By currency, USD16.6 billion was issued in US dollars, while EUR-denominated and JPY-denominated bonds amounted to USD0.9 billion and USD0.5 billion, respectively. Property developer Sun Hung Kai Properties issued USD0.5 billion of 10-year callable, USD-denominated bonds with a coupon rate of 2.75%. The issuance came as other real estate companies offered US dollar bonds in expectation of an economic rebound following the COVID-19 pandemic. CLP Power sold a USD1.0 billion dual-tranche bond in US dollars with tenors of 10 years and 15 years. The issuance was a defensive move by the utilities company amid political risks brought by the new national security law in Hong Kong, China.

G3 currency bond issuance among ASEAN member economies increased 68.1% y-o-y to USD57.2 billion in January–July from USD34.0 billion in the same period in 2019 as all ASEAN economies, except Viet Nam, ramped up issuance during the period. As a share of emerging East Asia's total during the review period, ASEAN's G3 currency bond issuance accounted for 26.4%, up from 16.2% during the same period in 2019. Indonesia and Malaysia led all ASEAN members in terms of G3 currency bond issuance, followed by the Philippines, Singapore, and Thailand, with issuances amounting to USD11.2 billion, USD7.0 billion, and USD3.6 billion, respectively.

Indonesia's G3 currency bond issuance in January–July accounted for 10.9% of the total in emerging East Asia, comprising USD21.6 billion in US dollars, the equivalent of USD1.2 billion in euros, and the equivalent of USD0.9 billion in Japanese yen. In June, Perusahaan Penerbit SBSN Indonesia III, a special purpose vehicle of the Government of Indonesia that issues Shariah-compliant securities in foreign currencies, issued a three-tranche bond denominated in US dollars totaling USD2.5 billion and with tenors of 5 years, 10 years, and 30 years. The bonds was structured following the *wakalah* principle wherein the Islamic bonds are backed by an agreement between an investor and an agent, and the bondholders are entitled to profits as agreed upon by the two parties. Guided by the government's green *sukuk* framework, proceeds from the 5-year tenor will be used in financing eligible green projects. In July, the Government of Indonesia issued USD0.9 billion worth of samurai bonds in five tranches with tenors ranging from 3 years to 20 years. Proceeds from the issuance will be used to cover

the government's budget deficit and fund efforts to battle the COVID-19 pandemic.

G3 currency bonds issued in Malaysia accounted for 5.4% of emerging East Asia's total, including USD-denominated bonds worth USD11.1 billion and JPY-denominated bonds worth USD0.6 billion. In June, Malayan Banking (Maybank) raised USD0.2 billion via a 40-year zero-coupon, callable bond denominated in US dollars. The issuance was made under the bank's USD15.0 billion multicurrency medium-term note program, the proceeds from which will be used for Maybank's working capital and other general business purposes. In July, Maybank issued another USD-denominated bond worth USD0.02 billion with a tenor of 3 years and a coupon rate 1.08675%.

The Philippines accounted for 5.2% of total G3 currency bond issuance in emerging East Asia during the January–July period, comprising bonds denominated in US dollars and euros amounting to USD9.8 billion and USD1.4 billion, respectively. In May, the Government of the Philippines issued two tranches of USD-denominated bonds worth USD2.4 billion and with tenors of 10 years and 25 years. Proceeds from the issuance will be used for general purposes including budgetary support. Jollibee Worldwide issued a dual-tranche, USD-denominated callable bond worth USD0.6 billion. Proceeds from the issuance will be used to support activities that may be affected by the COVID-19 pandemic.

Singapore's share of G3 currency bond issuance in emerging East Asia was 3.2% in January–July, comprising USD7.0 billion in US dollars and the equivalent of USD0.1 billion in euros. Global aircraft operating company BOC Aviation expanded its USD-denominated bonds with a 3.5-year bond worth USD0.8 billion and with a coupon rate of 2.75%. Proceeds from the issuance will be used for new capital expenditure, general corporate purposes, and debt financing. Telecommunications conglomerate Singtel Group raised USD0.8 billion through the issuance of a 10-year callable bond with a coupon rate of 1.875%. Proceeds from the issuance will be used to fund regular business activities.

During the January–July period, 1.7% of all G3 currency bonds issued in the region were from Thailand, comprising USD3.1 billion worth of bonds denominated in US dollars and USD0.5 billion in euros. Thaioil Treasury issued a dual-tranche, USD-denominated bond worth USD1.0 billion with tenors of 10 years and 30 years, and coupon rates of 2.50% and 3.75%, respectively. In July, state-owned oil and gas company PTT raised USD0.7 billion with a 50-year callable bond denominated in US dollars. The issuance, with a coupon rate of 3.7%, took advantage of global demand for long-dated debt securities. Proceeds from the issuance will be used for general corporate purposes.

Cambodia issued USD0.4 billion worth of G3 currency bonds in July, contributing a 0.2% share of such bonds issued in the region during the review period. The USD-denominated bond issuance from casino and resort operator Nagacorp has a tenor of 4 years and a coupon rate of 7.95%. Proceeds from the issuance will be used to redeem part of the company's outstanding bonds.

Monthly G3 currency issuance trends from May through July were the same as those observed from the same period in 2019 wherein issuances slowed in July after spiking in June (**Figure 6**). The relatively high level of issuance in June–July 2020 was mainly due to the PRC's increased pace after its limited G3 currency bond issuance activities in April and May. Also contributing to the jump in issuances during the months of June and July were Indonesia, the Philippines, and Thailand. The rebound in issuances may be attributed to companies taking advantage of low interest

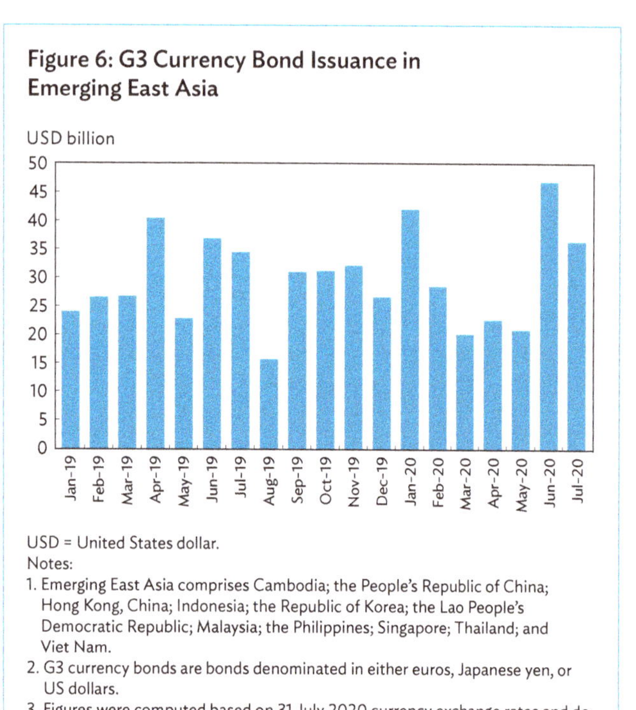

Figure 6: G3 Currency Bond Issuance in Emerging East Asia

USD = United States dollar.
Notes:
1. Emerging East Asia comprises Cambodia; the People's Republic of China; Hong Kong, China; Indonesia; the Republic of Korea; the Lao People's Democratic Republic; Malaysia; the Philippines; Singapore; Thailand; and Viet Nam.
2. G3 currency bonds are bonds denominated in either euros, Japanese yen, or US dollars.
3. Figures were computed based on 31 July 2020 currency exchange rates and do not include currency effects.
Source: *AsianBondsOnline* calculations based on Bloomberg LP data.

rates as advanced economy central banks implemented monetary policy easing to cope with the deleterious effects of the COVID-19 pandemic.

Government Bond Yield Curves

Government bond yields in emerging East Asia fell for most markets as the COVID-19 outbreak continued to dampen economic activities and governments sought to buttress their economies.

Between 15 June and 15 August, economic weakness in nearly all markets in emerging East Asia led to a continued decline in yields in most markets.

In the US, the Federal Reserve held monetary policy steady during its meetings on 9–10 June and 28–29 July. Forecasts from members of the Federal Open Market Operations showed that the current level of policy rates was expected to remain until 2022. Likewise, the European Central Bank and the Bank of Japan also left its existing monetary policy unchanged.

All three central banks indicated that they stood ready to act further as the economic situation warrants. However, monetary policy was largely left unchanged in advanced economies as past monetary easing was judged to be sufficient while financial volatility abated. Also, as quarantine measures are eased, some economic recovery is expected but is likely to be limited given the ongoing effects of the pandemic.

In emerging East Asia, economic weakness continued to drive yields downward, with some central banks implementing additional easing measures. This was most visible in 2-year yield movements, which trended downward across the region, with the sole exception being the PRC (**Figure 7a**). The rise in yields in the PRC was driven by its economic recovery that resulted from being one of the first economies to remove quarantine measures. While Thailand's 2-year yield trended downward (**Figure 7b**), concerns regarding an increased debt supply dampened the trend.

Across most of the region, 10-year yields followed a similar downward trend (**Figure 8a**). The PRC was once again an exception as domestic economic growth bolstered yield gains. While there was a downward trend in the 10-year yield in Hong Kong, China; the Republic of Korea;

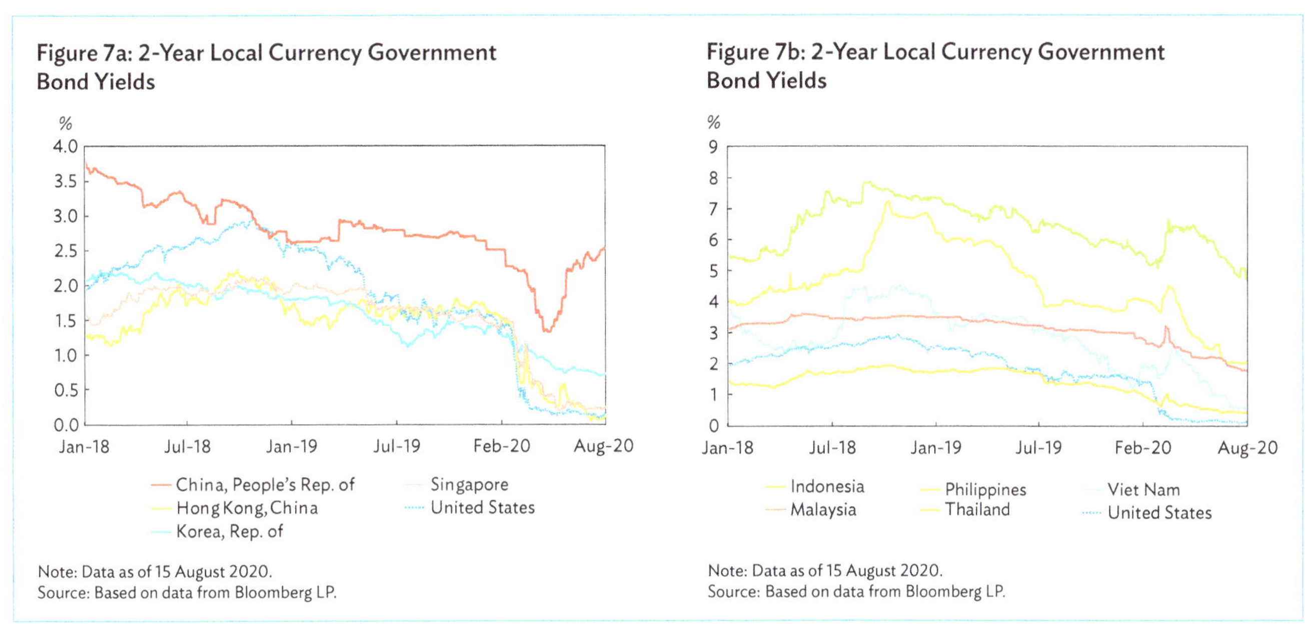

Figure 7a: 2-Year Local Currency Government Bond Yields

Note: Data as of 15 August 2020.
Source: Based on data from Bloomberg LP.

Figure 7b: 2-Year Local Currency Government Bond Yields

Note: Data as of 15 August 2020.
Source: Based on data from Bloomberg LP.

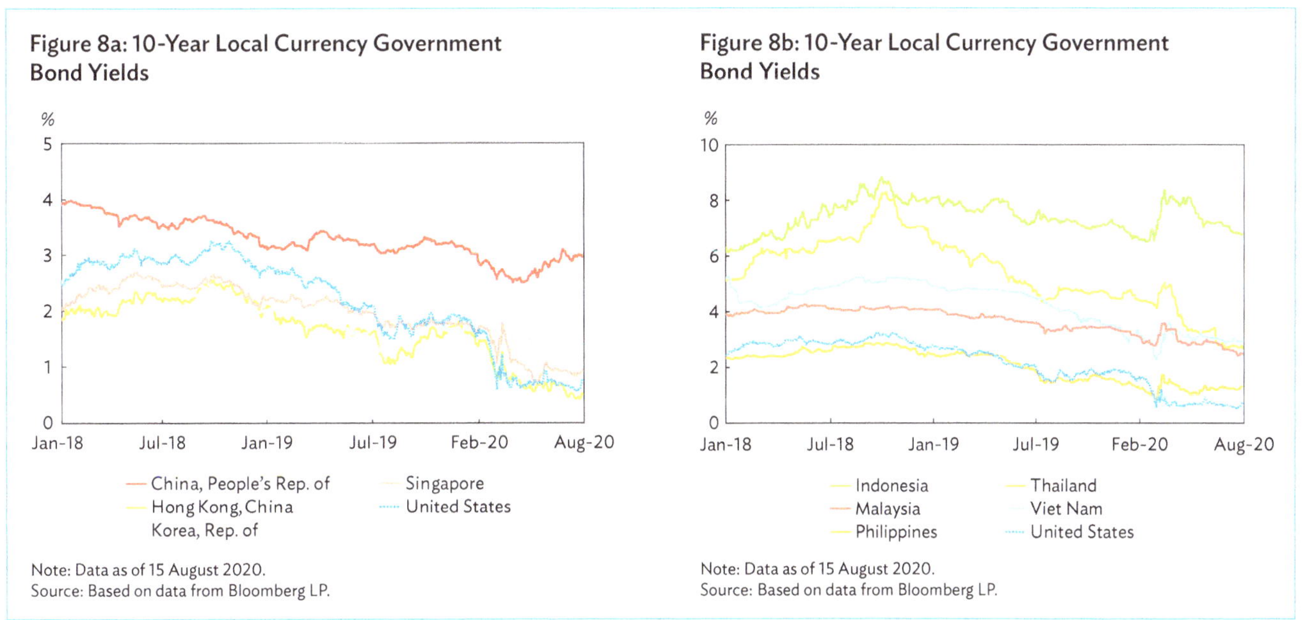

Figure 8a: 10-Year Local Currency Government Bond Yields

Note: Data as of 15 August 2020.
Source: Based on data from Bloomberg LP.

Figure 8b: 10-Year Local Currency Government Bond Yields

Note: Data as of 15 August 2020.
Source: Based on data from Bloomberg LP.

and Singapore, there was a small spike in these markets in August, which tracked closely with the movement of US Treasuries on expectations of improved economic growth following the release of favorable US payroll data in August. The 10-year yield rose in Thailand by 12 bps from 15 June to 15 August over concerns of rising debt supply as well as a lack of policy rate activity (**Figure 8b**).

Similar to movements in the 2-year and 10-year yields, the entire yield curve of the PRC shifted upward between

15 June and 15 August on the recovery of the domestic economy (**Figure 9**). The yield curve shifted downward for all tenors in Hong Kong China; Malaysia; the Philippines; and Viet Nam, and for all tenors except for the 6-year tenor in Indonesia. Excluding Viet Nam, these markets were also the ones whose central banks eased during the review period. The yield curve fell for most tenors in all other markets except in Singapore, where yield curve movements were mixed, and in Thailand, where the yield curve mostly shifted upward. In the case

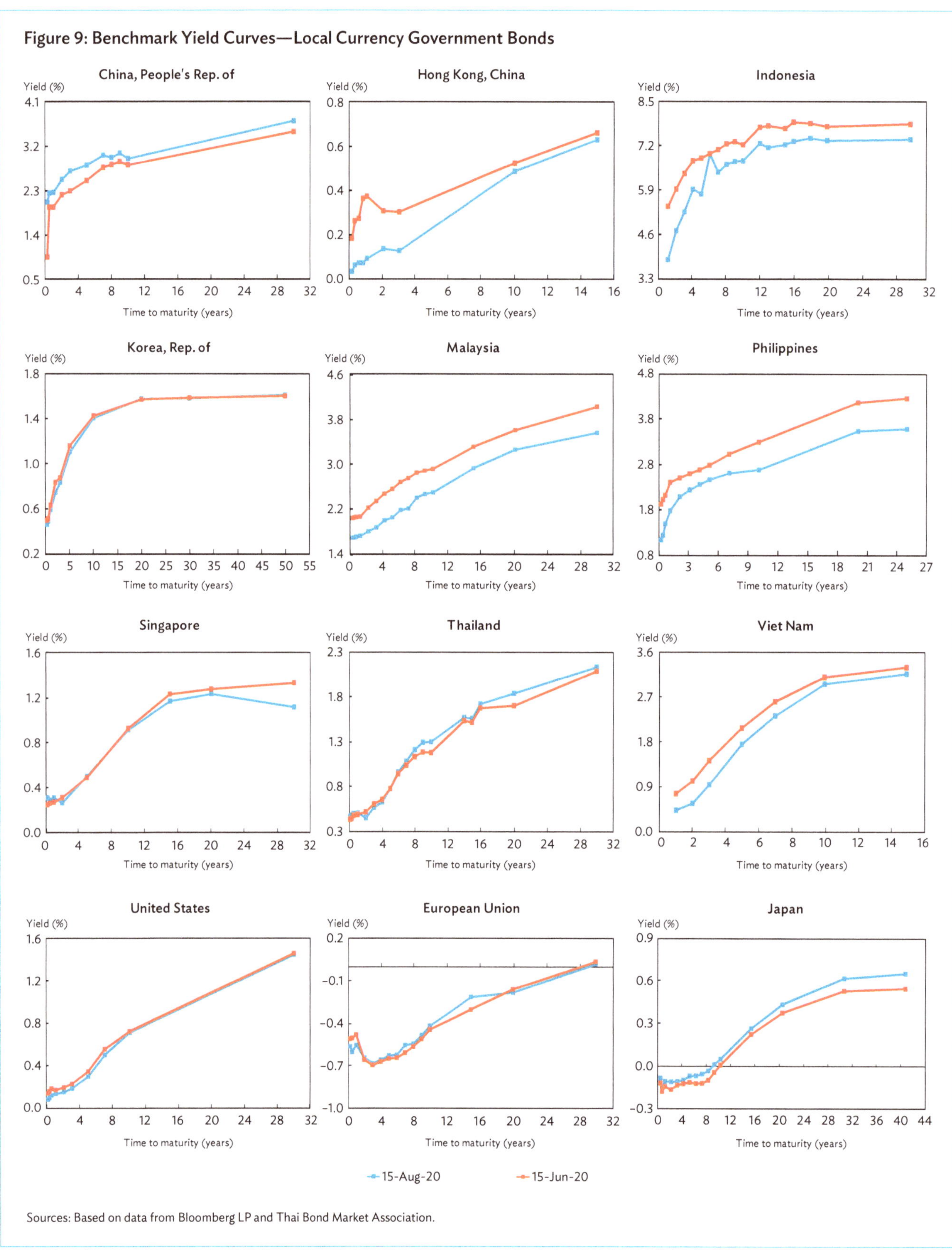

Sources: Based on data from Bloomberg LP and Thai Bond Market Association.

of Thailand, the rise in yields was driven by investor concerns over rising debt levels as the government sought to fund its stimulus program. A lack of easing from the central bank also contributed. The 2-year versus 10-year yield spread fell in the PRC and the Philippines between 15 June and 15 August, but rose in the region's remaining markets (**Figure 10**).

The COVID-19 outbreak led to reduced economic output due to quarantine measures imposed by governments as well as reduced demand from consumers. This resulted in GDP declines in most emerging East Asian economies in Q2 2020.

The PRC is one notable exception as it contained the outbreak earlier in the year and subsequently was able to ease restrictions ahead of most other economies. As a result, the PRC's GDP grew 3.2% y-o-y in Q2 2020 after declining 6.8% y-o-y in Q1 2020. Viet Nam was the only other market to post positive GDP growth in Q2 2020, albeit the expansion of 0.4% y-o-y was lower than the previous quarter's 3.8% y-o-y.

The region's largest decline in output was in Malaysia, where GDP fell 17.1% y-o-y in Q2 2020 after a small gain

of 0.7% y-o-y in Q1 2020. The next largest decline was in the Philippines, where GDP fell 16.5% y-o-y in Q2 2020 after falling 0.7% y-o-y in the previous quarter. Singapore and Thailand posted contractions of 13.2% y-o-y and 12.2% y-o-y, respectively, in Q2 2020 after declines of 0.3% y-o-y and 2.0% y-o-y in Q1 2020.

Hong Kong, China, which had already been affected by political unrest prior to the COVID-19 outbreak, posted GDP declines of 9.0% y-o-y and 9.1% y-o-y, respectively, in Q2 2020 and Q1 2020. Indonesia's GDP contracted 5.3% y-o-y in Q2 2020 after rising 3.0% y-o-y in Q1 2020. In the Republic of Korea, GDP fell 2.7% y-o-y in Q2 2020 after increasing 1.4% y-o-y in the previous quarter.

While most markets experienced deeper contractions or reversals of GDP growth in Q2 2020, there was some bottoming out of inflation, with most markets showing rising inflation in June after a downward trend previously. However, expectations are that inflation will remain soft through the remainder of the year given the impact of the COVID-19 pandemic.

The two exceptions to the trend of slightly rising inflation were Hong Kong, China, which posted a decline in inflation to –2.3% y-o-y in July from 0.7% y-o-y in June, and Indonesia, where the inflation rate fell to 1.5% y-o-y in July from 2.0% y-o-y in June (**Figure 11a**). The region's remaining markets showed a rise in inflation during the review period, including in the Republic of Korea where inflation of 0.3% y-o-y in July was recorded, up from 0.0% in the previous month (**Figure 11b**).

After previous rounds of monetary easing, a number of central banks opted to maintain existing monetary policy to allow the effects of previous easing to make their way through their respective economies. Bucking this trend, Malaysia reduced policy rates by 25 bps to 1.75% during its central bank meeting on 7 July (**Figure 12a**). While Bank Negara Malaysia expects business conditions to improve in the second half of the year, ongoing weaknesses make recovery uncertain. The Philippines likewise reduced by 50 bps its key policy rate to 2.25% on 25 June. The Bangko Sentral ng Pilipinas noted that even if the government eases quarantine policies, considerable uncertainty remains and recovery is likely to be slow. Bank Indonesia was the only central bank in the region that reduced policy rates twice during the period, each time by 25 bps on 18 June and 16 July (**Figure 12b**).

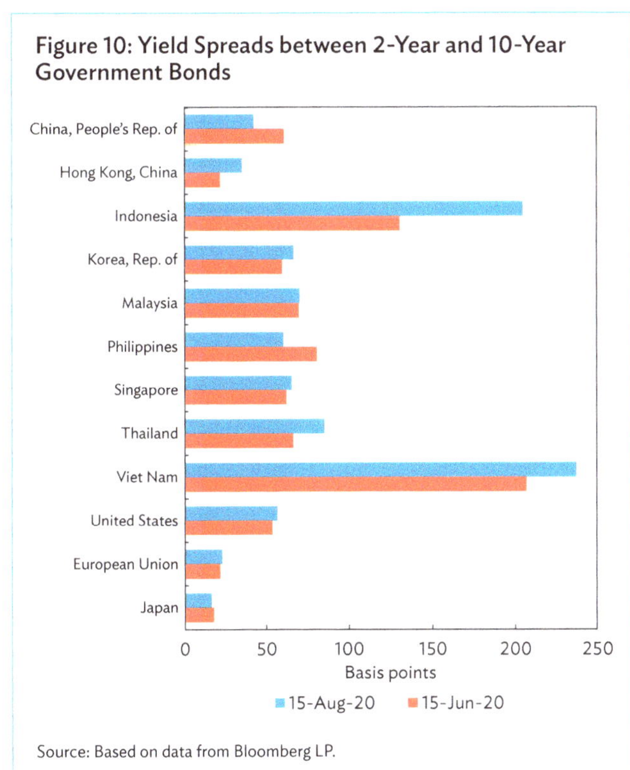
Figure 10: Yield Spreads between 2-Year and 10-Year Government Bonds

Source: Based on data from Bloomberg LP.

The AAA-rated corporate versus government bond yield spread fell in the PRC, the Republic of Korea, and Thailand, but rose in Malaysia.

The AAA-rated corporate versus government bond yield spread fell in the PRC, the Republic of Korea, and Thailand (**Figure 13a**). In the PRC, the spread declined as the economy showed signs of recovery, while the spread rose in Malaysia over falling oil prices.

For lower-rated corporate bond yields, spreads rose in the Republic of Korea, Malaysia, and Thailand, but fell in the PRC (**Figure 13b**).

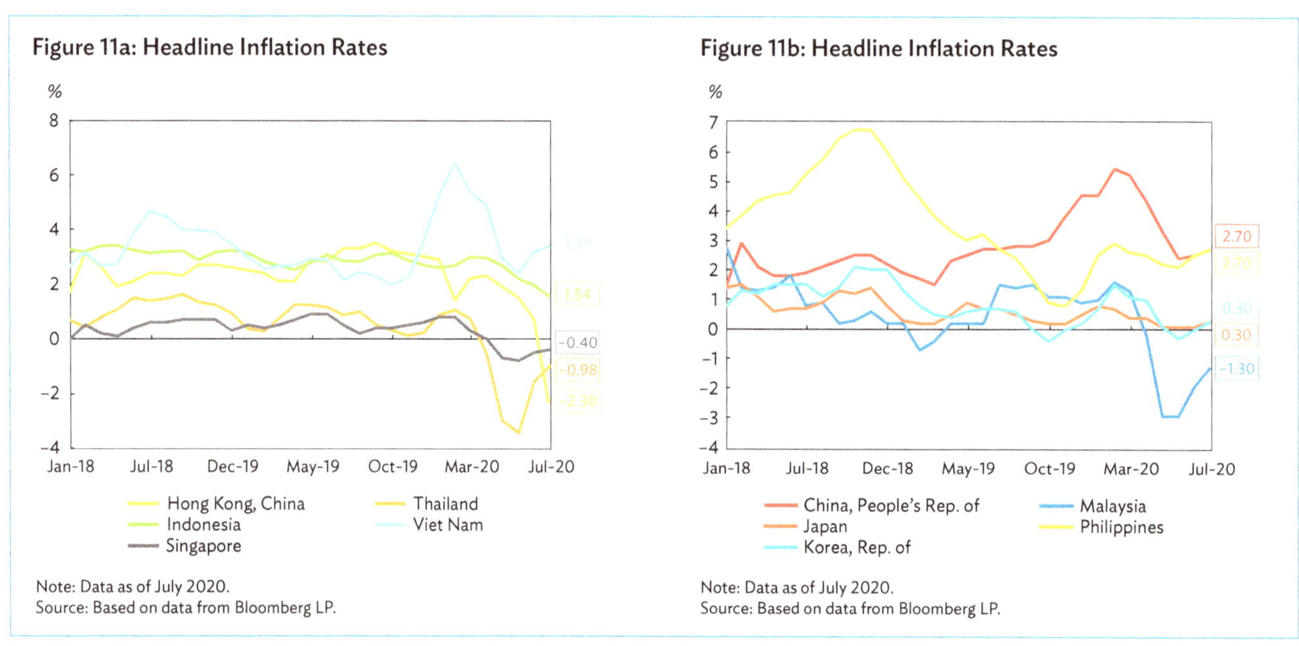

Figure 11a: Headline Inflation Rates

Note: Data as of July 2020.
Source: Based on data from Bloomberg LP.

Figure 11b: Headline Inflation Rates

Note: Data as of July 2020.
Source: Based on data from Bloomberg LP.

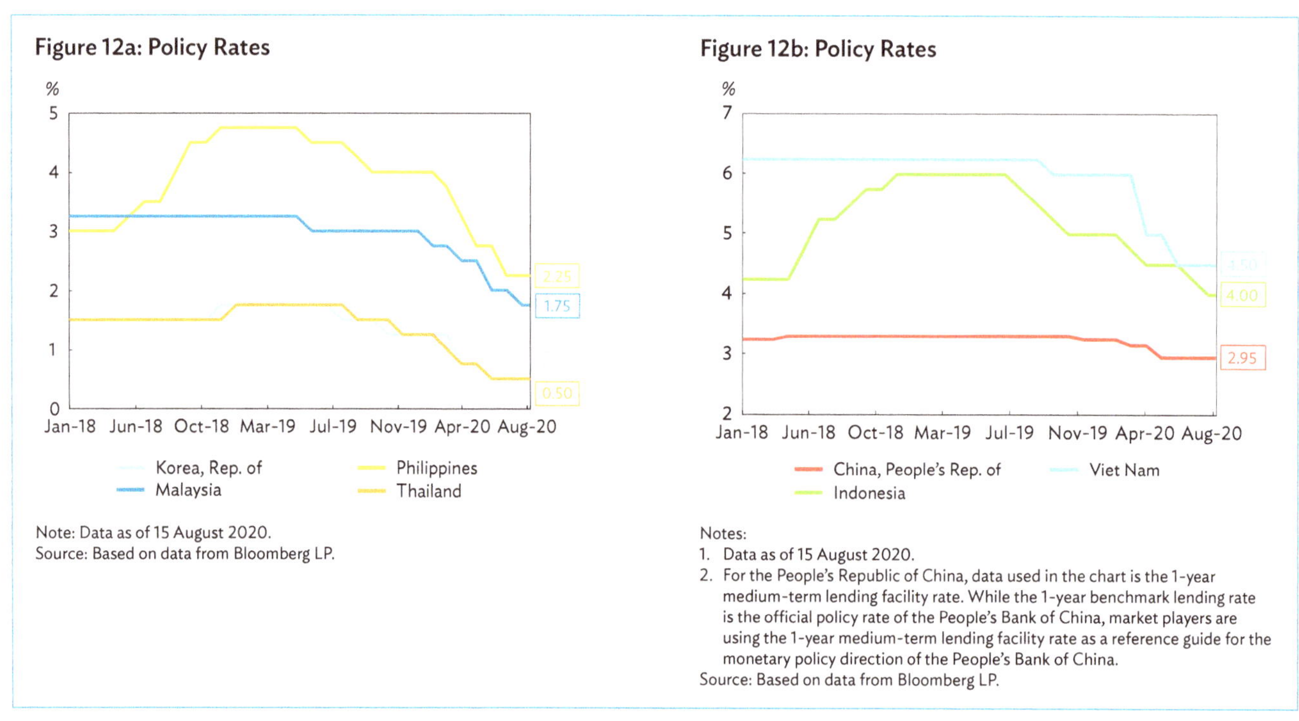

Figure 12a: Policy Rates

Note: Data as of 15 August 2020.
Source: Based on data from Bloomberg LP.

Figure 12b: Policy Rates

Notes:
1. Data as of 15 August 2020.
2. For the People's Republic of China, data used in the chart is the 1-year medium-term lending facility rate. While the 1-year benchmark lending rate is the official policy rate of the People's Bank of China, market players are using the 1-year medium-term lending facility rate as a reference guide for the monetary policy direction of the People's Bank of China.
Source: Based on data from Bloomberg LP.

Figure 13a: Credit Spreads—Local Currency Corporates Rated AAA vs. Government Bonds

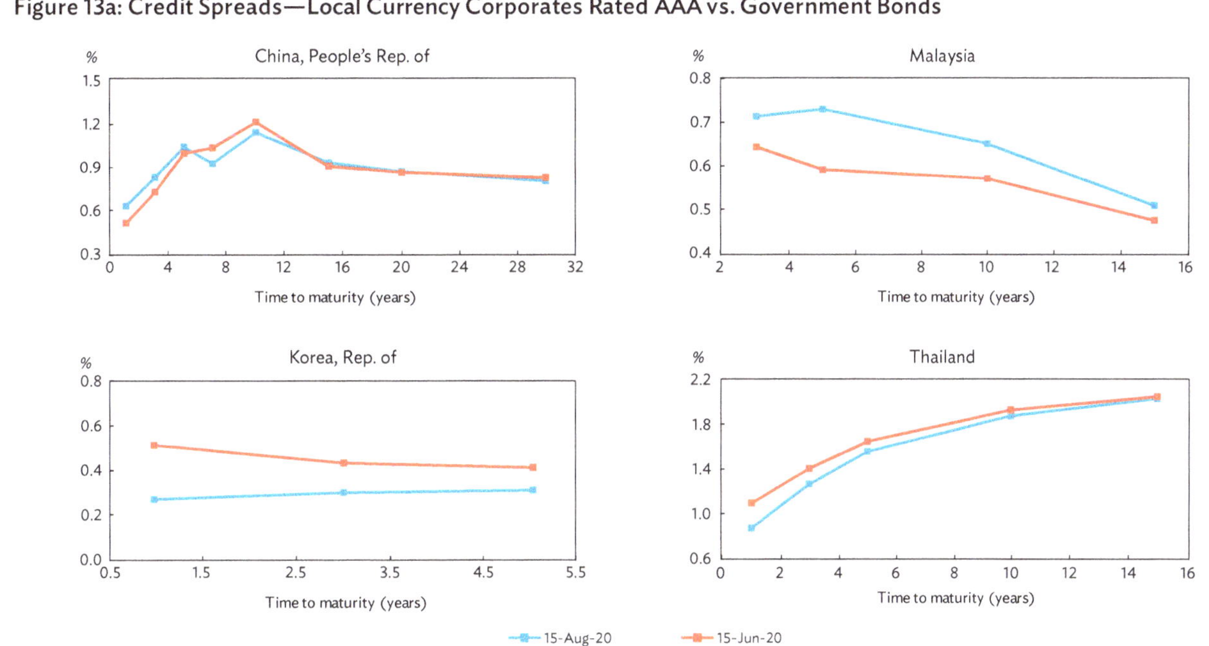

Notes:
1. Credit spreads are obtained by subtracting government yields from corporate indicative yields.
2. For Malaysia, data on corporate bonds yields are as of 12 June 2020 and 14 August 2020.
Sources: People's Republic of China (Bloomberg LP); Republic of Korea (*EDAILY BondWeb*); Malaysia (Fully Automated System for Issuing/Tendering Bank Negara Malaysia); and Thailand (Bloomberg LP).

Figure 13b: Credit Spreads—Lower-Rated Local Currency Corporates vs. AAA

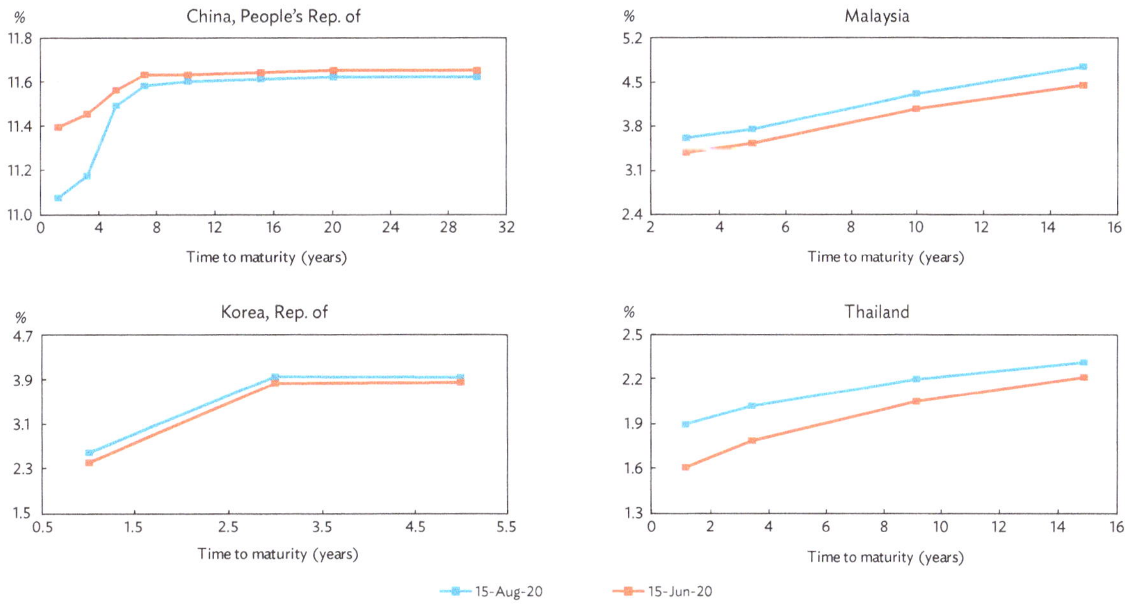

Notes:
1. For the People's Republic of China and the Republic of Korea, credit spreads are obtained by subtracting corporate indicative yields rated AAA from corporate indicative yields rated BBB+.
2. For Malaysia, data on corporate bonds yields are as of 12 June 2020 and 14 August 2020.
Sources: People's Republic of China (Bloomberg LP); Republic of Korea (*EDAILY BondWeb*); Malaysia (Fully Automated System for Issuing/Tendering Bank Negara Malaysia); and Thailand (Bloomberg LP).

Policy and Regulatory Developments

People's Republic of China

The People's Bank of China Issues Central Bank Bills in Hong Kong, China

In June and August, the People's Bank of China issued renminbi-denominated bills in Hong Kong, China to help manage offshore liquidity and control the renminbi yield curve. The issuance comprised of (i) CNY10 billion 6-month central bank bills at a yield of 2.21% in June, and (ii) CNY20 billion 3-month central bank bills at a yield of 2.70%, and (iii) CNY10 billion of 1-year bills at a yield of 2.70% in August.

Hong Kong, China

Hong Kong Monetary Authority Keeps Countercyclical Capital Buffer at 1.0%

On 7 July, the Hong Kong Monetary Authority (HKMA) decided to hold the countercyclical capital buffer (CCyB) at 1.00%. The HKMA noted that the latest data based on the first quarter of 2020 indicators signal a higher CCyB at 2.25%. However, the HKMA gauged that economic recovery will be protracted given the high level of uncertainty. The HKMA decided to hold the CCyB steady at 1.00% and continue monitoring the economic situation. A lower CCyB provides additional funds for banks, allowing them to extend credit to support financing needs in various sectors of the economy. The CCyB is an integral part of the Basel III regulatory capital framework designed to increase the resilience of the banking sector in periods of excess credit growth.

Indonesia

2020 State Budget Deficit Estimated to Reach 6.34% of Gross Domestic Product

In June, a second revision to the 2020 state budget was signed into law, which called for increased spending and a wider budget deficit to support the economy amid the coronavirus disease (COVID-19) outbreak. The second revision to the 2020 state budget estimates a deficit amounting to IDR1.03 quadrillion, which is equivalent to 6.34% of gross domestic product (GDP), up from an earlier revision announced in April of a deficit equivalent to 5.07% of GDP. The government expects state spending to hit IDR2.73 quadrillion in 2020, while state revenue is projected to be IDR1.69 quadrillion.

Republic of Korea

The Republic of Korea's National Assembly Passes Third Supplementary Budget

On 3 July, the National Assembly of the Republic of Korea passed the third supplementary budget worth KRW35.1 trillion. The amount approved was lower than the proposed KRW35.3 trillion, yet it was still the largest of the three supplementary budgets passed in 2020 in response to the economic impact of the COVID-19 pandemic, bringing the aggregate amount of supplementary budgets to KRW54.4 trillion and the total policy package to KRW277 trillion.

The Government of the Republic of Korea Submits 2021 Fiscal Budget

On 3 September, the Government of the Republic of Korea submitted the 2021 fiscal budget proposal totaling KRW555.8 trillion, primarily to aid in economic recovery and support the Korean New Deal. The 2021 budget is 8.5% higher than the original 2020 budget and 1.6% higher than the final 2020 budget that included three supplementary budgets in response to the COVID-19 pandemic. Government revenues in 2021 are projected to grow 1.2% to KRW483 trillion. A fiscal deficit equal to 5.4% of GDP and aggregate government debt equal to 46.7% of GDP are expected. In addition, the government also submitted to the National Assembly its 2020–2024 fiscal management plan.

Malaysia

The Fintech Booster Programme Launched to Support Malaysian Companies

On 4 August, the Fintech Booster Programme of the Malaysia Digital Economy Corporation was launched.

In cooperation with Bank Negara Malaysia, the program aims to help financial technology companies based in Malaysia in their capacity building. Participating companies are introduced to the following aspects of the financial technology industry: legal and compliance, business model, and technology. As a centralized hub, the program fosters collaboration between industry players—such as consultants, advisors, and solution providers—in supporting the industry's growth, development, and innovation.

Philippines

Bangko Sentral ng Pilipinas Cuts Reserve Requirements for Thrift Banks and Rural and Cooperative Banks

In July, the Bangko Sentral ng Pilipinas (BSP) reduced the reserve requirements for thrift banks, and rural and cooperative banks by 100 bps each to 3.0% and 2.0%, respectively. The central bank stated that the move is a part of its omnibus package of reforms to assist the banking public with their liquidity requirements during the ongoing COVID-19 pandemic and to support the transition toward a sustainable recovery after the crisis. The reserve requirement cuts are expected to increase the lending capacity of the banks and release approximately PHP10 billion in cash into the economy, which will support small businesses and rural community-based clients. The reduction is effective 31 July.

Bureau of the Treasury Launches Bonds.PH

In July, the Bureau of the Treasury launched Bonds.PH, the first mobile application in Asia for the distribution of government bonds enabled by distributed ledger technology. The system, which utilizes blockchain technology, allows tamper-proof record keeping and can facilitate complex transactions. Such technology supports financial inclusion in the economy as it makes investing, especially to the unbanked, easier and more secure. The Bureau of the Treasury's issuance of Retail Treasury Bonds in July utilized this technology.

Bangko Sentral ng Pilipinas Approves the Exclusion of Debt Held by Market-Makers from Single Borrower's Limit

In July, the BSP approved a new policy that excludes debt securities acquired from market-making activities of BSP-supervised financial institutions from the single borrower's limit (SBL) as part of initiatives to develop the capital market. According to the BSP's new policy, market-making activities from 1 August 2020 to 31 July 2021 will be excluded from the SBL computation for 90 calendar days from the time of acquisition of the securities. Beginning 1 August 2021, the debt securities will only be excluded from the SBL computation for a period of up to 60 calendar days. The BSP stated that this policy will promote liquidity and transparency in the market by giving market-makers latitude to continue providing prices for debt securities in the secondary market and to make available an exit mechanism for investors to liquidate their holdings.

Singapore

Monetary Authority of Singapore Announces Initiatives to Support Singapore Overnight Rate Average

On 5 August, Monetary Authority of Singapore (MAS) launched initiatives that boost the adoption of Singapore Overnight Rate Average (SORA) as a benchmark in the Singapore financial market. On 21 August, MAS began issuing SORA-based, floating-rate notes on a monthly basis to expand money market instruments and develop the use of SORA as a floating-rate benchmark. MAS will promote transparency by publishing key statistics on various tenors utilizing SORA. To ensure compliance and robustness in the use of SORA, MAS prescribed its use as a benchmark under the Securities and Futures Act. Finally, to meet international best practices and assure market confidence, MAS issued a statement of compliance with International Organization of Securities Commissions principles. These initiatives will help Singapore's financial industry transition from the use of the Swap Offer Rate to SORA.

Thailand

Public Debt Management Office Launches THB1 Savings Bonds via Blockchain

On June 24, the Ministry of Finance issued THB200 million worth of savings bonds at an unprecedented face value of THB1 each through Krungthai Bank's blockchain-based e-wallet. Using the blockchain system, the Public Debt Management Office was able to lower the amount of the savings bond face value from the regular THB1,000. The small-ticket bonds were part of the government's plan to encourage low-income earners to invest in risk-free assets. The bonds were divided into 5-year and 10-year tenors, with the 5-year bond carrying a coupon of 2.4% and the 10-year bond carrying a coupon of 3.0%. The bonds were sold in under 2 minutes, prompting the Public Debt Management Office to issue a second batch worth THB5,000 million on 25 August.

Viet Nam

Ministry of Finance Amends Decree to Tighten the Trading of Privately Placed Corporate Bonds

In July, Viet Nam's Ministry of Finance amended several points under Decree No. 163/2018/ND-CP to tighten the trading of privately placed corporate bonds in the domestic market. In the new version, depository organizations must provide information about corporate bond trading within 1 working day of the trade being completed. Regular updates about bond registration and depository must be provided to the stock exchange monthly, quarterly, and yearly. The amended decree will take effect on 1 September 2020.

Viet Nam Government Issues New Decree to Raise the Standards in the Corporate Bond Market

In July, the Government of Viet Nam issued Government Decree No. 81 to raise standards in the corporate bond market and ensure information transparency. In particular, the decree will limit private issuance to minimize risks for individual investors and will impose more responsibility on underwriters when evaluating the financial capacity of issuers. The decree also states that the total bond issuance of a company cannot exceed its equity capital by five times and that the gap between two bond issuances must be at least 6 months. The issuer must also declare the purpose of the funds and provide a business plan for proper monitoring by investors. The new decree takes effect on 1 September.

Market Summaries

People's Republic of China

Yield Movements

The People's Republic of China's (PRC) yield curve for local currency (LCY) bonds shifted upward between 15 June and 15 August (**Figure 1**). Yields rose more at the shorter-end of the curve, with tenors of 1 year or less rising by 56 basis points (bps). For tenors of between 2 years and 7 years, yields rose an average of 32 bps while yields rose an average of 17 bps for the remaining tenors. As a result, the spread for the 2-year versus 10-year yields fell to 42 bps from 60 bps between 15 June and 15 August.

Yields largely rose as economic data showed the PRC undergoing an economic recovery. The PRC's gross domestic product (GDP) grew 3.2% year-on-year (y-o-y) in the second quarter (Q2) of 2020 after a 6.8% y-o-y decline in the first quarter (Q1) of 2020. Among emerging East Asian economies, the PRC was only one of two markets that posted positive GDP growth in Q2 2020 and the only one that showed an improvement in GDP growth in the second quarter.

Industrial production in the PRC also showed improvement. After a 1.1% y-o-y decline in March, industrial production posted 4 months of positive growth, culminating in a 4.8% y-o-y expansion in July. Retail sales growth continued to be negative, but the declines have slowed. In March, retail sales declined 15.8% y-o-y, but in the succeeding months, the declines slowed, with a 1.8% y-o-y decline in June and a 1.1% y-o-y decline in July. Inflation also showed an uptick, with a 2.7% y-o-y inflation rate in July, up from 2.5% y-o-y in June. Producer prices also moved out of deflation, posting a 0.6% y-o-y increase in July after declining 0.1% in June.

Further contributing to the rise in yields was the People's Bank of China (PBOC) not engaging in broad-based monetary easing since it last adjusted its medium-term lending facility and other interest rates last April. However, fiscal stimulus measures are still ongoing as the central government targeted a higher budget deficit target in 2020 and directed local governments to issue more

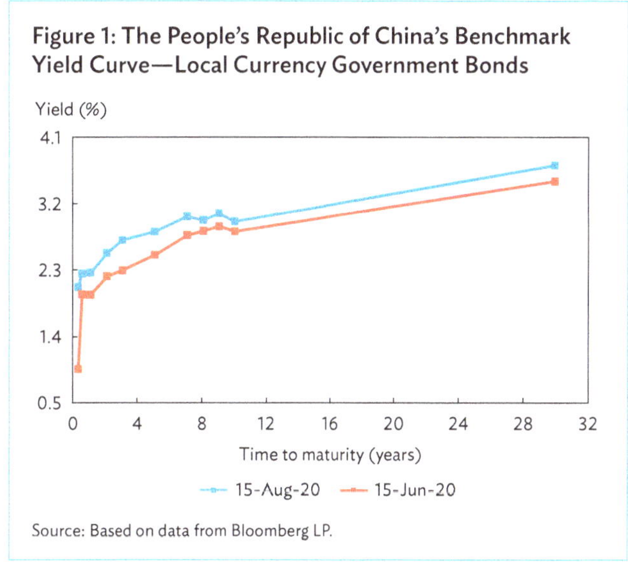

Figure 1: The People's Republic of China's Benchmark Yield Curve—Local Currency Government Bonds

Source: Based on data from Bloomberg LP.

bonds and ensure they are quickly utilized. The expected increased supply of bonds also put upward pressure on yields.

Size and Composition

The PRC's outstanding LCY bonds rose 5.6% quarter-on-quarter (q-o-q) in Q2 2020, after rising 4.9% q-o-q in Q1 2020, to reach CNY93.2 trillion (USD13.2 trillion). LCY bonds grew 17.9% y-o-y in Q1 2020 (**Table 1**).

Government bonds. Growth in the LCY government bond market in the PRC accelerated to 5.4% q-o-q in Q2 2020 from 3.5% q-o-q in Q1 2020. Growth was driven by an increase in Treasury bonds and other government bonds and in local government bonds. Treasury bonds and other governments rose 5.5% q-o-q after a decline of 0.9% in the previous quarter, while local government bonds outstanding grew 6.2% q-o-q, nearly the same pace as the 6.6% q-o-q growth in the previous quarter.

The rise in government bonds outstanding was due to the PRC's efforts to stabilize the economy through fiscal stimulus measures. The budget deficit is projected to

Table 1: Size and Composition of the Local Currency Bond Market in the People's Republic of China

| | Outstanding Amount (billion) | | | | | | Growth Rates (%) | | | |
| | Q2 2019 | | Q1 2020 | | Q2 2020 | | Q2 2019 | | Q2 2020 | |
	CNY	USD	CNY	USD	CNY	USD	q-o-q	y-o-y	q-o-q	y-o-y
Total	79,049	11,512	88,270	12,464	93,187	13,189	4.0	16.7	5.6	17.9
Government	51,135	7,447	55,852	7,886	58,867	8,332	4.2	15.9	5.4	15.1
Treasury Bonds and Other Government Bonds	15,461	2,252	16,850	2,379	17,775	2,516	3.9	11.7	5.49	15.0
Central Bank Bonds	4	1	19	3	15	2	166.7	–	(18.9)	275.0
Policy Bank Bonds	15,213	2,215	15,985	2,257	16,662	2,358	3.0	8.6	4.2	9.5
Local Government Bonds	20,457	2,979	22,999	3,247	24,415	3,456	5.4	25.7	6.2	19.3
Corporate	27,914	4,065	32,418	4,577	34,320	4,857	3.6	18.3	5.9	22.9
Policy Bank Bonds										
China Development Bank	8,580	1,250	8,875	1,253	9,138	1,293	3.0	10.8	3.0	6.5
Export–Import Bank of China	2,533	369	2,858	404	3,086	437	3.6	7.0	8.0	21.8
Agricultural Devt. Bank of China	4,100	597	4,252	600	4,438	628	2.4	5.3	4.4	8.2

( ) = negative, – = not applicable, CNY = Chinese yuan, q-o-q = quarter-on-quarter, Q1 = first quarter, Q2 = second quarter, USD = United States dollar, y-o-y = year-on-year.
Notes:
1. Calculated using data from national sources.
2. Treasury bonds include savings bonds and local government bonds.
3. Bloomberg LP end-of-period local currency–USD rates are used.
4. Growth rates are calculated from local currency base and do not include currency effects.
Sources: CEIC and Bloomberg LP.

Table 2: Corporate Bonds Outstanding in Key Categories

| | Amount (CNY billion) | | | Growth Rate (%) | | | |
| | | | | Q2 2019 | | Q2 2020 | |
	Q2 2019	Q1 2020	Q2 2020	q-o-q	y-o-y	q-o-q	y-o-y
Financial Bonds	5,042	6,364	6,803	1.1	30.8	6.9	34.9
Enterprise Bonds	3,834	3,707	3,771	1.0	(8.8)	1.7	(1.6)
Listed Corporate Bonds	7,024	8,328	8,996	1.1	22.0	8.0	28.1
Commercial Paper	2,197	2,671	2,825	1.0	26.2	5.8	28.6
Medium-Term Notes	5,919	6,829	7,300	1.0	17.1	6.9	23.3
Asset-Backed Securities	1,924	2,388	2,406	1.1	65.3	0.8	25.0

( ) = negative, CNY = Chinese yuan, q-o-q = quarter-on-quarter, Q1 = first quarter, Q2 = second quarter, y-o-y = year-on-year.
Source: CEIC.

be at least CNY1.0 trillion higher in 2020 than in 2019, with the budget deficit expected to exceed 3.6% of GDP, up from 2.8%. In addition, the PRC announced that it will issue CNY1.0 trillion of special government bonds specifically earmarked for coronavirus disease (COVID-19) measures; these bonds are considered off-book and not counted as part of the government's budget. The PRC also set a target of CNY3.75 trillion for local government bond issuance in 2020, which is CNY1.6 trillion higher than last year.

Corporate bonds. The PRC's corporate bond market growth decelerated to 5.9% in Q2 2020 from 7.3% q-o-q in Q1 2020. Financial bonds grew the fastest, rising 6.9% q-o-q (**Table 2**). While growth slowed in Q2 2020, it was still relatively high as the PRC has sought to make issuances of bonds easier in 2020. In addition, better economic conditions in the PRC helped improve the environment for issuing corporate bonds as well.

As a result, issuance of all major corporate bond categories increased in Q2 2020, except for commercial paper, which fell 2.7% q-o-q (**Figure 2**).

The PRC's LCY corporate bond market continued to be dominated by a few big issuers (**Table 3**). At the end of Q2 2020, the top 30 corporate bond issuers accounted for a combined CNY9.4 trillion worth of corporate

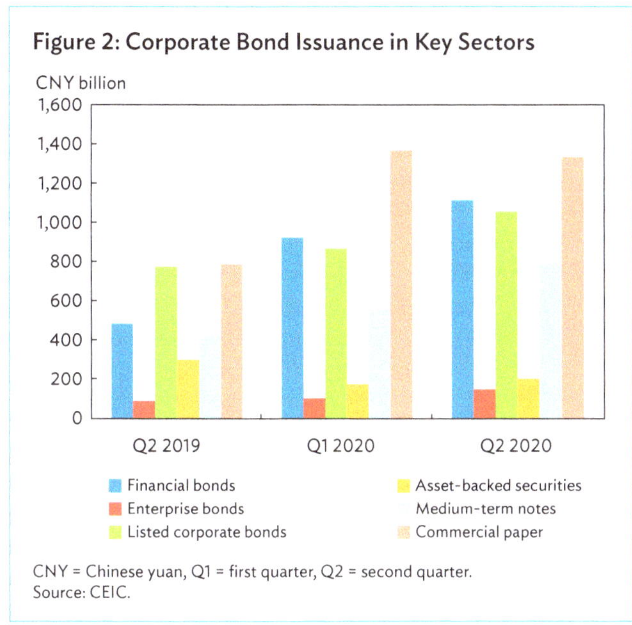

Figure 2: Corporate Bond Issuance in Key Sectors

CNY = Chinese yuan, Q1 = first quarter, Q2 = second quarter.
Source: CEIC.

bonds outstanding, or about 27.4% of the total market. Of the top 30, the 10 largest issuers accounted for an aggregate CNY6.1 trillion. China Railway, the top issuer, had nearly four times the outstanding amount of bonds as Agricultural Bank of China, the second-largest issuer. The top 30 issuers included 15 banks, which continued to generate funding to strengthen their capital bases, improve liquidity, and lengthen their maturity profiles given the ongoing uncertainty.

Table 4 lists the largest corporate bond issuances in Q2 2020. The top issuers consisted largely of financial institutions as they seek to improve their capital base and liquidity in light of the ongoing economic impact of COVID-19.

Investor Profile

Government bonds. Among the major government bond categories, banks were the single-largest holder at the end of June (**Figure 3**), with banks owning 72.7% of all outstanding government bonds. The concentration of bank ownership was the highest for local government bonds (87.9%), as banks have been asked by the central government to help support the funding efforts of local governments, followed by policy banks as the next largest holder of local government bonds. Unincorporated products are the second-largest holder of policy bank bonds after banks.[6]

Liquidity

The volume of interest rate swaps fell 10.2% q-o-q in Q2 2020. The 7-day repurchase remained the most used interest rate swap, comprising a 79.2% share of the total interest rate swap volume during the quarter (**Table 5**).

Policy, Institutional, and Regulatory Developments

The People's Bank of China Issues Central Bank Bills in Hong Kong, China

In June and August, the PBOC issued renminbi-denominated bills in Hong Kong, China to help manage offshore liquidity and control the renminbi yield curve. The issuance comprised of (i) CNY10 billion 6-month central bank bills at a yield of 2.21% in June, and (ii) CNY20 billion 3-month central bank bills at a yield of 2.70%, and (iii) CNY10 billion of 1-year bills at a yield of 2.70% in August.

---

[6] Unincorporated products include banks' wealth management products, securities investment funds, trust funds, and insurance products.

Table 3: Top 30 Issuers of Local Currency Corporate Bonds in the People's Republic of China

	Issuers	Outstanding Amount		State-Owned	Listed Company	Type of Industry
		LCY Bonds (CNY billion)	LCY Bonds (USD billion)			
1.	China Railway	2,243.5	317.5	Yes	No	Transportation
2.	Agricultural Bank of China	645.1	91.3	Yes	Yes	Banking
3.	Bank of China	530.6	75.1	Yes	Yes	Banking
4.	Industrial and Commercial Bank of China	517.6	73.3	Yes	Yes	Banking
5.	Central Huijin Investment	476.0	67.4	Yes	No	Asset Management
6.	Bank of Communications	391.6	55.4	No	Yes	Banking
7.	Shanghai Pudong Development Bank	353.7	50.1	No	Yes	Banking
8.	State Grid Corporation of China	352.5	49.9	Yes	No	Public Utilities
9.	China Construction Bank	307.1	43.5	Yes	Yes	Banking
10.	China National Petroleum	294.9	41.7	Yes	No	Energy
11.	Industrial Bank	273.4	38.7	No	Yes	Banking
12.	China Minsheng Banking	264.0	37.4	No	Yes	Banking
13.	China CITIC Bank	223.2	31.6	No	Yes	Banking
14.	State Power Investment	210.6	29.8	Yes	No	Energy
15.	Ping An Bank	193.7	27.4	No	Yes	Banking
16.	PetroChina	180.0	25.5	Yes	Yes	Energy
17.	Tianjin Infrastructure Construction and Investment Group	170.0	24.1	Yes	No	Industrial
18.	China Southern Power Grid	167.0	23.6	Yes	No	Energy
19.	Huaxia Bank	165.0	23.4	Yes	No	Banking
20.	China Everbright Bank	163.8	23.2	Yes	Yes	Banking
21.	Postal Savings Bank of China	155.0	21.9	Yes	Yes	Banking
22.	China Merchants Bank	151.4	21.4	Yes	Yes	Banking
23.	CITIC Securities	147.7	20.9	Yes	Yes	Brokerage
24.	Datong Coal Mine Group	139.4	19.7	Yes	No	Coal
25.	Shaanxi Coal and Chemical Industry Group	137.5	19.5	Yes	No	Energy
26.	China Three Gorges Corporation	114.0	16.1	Yes	No	Power
27.	Shougang Group	113.4	16.1	Yes	No	Steel
28.	China Datang	105.1	14.9	Yes	Yes	Energy
29.	China Cinda Asset Management	103.0	14.6	Yes	Yes	Asset Management
30.	Bank of Beijing	102.9	14.6	No	Yes	Banking
	Total Top 30 LCY Corporate Issuers	**9,392.5**	**1,329.4**			
	Total LCY Corporate Bonds	**34,319.6**	**4,857.4**			
	Top 30 as % of Total LCY Corporate Bonds	**27.4%**	**27.4%**			

CNY = Chinese yuan, LCY = local currency, USD = United States dollar.
Notes:
1. Data as of 30 June 2020.
2. State-owned firms are defined as those in which the government has more than a 50% ownership stake.
Source: *AsianBondsOnline* calculations based on Bloomberg LP data.

Table 4: Notable Local Currency Corporate Bond Issuance in the Second Quarter of 2020

Corporate Issuers	Coupon Rate (%)	Issued Amount (CNY billion)
China State Railway Group		
1-year bond	1.64	15
1-year bond	1.74	10
5-year bond	3.07	20
5-year bond	3.07	20
5-year bond	3.07	20
10-year bond	3.58	12
10-year bond	3.58	12
10-year bond	3.58	12
20-year bond	3.97	8
Central Huijin Investment		
3-year bond	2.15	15
3-year bond	2.28	15
3-year bond	2.92	15
5-year bond	2.71	6
5-year bond	3.29	6
5-year bond	2.61	6

Corporate Issuers	Coupon Rate (%)	Issued Amount (CNY billion)
Agricultural Bank of China		
3-year bond	1.99	20
10-year bond	3.10	40
Industrial Bank		
3-year bond	2.17	23
3-year bond	2.58	22
5-year bond	2.67	7
5-year bond	2.95	5
Shanghai Pudong Development Bank		
3-year bond	2.08	50

CNY = Chinese yuan.
Source: Based on data from Bloomberg LP.

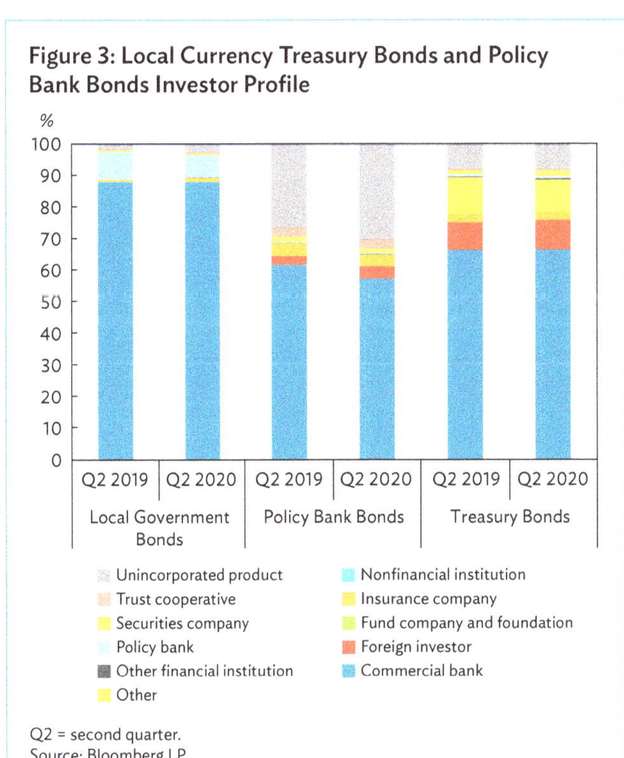

Figure 3: Local Currency Treasury Bonds and Policy Bank Bonds Investor Profile

Q2 = second quarter.
Source: Bloomberg LP.

Table 5: Notional Values of the People's Republic of China's Interest Rate Swap Market in the Second Quarter of 2020

Interest Rate Swap Benchmarks	Notional Amount (CNY billion)	Share of Total Notional Amount (%)	Growth Rate (%)
	Q2 2020		q-o-q
7-Day Repo Rate	2.0	0.0	0.0
7-Day Repo Rate (Deposit Institutions)	33,950.5	79.2	3.7
Overnight SHIBOR	234.0	0.5	170.5
3-Month SHIBOR	7,799.3	18.2	(45.2)
1-Year Lending Rate	728.5	1.7	77.8
5-Year Lending Rate	25.6	0.1	39.7
10-Year Treasury Yield	62.0	0.1	(61.1)
10-Year Bond Yield/10-Year Government Bond Yield	61.0	0.1	(34.1)
Total	42,862.9	100.0	(10.2)

( ) = negative, CNY = Chinese yuan, q-o-q = quarter-on-quarter, Q2 = second quarter, Repo = repurchase, SHIBOR = Shanghai Interbank Offered Rate.
Note: Growth rate computed based on notional amounts.
Sources: *AsianBondsOnline* and *ChinaMoney*.

Hong Kong, China

Yield Movements

Between 15 June and 15 August, local currency (LCY) bond market yields in Hong Kong, China fell across all tenors, shifting the yield curve downward (**Figure 1**). The downward shift was more evident at the shorter-end of the curve, as tenors with maturities of 1 year or less shed an average of 22 basis points (bps). Bond yields for maturities of 2 years or more fell an average of 10 bps, with the 15-year yield showing the smallest dip at 3 bps. During the review period, the spread between 2-year and 10-year bond yields widened from 22 bps to 35 bps.

Hong Kong, China's government bond yields tracked United States (US) Treasury yields during the review period. US Treasury yields fell an average of 4 bps from 15 June to 15 August: yields for maturities of 1 year or below fell an average of 6 bps, while those for maturities of 2 years and longer dropped an average of 4 bps. The fall in US Treasury yields was partly driven by weakened investor sentiment regarding the US economy amid the coronavirus disease (COVID-19) pandemic, the slow progress of the latest fiscal relief package in the US Congress, and uncertainties over the upcoming election. Moreover, the Federal Reserve continued its bond-buying policy to keep rates low.

Demand for the Hong Kong dollar surged during the review period, fueled by carry trade and equity-related activities. The heightened demand for the Hong Kong dollar pushed the strong-side of its trading band against the US dollar in July, prompting the Hong Kong Monetary Authority (HKMA) to spend a total of HKD23.2 billion to maintain the Hong Kong dollar's peg to the US dollar. The HKMA's interventions brought the aggregate balance— an indicator of liquidity in the financial system—from HKD122.1 billion (USD15.8 billion) to HKD187.7 billion (USD24.2 billion) during the review period.

Declining yields also reflected the continuing contraction in Hong Kong, China's economy. Based on advanced estimates, Hong Kong, China's gross domestic product plunged 9.0% year-on-year (y-o-y) in the second quarter (Q2) of 2020 following a 9.1% y-o-y drop in the first quarter (Q1). The economy has been in a technical recession since the third quarter of 2019. Depressed

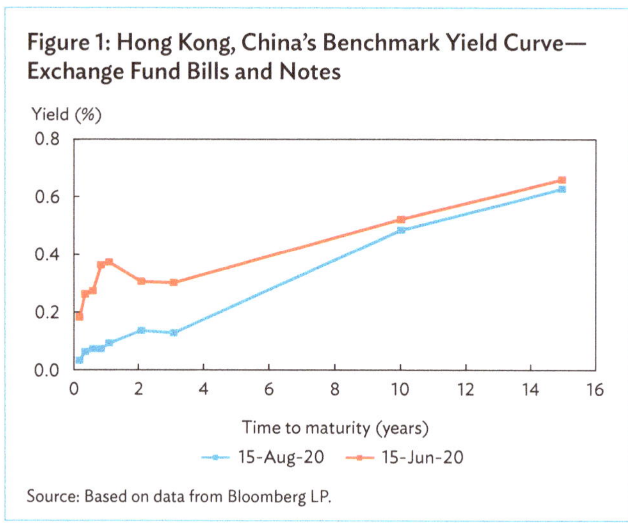

Figure 1: Hong Kong, China's Benchmark Yield Curve— Exchange Fund Bills and Notes

Source: Based on data from Bloomberg LP.

domestic and external demand continued to batter the economy. Private consumption slid further, dropping 14.5% y-o-y in Q2 2020 after a 10.6% y-o-y decrease in the previous quarter. Exports of goods dropped 2.1% y-o-y, while exports of services plummeted 46.6% y-o-y in Q2 2020. Gross fixed capital formation dropped 20.6% y-o-y in Q2 2020 following a 15.8% y-o-y decline in the previous quarter. Due to increased spending on fiscal stimulus to combat the effects of COVID-19 on the economy, government consumption rose 9.6% y-o-y in Q2 2020 after rising 8.8% y-o-y in the prior quarter.

Heightened downside risks—brought about by the combined effects of political unrest, COVID-19, and worsening trade and political tensions between the People's Republic of China and the US—was exacerbated by the new security law that came into effect in Q2 2020. Uncertainties remain as to how the new security law will affect Hong Kong, China's financial system in the long run.

Hong Kong, China posted deflation of 2.3% y-o-y in July, the largest negative reading since November 2003. July's deflation, which reversed the 0.7% y-o-y uptick in June, stemmed mainly from the government's public housing rental payments. Netting out the effects of government one-off relief measures, consumer price inflation in July rose 0.2% y-o-y, which was down from 1.2% y-o-y in June. On a seasonally adjusted month-on-month basis, the average monthly inflation from May to July was –0.1%.

Size and Composition

Hong Kong, China's LCY bond outstanding reached HKD2,267.6 billion at the end of June, up from HKD2,255.5 at the end of March (**Table 1**). The 0.5% quarter-on-quarter (q-o-q) growth in Q2 2020 reversed the 0.5% q-o-q decline in Q1 2020. The q-o-q growth was primarily driven by a 2.3% q-o-q rise in the corporate bond segment as the government bond segment contracted 1.1% q-o-q in Q2 2020, the same rate of decline in Q1 2020. On a y-o-y basis, aggregate bonds outstanding dropped 0.8% in Q2 2020, reversing the tepid 0.3% growth in the prior quarter. Government bonds accounted for a 51.0% share of total LCY bonds outstanding at the end of June.

Government bonds. At the end of June, LCY government bonds outstanding amounted to HKD1,156.2 billion, down from HKD1,169.5 billion at the end of March. The stock of government bonds dropped 1.1% q-o-q in Q2 2020 due to the combined reduction in outstanding Exchange Fund Bills (EFBs) and Exchange Fund Notes (EFNs), which outpaced the growth of outstanding Hong Kong Special Administrative Region (HKSAR) bonds. On an annual basis, outstanding LCY government bonds dropped 0.7% y-o-y in Q2 2020, reversing the 0.7% y-o-y growth in Q1 2020. Government bond issuance contracted 0.8% q-o-q in Q2 2020, mainly due to a contraction in EFB issuance, which outpaced the expansion in EFN and HKSAR bond issuance.

Exchange Fund Bills. The outstanding stock of EFBs stood at HKD1,041.9 billion in Q2 2020, down from HKD1,059.7 billion in Q1 2020. The 1.7% q-o-q contraction in Q2 2020 reversed the modest 0.4% q-o-q gain posted in the previous quarter. Issuance of EFBs amounted to HKD821.6 billion in Q2 2020, contracting 1.5% q-o-q.

Exchange Fund Notes. Since 2015, the HKMA has limited its issuance of EFNs to 2-year tenors. In May, the HKMA issued a 2-year EFN worth HKD1.2 billion. Due to maturities, the amount of outstanding EFNs dropped 3.0% q-o-q and 12.2% y-o-y to reach HKD25.8 billion at the end of June.

HKSAR bonds. HKSAR bonds outstanding rose 6.4% q-o-q to reach HKD88.5 billion at the end of Q2 2020. The government issued a 3-year bond worth HKD4.0 billion in April, a 5-year bond worth HKD2.5 billion in May, and a 10-year bond worth HKD1.7 billion in June under the Institutional Bond Issuance Programme.

Corporate bonds. Corporate bonds outstanding reached HKD1,111.3 billion at the end of June. Growth in the corporate bond segment accelerated to 2.3% q-o-q in Q2 2020 from 0.2% q-o-q in Q1 2020. On a y-o-y basis, corporate bonds outstanding declined 0.9% in Q2 2020 following a 0.2% contraction in the previous quarter.

Hong Kong, China's top 30 nonbank issuers had a combined HKD249.9 billion of LCY bonds outstanding at the end of June, accounting for 22.5% of the total corporate bond market (**Table 2**). Government-owned Hong Kong Mortgage Corporation maintained

Table 1: Size and Composition of the Local Currency Bond Market in Hong Kong, China

| | Outstanding Amount (billion) | | | | | | Growth Rate (%) | | | |
| | Q2 2019 | | Q1 2020 | | Q2 2020 | | Q2 2019 | | Q2 2020 | |
	HKD	USD	HKD	USD	HKD	USD	q-o-q	y-o-y	q-o-q	y-o-y
Total	2,285	293	2,255	291	2,268	293	1.6	5.1	0.5	(0.8)
Government	1,164	149	1,170	151	1,156	149	0.2	0.5	(1.1)	(0.7)
Exchange Fund Bills	1,042	133	1,060	137	1,042	134	0.6	2.3	(1.7)	0.003
Exchange Fund Notes	29	4	27	3	26	3	(5.8)	(16.0)	(3.0)	(12.2)
HKSAR Bonds	93	12	83	11	89	11	(2.1)	(11.4)	6.4	(4.5)
Corporate	1,121	144	1,086	140	1,111	143	3.1	10.3	2.3	(0.9)

( ) = negative, – = not applicable, HKD = Hong Kong dollar, HKSAR = Hong Kong Special Administrative Region, q-o-q = quarter-on-quarter, Q1 = first quarter, Q2 = second quarter, USD = United States dollar, y-o-y = year-on-year.
Notes:
1. Calculated using data from national sources.
2. Bloomberg LP end-of-period local currency–USD rates are used.
3. Growth rates are calculated from local currency base and do not include currency effects.
Source: Hong Kong Monetary Authority.

Table 2: Top 30 Nonbank Corporate Issuers of Local Currency Corporate Bonds in Hong Kong, China

	Issuers	Outstanding Amount		State-Owned	Listed Company	Type of Industry
		LCY Bonds (HKD billion)	LCY Bonds (USD billion)			
1.	Hong Kong Mortgage Corporation	38.7	5.0	Yes	No	Finance
2.	Sun Hung Kai & Co.	18.0	2.3	No	Yes	Finance
3.	The Hong Kong and China Gas Company	15.2	2.0	No	Yes	Utilities
4.	MTR Corporation	13.6	1.8	Yes	Yes	Transportation
5.	Link Holdings	12.9	1.7	No	Yes	Finance
6.	New World Development	12.1	1.6	No	Yes	Diversified
7.	Henderson Land Development	11.6	1.5	No	Yes	Real Estate
8.	Hongkong Land	11.3	1.5	No	No	Real Estate
9.	Swire Pacific	10.3	1.3	No	Yes	Diversified
10.	Hang Lung Properties	8.2	1.1	No	Yes	Real Estate
11.	Hongkong Electric	8.1	1.0	No	No	Utilities
12.	CLP Power Hong Kong Financing	7.7	1.0	No	No	Finance
13.	Swire Properties	7.6	1.0	No	Yes	Diversified
14.	Wharf Real Estate Investment	6.9	0.9	No	Yes	Real Estate
15.	Smart Edge	6.8	0.9	No	No	Finance
16.	Airport Authority Hong Kong	6.6	0.9	Yes	No	Transportation
17.	AIA Group	6.3	0.8	No	Yes	Insurance
18.	Hysan Development Corporation	6.3	0.8	No	Yes	Real Estate
19.	CK Asset Holdings	6.2	0.8	No	Yes	Real Estate
20.	Guotai Junan International Holdings	5.9	0.8	No	Yes	Finance
21.	The Wharf Holdings	5.8	0.7	No	Yes	Finance
22.	Future Days	5.5	0.7	No	No	Transportation
23.	Lerthai Group	3.0	0.4	No	Yes	Real Estate
24.	China Dynamics Holdings	2.4	0.3	No	Yes	Automotive
25.	Champion REIT	2.3	0.3	No	Yes	Real Estate
26.	South Shore Holdings	2.2	0.3	No	Yes	Industrial
27.	Emperor Capital Group	2.2	0.3	No	Yes	Finance
28.	Emperor International Holdings	2.2	0.3	No	Yes	Finance
29.	Cathay Pacific	2.1	0.3	No	Yes	Transportation
30.	IFC Development	2.0	0.3	No	No	Finance
Total Top 30 Nonbank LCY Corporate Issuers		**249.9**	**32.2**			
Total LCY Corporate Bonds		**1,111.3**	**143.4**			
Top 30 as % of Total LCY Corporate Bonds		**22.5%**	**22.5%**			

HKD = Hong Kong dollar, LCY = local currency, REIT = real estate investment trust, USD = United States dollar.
Notes:
1. Data as of 30 June 2020.
2. State-owned firms are defined as those in which the government has more than a 50% ownership stake.
Source: *AsianBondsOnline* calculations based on Bloomberg LP data.

its position as the top issuer with bonds outstanding amounting to HKD38.7 billion at the end of June. Sung Hung Kai & Co., a finance firm, also retained its position as the second-largest issuer with bonds outstanding of HKD18.0 billion at the end of Q2 2020. The Hong Kong and China Gas Company became the third-largest issuer in Q2 2020 with an outstanding amount of HKD15.2 billion, overtaking MTR Corporation, which had HKD13.6 billion of outstanding bonds. The top 30 issuers were predominantly finance and real estate companies. A majority of them were listed in the Hong Kong Stock Exchange and only three were state-owned companies.

Corporate bond issuance reached HKD234.5 billion at the end of June. Issuance growth moderated to 9.8% q-o-q in Q2 2020 from 44.3% q-o-q in Q1 2020. Among the largest issuances during the quarter were bonds issued by the Airport Authority Hong Kong, Hong Kong Mortgage Corporation, and Hong Kong and China Gas Company. The Airport Authority Hong Kong, the state-owned operator of Hong Kong International Airport, issued bonds amounting to HKD5.2 billion, including a 5-year bond with a 1.62% coupon worth HKD0.7 billion, a 7-year bond with a 1.95% coupon worth HKD0.80 billion, and a 10-year bond with a 2.30% coupon worth HKD0.9 billion (**Table 3**).

Government-owned Hong Kong Mortgage Corporation's issuances included a zero coupon 1-year bond worth HKD1.0 billion, a 3-year bond with a 0.97% coupon worth HKD1.0 billion, and a 4-year bond with a 1.31% coupon worth HKD0.25 billion.

Goutai Junan International Holdings, a financial firm, issued a total of HKD4.0 billion worth of bonds including a 1-year bond with a 2.53% coupon worth HKD0.8 billion and a 1-year bond with a 2.50% coupon worth HKD0.5 billion.

There were several issuances of long-dated bonds in Q2 2020, including two 30-year bonds issued by the Hong Kong and China Gas Company, which carried coupons of 2.57% each and were worth a total of HKD1.92 billion. Among Hong Kong Electric's issuances during the quarter was a 30-year bond with a 2.59% coupon worth HKD1.24 billion. MTR Corporation issued the longest-dated bond during the quarter: a 35-year bond with a 2.55% coupon worth HKD0.5 billion.

Policy, Institutional, and Regulatory Developments

The People's Bank of China, Hong Kong Monetary Authority, and Monetary Authority of Macao Launch Cross-Boundary Wealth Management Pilot Scheme

On 29 June, the People's Bank of China, the HKMA, and the Monetary Authority of Macao launched a pilot scheme for cross-boundary wealth management in the Greater Bay Area. Wealth Management Connect is an arrangement wherein residents in the Greater Bay Area can undertake cross-boundary investment in wealth management products managed by banks in the Greater Bay Area. The arrangement will be governed by the respective laws and regulations on retail wealth management products applicable in the three areas as well as international standards and practices. Cross-boundary remittances under the scheme will be carried out in renminbi, with currency conversion conducted in the offshore markets. Relevant regulators in the People's Republic of China; Hong Kong, China; and Macau, China will agree on supervisory cooperation to protect investor interests and maintain fair trading.

Table 3: Notable Local Currency Corporate Bond Issuance in the Second Quarter of 2020

Corporate Issuers	Coupon Rate (%)	Issued Amount (HKD million)
Airport Authority Hong Kong		
5-year bond	1.62	0.70
7-year bond	1.95	0.80
10-year bond	2.30	0.90
Hong Kong Mortgage Corporation		
1-year bond	0.00	1.00
3-year bond	0.97	1.00
4-year bond	1.31	0.25
The Hong Kong and China Gas Company		
30-year bond	2.57	1.51
30-year bond	2.57	0.41
Hongkong Electric		
15-year bond	2.59	0.56
30-year bond	2.59	1.24
Goutai Junan International Holdings		
1-year bond	2.53	0.83
1-year bond	2.50	0.50
MTR Corporation		
35-year bond	2.55	0.50

HKD = Hong Kong dollar.
Source: Bloomberg LP.

Hong Kong Monetary Authority Keeps Countercyclical Capital Buffer at 1.0%

On 7 July, the HKMA decided to hold the countercyclical capital buffer (CCyB) at 1.00%. The HKMA noted that the latest data based on Q1 2020 indicators signal a higher CCyB at 2.25%. However, the HKMA gauged that economic recovery will be protracted given the high level of uncertainty. The HKMA decided to hold the CCyB steady at 1.00% and continue monitoring the economic situation. A lower CCyB provides additional funds for banks, allowing them to extend credit to support financing needs in various sectors of the economy. The CCyB is an integral part of the Basel III regulatory capital framework designed to increase the resilience of the banking sector in periods of excess credit growth.

Indonesia

Yield Movements

Between 15 June and 15 August, local currency (LCY) government bond yields in Indonesia fell for all tenors except the 6-year maturity, which was unchanged (**Figure 1**). Bond yields declined more at the shorter-end of the curve than at the longer-end. Yields shed an average of 116 basis points (bps) for maturities of 1 year to 5 years, while they fell an average of 52 bps for maturities of 7 years to 30 years. The spread between the 2-year and 10-year tenors widened from 130 bps on 15 June to 205 bps on 15 August.

The overall decline in yields was largely influenced by Bank Indonesia's accommodative monetary stance. During the review period, Bank Indonesia reduced its key policy rate by 25 bps once in June and again in July, which brought the 7-day reverse repurchase rate to a 4-year low of 4.0%. Bank Indonesia said that the moves were in line with efforts to preserve economic stability and support economic growth. The central bank had reduced its policy rate by a cumulative 100 bps since the start of the year through the middle of August. Bank Indonesia was among emerging East Asia's central banks that have reduced policy rates substantially this year. In its Board of Governors meeting held on 18–19 August, the central bank decided to leave the 7-day reverse repurchase rate at its current level. It also left unchanged the deposit facility rate at 3.25% and the lending facility rate at 4.75%. Bank Indonesia noted that the current level was appropriate and that it would work on other measures to promote economic recovery by improving liquidity conditions.

The drop in bond yields was also driven by the bleak economic outlook amid the coronavirus disease (COVID-19) outbreak. Economic activities were halted due to lockdowns and social restrictions to curb the transmission of the virus. As a result, the Indonesian economy recorded a contraction in the second quarter (Q2) of 2020, with real gross domestic product (GDP) growth falling 5.3% year-on-year (y-o-y) after rising 3.0% y-o-y in the first quarter (Q1) of 2020. In August, the Ministry of Finance revised downward its economic growth projection for 2020 to a range of between –1.1% to 0.2% from an earlier estimate of –0.4% to 2.3%.

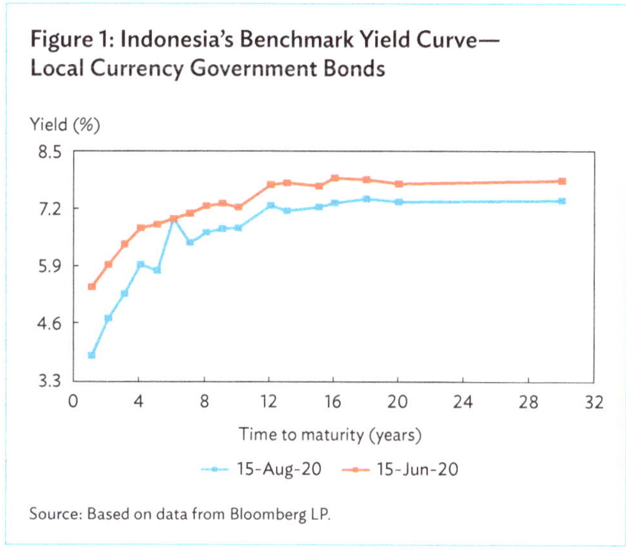

Figure 1: Indonesia's Benchmark Yield Curve—Local Currency Government Bonds

Source: Based on data from Bloomberg LP.

Investment sentiment remained weak over concerns of an increased debt supply as well as debt monetization. A wider budget deficit set at a ceiling of 6.34% of GDP is expected to help fund the government's large-scale stimulus and recovery measures. Regulations allowing the central bank to purchase bonds directly from the government also raised investor concerns. Since April, the government has allowed Bank Indonesia to purchase government bonds during weekly Treasury auctions.

These factors also contributed to the overall weakness in the Indonesian rupiah during the review period. The rupiah recorded the fastest depreciation among emerging East Asian currencies. Despite the overall weakness of the United States dollar since May of this year, the Indonesian rupiah weakened by 4.6% versus the dollar between 15 June and 15 August.

Size and Composition

Indonesia's LCY bond market surged to a size of IDR3,585.2 trillion (USD251.3 billion) at the end of June, with growth accelerating to 7.8% quarter-on-quarter (q-o-q) from only 0.4% q-o-q in Q1 2020 (**Table 1**). Indonesia posted the fastest q-o-q growth among emerging East Asian LCY bond markets at the end of June. Growth was largely driven by increases in the stock of government bonds, particularly Treasury bills and Treasury bonds. Central bank instruments also

Table 1: Size and Composition of the Local Currency Bond Market in Indonesia

| | Outstanding Amount (billion) | | | | | | Growth Rate (%) | | | |
| | Q2 2019 | | Q1 2020 | | Q2 2020 | | Q2 2019 | | Q2 2020 | |
	IDR	USD	IDR	USD	IDR	USD	q-o-q	y-o-y	q-o-q	y-o-y
Total	3,069,867	217	3,324,692	204	3,585,233	251	(0.5)	17.6	7.8	16.8
Government	2,652,610	188	2,881,782	177	3,155,519	221	(0.3)	20.1	9.5	19.0
Central Govt. Bonds	2,531,039	179	2,833,359	174	3,105,895	218	0.1	15.2	9.6	22.7
of which: Sukuk	420,064	30	478,152	29	579,263	41	(1.7)	18.6	21.1	37.9
Central Bank Bonds	121,571	9	48,423	3	49,624	3	(7.7)	915.9	2.5	(59.2)
of which: Sukuk	21,938	2	36,173	2	38,874	3	(11.9)	83.3	7.5	77.2
Corporate	417,257	30	442,909	27	429,715	30	(1.6)	3.7	(3.0)	3.0
of which: Sukuk	24,133	2	30,200	2	29,382	2	(1.9)	64.3	(2.7)	21.8

( ) = negative, IDR = Indonesian rupiah, q-o-q = quarter-on-quarter, Q1 = first quarter, Q2 = second quarter, USD = United States dollar, y-o-y = year-on-year.
Notes:
1. Calculated using data from national sources.
2. Bloomberg LP end-of-period local currency–USD rates are used.
3. Growth rates are calculated from local currency base and do not include currency effects.
4. The total stock of nontradable bonds as of 30 June 2020 stood at IDR176.1 trillion.
Sources: Bank Indonesia; Directorate General of Budget Financing and Risk Management, Ministry of Finance; Indonesia Stock Exchange; and Bloomberg LP.

contributed to overall growth but to a lesser extent, while corporate bonds posted contractions during the quarter. On an annual basis, LCY bond market growth accelerated to 16.8% y-o-y in Q2 2020 from 7.8% y-o-y in Q1.

The LCY bond market in Indonesia is dominated by government bonds, which accounted for a share of 88.0% of the aggregate bond total at the end of June. Corporate bonds accounted for the remaining 12.0% share. Conventional bonds accounted for a majority share of the total bond stock, representing 81.9% of the total bond stock at the end of June. The share of sukuk (Islamic bonds) inched up to 18.1% in the same period.

Government bonds. The total stock of government bonds at the end of June stood at IDR3,155.5 trillion on growth of 9.5% q-o-q and 19.0% y-o-y. Much of the growth stemmed from expansions in the stock of central government bonds during the review period.

Central government bonds. At the end of June, the size of central government bonds reached IDR3,105.9 trillion, as growth quickened to 9.6% q-o-q and 22.7% y-o-y in Q2 2020 from 2.9% q-o-q and 12.1% y-o-y in Q1 2020. The Ministry of Finance issued Treasury instruments during the quarter at an increased pace to help fund the government's wider budget deficit.

In Q2 2020, issuance of Treasury bills and Treasury bonds totaled IDR326.2 trillion, higher by 84.5% q-o-q and 116.9% y-o-y. The government accepted more bids than its targeted amount in most of its Treasury auctions during the quarter. In addition to the weekly Treasury auctions, the government undertook private placements of select conventional bonds and sukuk during the quarter.

Central bank bonds. Central bank bonds outstanding, which comprised Sertifikat Bank Indonesia and Sukuk Bank Indonesia, tallied IDR49.6 trillion at the end of June. This represented a hike of 2.5% q-o-q but was down by 59.2% y-o-y. Issuance of central bank instruments during Q2 2020 totaled IDR113 trillion, slightly down from IDR115 trillion in Q1 2020.

Corporate bonds. At the end of June, the total corporate bond stock reached IDR429.7 trillion on a decline of 3.0% q-o-q but an increase of 3.0% y-o-y. The amount of corporate bonds outstanding declined on weak issuance since the start of this year.

The aggregate bond stock of Indonesia's 30 largest corporate bond issuers slipped to IDR318.7 trillion at the end of June (**Table 2**). This was down from IDR330.3 trillion recorded at the end of March. Together, the top 30 issuers represented a 74.2% share of the total bond stock at the end of June. Out of the 30 firms on the list, 17 institutions were from the banking and financial industry. Other corporates on the list were from the telecommunications, construction, and transportation sectors. Similar to Q1 2020, 17 firms from the top 30 list were state-owned companies, and 17 institutions were listed on the Indonesia Stock Exchange.

Table 2: Top 30 Issuers of Local Currency Corporate Bonds in Indonesia

	Issuers	Outstanding Amount		State-Owned	Listed Company	Type of Industry
		LCY Bonds (IDR billion)	LCY Bonds (USD billion)			
1.	Perusahaan Listrik Negara	34,412	2.41	Yes	No	Energy
2.	Indonesia Eximbank	32,110	2.25	Yes	No	Banking
3.	Bank Rakyat Indonesia	23,282	1.63	Yes	Yes	Banking
4.	Sarana Multi Infrastruktur	21,866	1.53	Yes	No	Finance
5.	Bank Tabungan Negara	18,197	1.28	Yes	Yes	Banking
6.	Sarana Multigriya Finansial	15,596	1.09	Yes	No	Finance
7.	Indosat	14,437	1.01	No	Yes	Telecommunications
8.	Bank Mandiri	14,000	0.98	Yes	Yes	Banking
9.	Bank Pan Indonesia	13,427	0.94	No	Yes	Banking
10.	Waskita Karya	12,960	0.91	Yes	Yes	Building Construction
11.	Bank CIMB Niaga	10,350	0.73	No	Yes	Banking
12.	Telekomunikasi Indonesia	8,995	0.63	Yes	Yes	Telecommunications
13.	Permodalan Nasional Madani	8,439	0.59	Yes	No	Finance
14.	Adira Dinamika Multifinance	8,232	0.58	No	Yes	Finance
15.	Pupuk Indonesia	7,945	0.56	Yes	No	Chemical Manufacturing
16.	Semen Indonesia	7,078	0.50	Yes	Yes	Cement Manufacturing
17.	Astra Sedaya Finance	6,958	0.49	No	No	Finance
18.	Hutama Karya	6,500	0.46	Yes	No	Nonbuilding Construction
19.	Medco-Energi Internasional	6,183	0.43	No	Yes	Petroleum and Natural Gas
20.	Perum Pegadaian	6,151	0.43	Yes	No	Finance
21.	Federal International Finance	5,910	0.41	No	No	Finance
22.	Bank Maybank Indonesia	5,423	0.38	No	Yes	Banking
23.	Bank Pembangunan Daerah Jawa Barat Dan Banten	5,000	0.35	Yes	Yes	Banking
24.	Mandiri Tunas Finance	4,120	0.29	No	No	Finance
25.	Adhi Karya	4,027	0.28	Yes	Yes	Building Construction
26.	Kereta Api	4,000	0.28	Yes	No	Transportation
27.	Maybank Indonesia Finance	3,550	0.25	No	No	Finance
28.	XL Axiata	3,413	0.24	No	Yes	Telecommunications
29.	Chandra Asri Petrochemicals	3,139	0.22	No	Yes	Petrochemicals
30.	Tower Bersama Infrastructure	3,038	0.21	No	Yes	Telecommunications Infrrastructure Provider
	Total Top 30 LCY Corporate Issuers	318,735	22.34			
	Total LCY Corporate Bonds	429,715	30.12			
	Top 30 as % of Total LCY Corporate Bonds	74.2%	74.2%			

IDR = Indonesian rupiah, LCY = local currency, USD = United States dollar.
Notes:
1. Data as of 30 June 2020.
2. State-owned firms are defined as those in which the government has more than a 50% ownership stake.
Source: *AsianBondsOnline* calculations based on Indonesia Stock Exchange data.

The composition of the top five firms on the list was unchanged from that at the end of March. State-owned energy firm Perusahaan Listrik Negara (PLN) remained in the top spot with outstanding bonds of IDR34.4 trillion. The second through fifth spots were occupied by state-owned firms from the banking and financial sector: Indonesia Eximbank (IDR32.1 trillion), Bank Rakyat Indonesia (IDR23.3 trillion), Sarana Multi Infrastruktur (IDR21.9 trillion), and Bank Tabungan Negara (IDR18.2 trillion).

Total corporate bond issuance reached IDR8.6 trillion in Q2 2020, down by 54.6% q-o-q and 70.2% y-o-y. Some companies reconsidered their issuance plans given the economic slowdown resulting from the COVID-19 outbreak. In addition, market conditions were not yet conducive for issuing bonds due to higher costs. While Bank Indonesia has reduced policy rates, government bond yields, which are used as benchmark reference pricing, remain elevated.

During the quarter, 15 firms raised funds from the bond market, adding 29 new bond series to the corporate bond stock. Of the new bond series, only two were *sukuk*, both of which were issued by state-owned Perum Pegadaian and structured as *sukuk mudharabah* (Islamic bonds backed by a profit-sharing scheme from a business venture or partnership). The longest-dated new corporate bond issue in Q2 2020 was PLN's 10-year bond issue.

Leading the list of new corporate issuance during the quarter was PLN, with issuance valued at IDR1,737.1 billion in four tranches (**Table 3**). It was followed by Indah Kiat Pulp and Paper, with issuance totaling IDR1,391.1 billion in three tranches. Taking the third spot was Bank Mandiri's aggregate issuance worth IDR1,000 billion in two tranches.

Investor Profile

Heightened risk aversion brought about by the COVID-19 outbreak led to net outflows of foreign funds from the LCY government bond market in the first half of 2020; however, net inflows were noted in May and June. As a result, the foreign investors' share, which used to comprise the largest share of government bonds, fell to 30.2% at the end of June from 39.1% a year earlier (**Figure 2**). The total amount of bonds held by foreign investors fell to IDR937.0 trillion from IDR988.8 trillion at the end of June 2019.

Table 3: Notable Local Currency Corporate Bond Issuance in the Second Quarter of 2020

Corporate Issuers	Coupon Rate (%)	Issued Amount (IDR billion)
Perusahaan Listrik Negara		
3-year bond	7.92	316.70
5-year bond	8.25	99.16
7-year bond	8.55	312.18
10-year bond	9.10	1,009.10
Indah Kiat Pulp & Paper		
370-day bond	9.00	495.50
3-year bond	10.25	883.48
5-year bond	11.00	12.10
Bank Mandiri		
5-year bond	7.75	350.00
7-year bond	8.30	650.00
SMART		
3-year bond	8.50	608.50
5-year bond	9.00	166.50
Toyota Astra Financial		
370-day bond	7.10	206.00
3-year bond	8.25	539.05

IDR = Indonesian rupiah.
Source: Indonesia Stock Exchange.

A relatively larger share of foreign investor holdings of government bonds is in longer-term maturities (**Figure 3**). Among foreign investor holdings, the share of bonds with maturities longer than 10 years stood at 36.4% at the end of June 2020. Bonds with maturities of between 5 years and 10 years were the second most popular, comprising 28.6% of foreign holdings. Only 3.3% of bonds held by foreign investors carried a maturity of less than a year.

As a result of the foreign investor outflows, banks became the dominant holder of government bonds, with their share rising from 23.3% at the end of June 2019 to 33.3% at the end of June 2020. Banks were aggressive buyers, with the total amount of government bonds held rising to IDR1,034.3 trillion at the end of June 2020 from IDR588.8 trillion a year earlier.

Other domestic investors that posted increases in their holdings of government bonds during the review period were insurance firms, mutual funds, and Bank Indonesia. The government bond holdings of insurance firms inched up to a share of 8.9% of the total at the end of June 2020 from 8.4% in the same period a year earlier. Mutual fund holdings of government bonds rose to a share of 4.4% from 4.2% in the same period, while Bank Indonesia's share rose to 6.7% from 6.1%.

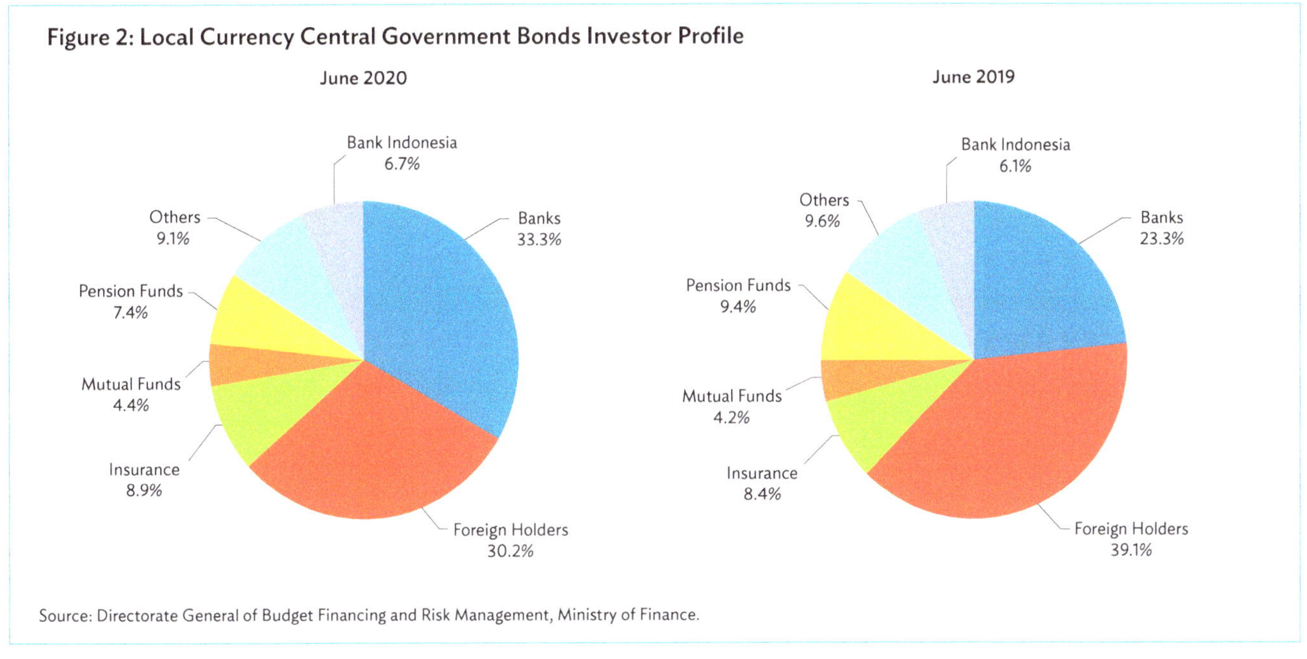

Figure 2: Local Currency Central Government Bonds Investor Profile

June 2020

June 2019

Source: Directorate General of Budget Financing and Risk Management, Ministry of Finance.

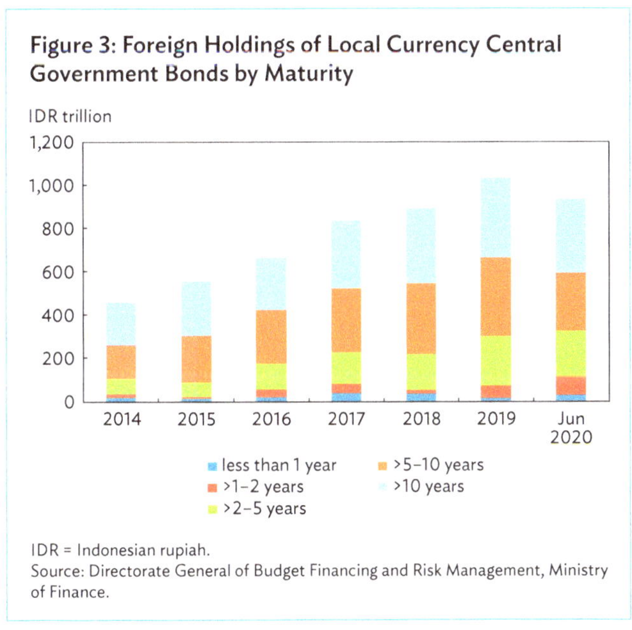

Figure 3: Foreign Holdings of Local Currency Central Government Bonds by Maturity

IDR = Indonesian rupiah.
Source: Directorate General of Budget Financing and Risk Management, Ministry of Finance.

The share of other investors fell to 9.1% at the end of June 2020 from 9.6% at the end of June 2019. The share of pension funds declined, falling to 7.4% from 9.4% in the same review period as pension funds reduced their holdings of government bonds to IDR230.2 trillion from IDR237.0 trillion.

Ratings Update

On 10 August, Fitch Ratings (Fitch) affirmed the sovereign credit rating of Indonesia at BBB. The rating was given a stable outlook. Fitch cited the sovereign's favorable growth outlook in the medium term and low debt-to-GDP ratio as the factors for the rating affirmation. The rating agency also noted the challenges faced by Indonesia including (i) high dependence on external financing, (ii) low government revenue, and (iii) lagging structural features compared with other similarly-rated sovereigns.

Policy, Institutional, and Regulatory Developments

2020 State Budget Deficit Estimated to Reach 6.34% of Gross Domestic Product

In June, a second revision to the 2020 state budget was signed into law, which called for increased spending and a wider budget deficit to support the economy amid the COVID-19 outbreak. The second revision to the 2020 state budget estimates a deficit amounting to IDR1.03 quadrillion, which is equivalent to 6.34% of GDP, up from an earlier revision announced in April of a deficit equivalent to 5.07% of GDP. The government expects state spending to hit IDR2.73 quadrillion in 2020, while state revenue is projected to be IDR1.69 quadrillion.

Bank Indonesia and the Ministry of Finance of Japan Establish Framework for Cooperation

On 31 August, Bank Indonesia and the Ministry of Finance of Japan launched a framework for cooperation on the use of the Indonesian rupiah and the Japanese yen in the settlement of bilateral trade and direct investment. The establishment of the framework was part of the memorandum of cooperation between the two parties, which was signed on 5 December 2019. Under the framework, direct quotation between the Indonesian rupiah and the Japanese yen will be made available, and certain regulations will be relaxed, to encourage the use of the two currencies. Certain banks were also selected to serve as the appointed cross-currency dealers.

Republic of Korea

Yield Movements

The Republic of Korea's local currency (LCY) government bond yields remained range-bound between 15 June and 15 August (**Figure 1**). The yields for short-term tenors from 3 months to 1 year fell 3 basis points (bps) on average. The 2-year tenor fell the most, dipping 9 bps, while for tenors of 3–10 years the average decline was 4 bps. Yields for long-term tenors of 20–50 years moved either up or down by less than 1 bp. The spread between the 2-year and 10-year yields slightly rose to 66 bps from 59 bps during the review period.

Yields moved marginally during the review period given market expectations that the Bank of Korea would maintain the base rate at its 16 July meeting following a 50-bps rate cut in May. In particular, the prior rise in yields for long-term paper observed from March to May tapered during the current review period as increased bond supply concerns, generated by the passage of the first two supplementary government budgets, abated. The rise in yields were tempered by expectations of a Bank of Korea bond purchase program to address the oversupply of bonds in the market. However, a rise in yields at the long-end of the curve was observed in August due to talks over a fourth supplementary budget and as the market anticipated the release of the 2021 fiscal budget.

On 16 July, the Bank of Korea decided to leave its base rate unchanged at 0.50%. The central bank noted a moderate rebound in global economic growth and a reduction in financial market volatility, while also noting the ongoing effects of the coronavirus disease (COVID-19) pandemic. Domestic economic growth remained weak despite the rebound in consumption, as exports continued to contract. Given this, the Bank of Korea stated that growth for 2020 is projected to be below the May forecast of 0.2% year-on-year (y-o-y). Consumer price inflation is expected to be in the lower 0% level as a result of low global oil prices and weak demand.

The contraction of the Republic of Korea's real gross domestic product (GDP) accelerated to 3.2% quarter-on-quarter (q-o-q) in the second quarter (Q2) of 2020 from 1.3% q-o-q in the first quarter (Q1), based on preliminary estimates from the Bank of Korea. The sharper decline

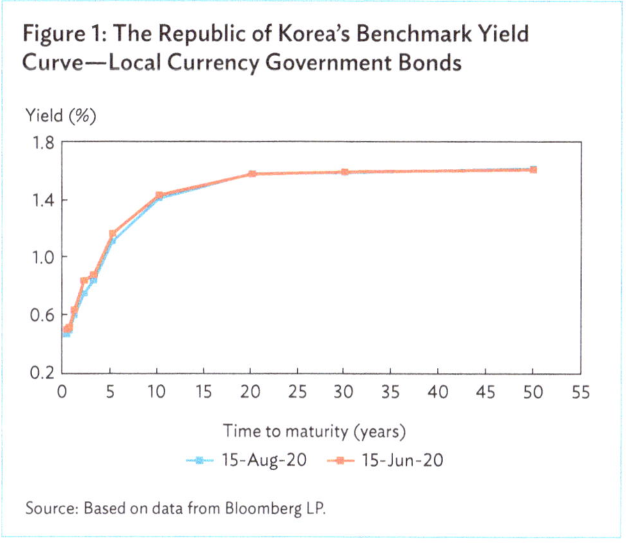

Figure 1: The Republic of Korea's Benchmark Yield Curve—Local Currency Government Bonds

Source: Based on data from Bloomberg LP.

of 16.1% q-o-q in exports in Q2 2020 from 1.4% q-o-q in Q1 2020 drove the Republic of Korea into a technical recession, highlighting the economic impact of the pandemic. Gross fixed capital formation also contracted 0.4% q-o-q in Q2 2020 after a marginal increase of 0.5% q-o-q in the previous quarter, while government spending growth slowed to 1.1% q-o-q from 1.4% q-o-q. Meanwhile, private consumption rebounded in Q2 2020, posting growth of 1.5% q-o-q after a decline of 6.5% q-o-q in Q1 2020. The Republic of Korea's economy fell 2.7% y-o-y in Q2 2020 following growth of 1.4% y-o-y in the previous quarter. Consumer prices fell 0.3% y-o-y in May, were flat in June, and increased 0.3% y-o-y in July.

The Republic of Korea continued to register monthly net foreign inflows from May to July. Foreign demand remained strong, as the economy is considered a safe haven relative to its peers, and on the back of government policies to reduce volatility in financial markets and maintain a stable Korean won. Moreover, LCY government bonds continued to offer higher yields compared to other markets in the region and similarly rated developed markets.

The Korean won strengthened during the review period, appreciating 2.7% to KRW1,198.47 per USD1 as of 15 August. This was primarily due to the weakness of the United States (US) dollar, and the additional support from the extended currency swap agreement between the Bank of Korea and the US Federal Reserve.

Size and Composition

The Republic of Korea's LCY bond market grew 3.1% q-o-q to KRW2,553.7 trillion (USD2,123.3 billion) at the end of June (**Table 1**), up from the 2.8% q-o-q growth posted in Q1 2020. Growth in the domestic bond market continued to be driven by the rising stock of government bonds, particularly central government bonds. Corporate bonds also posted growth but at a slower pace. The Republic of Korea's LCY bond market expanded 9.5% y-o-y in Q2 2020, up from the 8.7% y-o-y growth posted in Q1 2020.

Government bonds. The Republic of Korea's LCY government bonds outstanding were up 4.6% q-o-q and 9.7% y-o-y at the end of June, breaching the KRW1,000 trillion level to reach KRW1,038.1 trillion. Growth continued to stem from the rising stock of central government bonds, which were up 5.1% q-o-q on a sustained increase in issuance in Q2 2020. Government agency bonds outstanding also posted rapid growth of 5.3% q-o-q to KRW190.2 trillion as they have been part of the government's funding source for COVID-19 economic response programs. Monetary Stabilization Bonds issued by the Bank of Korea inched up 1.9% q-o-q to KRW168.9 trillion.

The issuance pace of central government bonds slowed in Q2 2020 but still rose to KRW49.1 trillion from KRW42.5 trillion in Q1 2020. The sustained high level of issuance was needed to fund the larger annual fiscal budget and the two supplementary budgets approved in the first half of the year. The same trend is expected to continue in the remainder of the year to finance the third supplementary budget passed in July and other programs to boost economic growth.

Corporate bonds. The Republic of Korea's LCY corporate bond market posted marginal growth of 2.1% q-o-q to reach a size of KRW1,515.6 trillion at the end of June as issuance for the quarter remained tepid. **Table 2** lists the top 30 LCY corporate bond issuers in the Republic of Korea with aggregate total bonds outstanding of KRW936.7 trillion at the end of Q2 2020, which comprised 61.8% of the LCY corporate bond market. Financial companies such as banks and securities and investment firms continued to dominate the list of the 30 largest corporate bond issuers. State-owned Korea Housing Finance Corporation remained the largest issuer with outstanding bonds of KRW137.8 trillion. Private firm Mirae Asset Daewoo Corporation was the second largest with bonds outstanding of KRW72.6 trillion.

Issuance of corporate bonds in the Republic of Korea remained tepid in Q2 2020, particularly in April and May, declining 4.1% q-o-q due to the contraction in economic activity as a result of the COVID-19 pandemic. **Table 3** lists notable corporate bond issuances in Q2 2020, which mainly came from financial institutions such as NongHyup Bank, Sinbo Securitization, and Kookmin Bank.

Table 1: Size and Composition of the Local Currency Bond Market in the Republic of Korea

| | Outstanding Amount (billion) | | | | | | Growth Rate (%) | | | |
| | Q2 2019 | | Q1 2020 | | Q2 2020 | | Q2 2019 | | Q2 2020 | |
	KRW	USD	KRW	USD	KRW	USD	q-o-q	y-o-y	q-o-q	y-o-y
Total	2,331,705	2,019	2,476,170	2,032	2,553,743	2,123	2.4	5.0	3.1	9.5
Government	946,417	820	992,346	814	1,038,139	863	1.7	1.0	4.6	9.7
Central Government Bonds	599,552	519	645,928	530	679,020	565	2.7	1.7	5.1	13.3
Central Bank Bonds	171,580	149	165,710	136	168,870	140	0.3	(1.7)	1.9	(1.6)
Others	175,285	152	180,708	148	190,249	158	(0.3)	1.2	5.3	8.5
Corporate	1,385,288	1,200	1,483,824	1,218	1,515,604	1,260	2.9	7.9	2.1	9.4

( ) = negative, KRW = Korean won, q-o-q = quarter-on-quarter, Q1 = first quarter, Q2 = second quarter, USD = United States dollar, y-o-y = year-on-year.
Notes:
1. Calculated using data from national sources.
2. Bloomberg LP end-of-period local currency–USD rates are used.
3. Growth rates are calculated from local currency base and do not include currency effects.
4. "Others" comprise Korea Development Bank Bonds, National Housing Bonds, and Seoul Metro Bonds.
5. Corporate bonds include equity-linked securities and derivatives-linked securities.
Sources: The Bank of Korea and *EDAILY BondWeb*.

Table 2: Top 30 Issuers of Local Currency Corporate Bonds in the Republic of Korea

| | | Outstanding Amount | | | Listed on | | |
	Issuers	LCY Bonds (KRW billion)	LCY Bonds (USD billion)	State-Owned	KOSPI	KOSDAQ	Type of Industry
1.	Korea Housing Finance Corporation	137,831	114.6	Yes	No	No	Housing Finance
2.	Mirae Asset Daewoo Co.	72,611	60.4	No	Yes	No	Securities
3.	Korea Investment and Securities	65,838	54.7	No	No	No	Securities
4.	Industrial Bank of Korea	64,280	53.4	Yes	Yes	No	Banking
5.	KB Securities	54,861	45.6	No	No	No	Securities
6.	Hana Financial Investment	51,210	42.6	No	No	No	Securities
7.	NH Investment & Securities	44,743	37.2	Yes	Yes	No	Securities
8.	Samsung Securities	34,966	29.1	No	Yes	No	Securities
9.	Korea Land & Housing Corporation	29,641	24.6	Yes	No	No	Real Estate
10.	Korea Electric Power Corporation	29,060	24.2	Yes	Yes	No	Electricity, Energy, and Power
11.	Shinhan Bank	28,762	23.9	No	No	No	Banking
12.	Korea Expressway	24,210	20.1	Yes	No	No	Transport Infrastructure
13.	The Export-Import Bank of Korea	24,135	20.1	Yes	No	No	Banking
14.	Shinhan Investment Corporation	23,145	19.2	No	No	No	Securities
15.	Woori Bank	19,770	16.4	Yes	Yes	No	Banking
16.	Shinyoung Securities	19,471	16.2	No	Yes	No	Securities
17.	Korea Rail Network Authority	19,070	15.9	Yes	No	No	Transport Infrastructure
18.	Kookmin Bank	18,324	15.2	No	No	No	Banking
19.	NongHyup Bank	17,450	14.5	Yes	No	No	Banking
20.	Hanwha Investment and Securities	16,814	14.0	No	No	No	Securities
21.	KEB Hana Bank	16,200	13.5	No	No	No	Banking
22.	Korea SMEs and Startups Agency	15,888	13.2	Yes	No	No	SME Development
23.	Shinhan Card	15,375	12.8	No	No	No	Credit Card
24.	Meritz Securities	15,101	12.6	No	Yes	No	Securities
25.	Hyundai Capital Services	14,355	11.9	No	No	No	Consumer Finance
26.	KB Kookmin Bank Card	13,600	11.3	No	No	No	Consumer Finance
27.	Standard Chartered Bank Korea	13,170	10.9	No	No	No	Banking
28.	Korea Deposit Insurance Corporation	12,720	10.6	Yes	No	No	Insurance
29.	Korea Gas Corporation	12,129	10.1	Yes	Yes	No	Gas Utility
30.	NongHyup	11,980	10.0	Yes	No	No	Banking
	Total Top 30 LCY Corporate Issuers	**936,710**	**778.8**				
	Total LCY Corporate Bonds	**1,515,604**	**1,260.1**				
	Top 30 as % of Total LCY Corporate Bonds	**61.8%**	**61.8%**				

KOSDAQ = Korean Securities Dealers Automated Quotations, KOSPI = Korea Composite Stock Price Index, KRW = Korean won, LCY = local currency, SME = small and medium-sized enterprise, USD = United States dollar.
Notes:
1. Data as of 30 June 2020.
2. State-owned firms are defined as those in which the government has more than a 50% ownership stake.
3. Corporate bonds include equity-linked securities and derivatives-linked securities.
Sources: *AsianBondsOnline* calculations based on Bloomberg LP and *EDAILY BondWeb* data.

Investor Profile

Insurance companies and pension funds remained the largest investor group in the Republic of Korea's LCY government bond market at the end of March with a share of 35.1%, up from a 34.6% share a year earlier (**Figure 2**). Banks surpassed the general government as the second-largest holder of government bonds with a share of 17.7%, which was only marginally changed from 17.2% in March 2019. The share of the general government fell to 16.9% from 18.1% during the same period. The share of other financial institutions slightly fell to 14.5% from 14.9%, while that of foreign investors rose to 12.8% from 11.0%.

At the end of March 2020, other financial institutions topped insurance companies and pension funds as the largest investor group in the Republic of Korea's LCY corporate bond market, with its share rising to 37.5% from

Table 3: Notable Local Currency Corporate Bond Issuance in the Second Quarter of 2020

Corporate Issuers	Coupon Rate (%)	Issued Amount (KRW billion)
NongHyup Bank		
5-month bond		400
1-year bond	0.89	700
1-year bond	0.91	330
1-year bond	1.01	550
1-year bond	1.03	250
3-year bond	1.19	360
Sinbo Securitization		
2-year bond	1.34	250
3-year bond	1.28	675
3-year bond	1.28	315
3-year bond	1.35	491
3-year bond	1.39	412
Kookmin Bank		
1-year bond	0.76	350
1-year bond	1.15	400
2-year bond	0.99	400
10-year bond	2.13	450

Corporate Issuers	Coupon Rate (%)	Issued Amount (KRW billion)
HMM Company		
30-year bond	3.00	720
Kia Motors		
3-year bond	2.02	480
Hana Financial Group		
Perpetual Bonds	3.20	450
Citibank Korea		
2-year bond	1.13	410
Standard Chartered		
1-year bond	0.85	400
Hyundai Motor		
3-year bond	1.74	390
Lotte Shopping		
3-year bond	2.33	350
SK Energy		
3-year bond	1.95	340

KRW = Korean won.
Source: Based on data from Bloomberg LP.

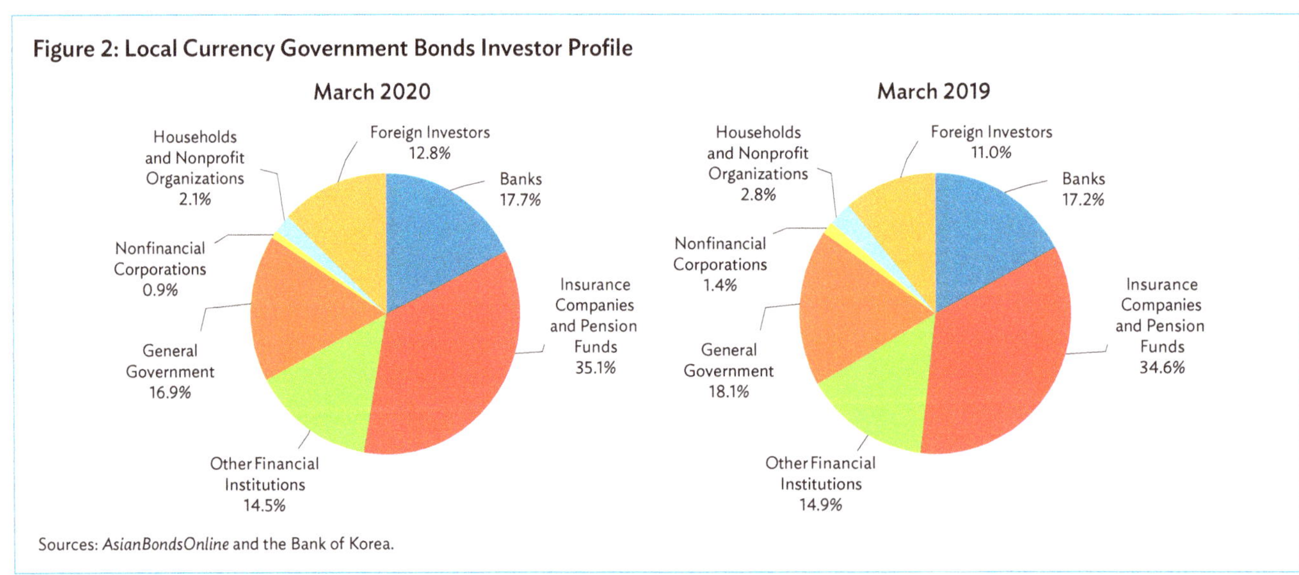

Figure 2: Local Currency Government Bonds Investor Profile

Sources: *AsianBondsOnline* and the Bank of Korea.

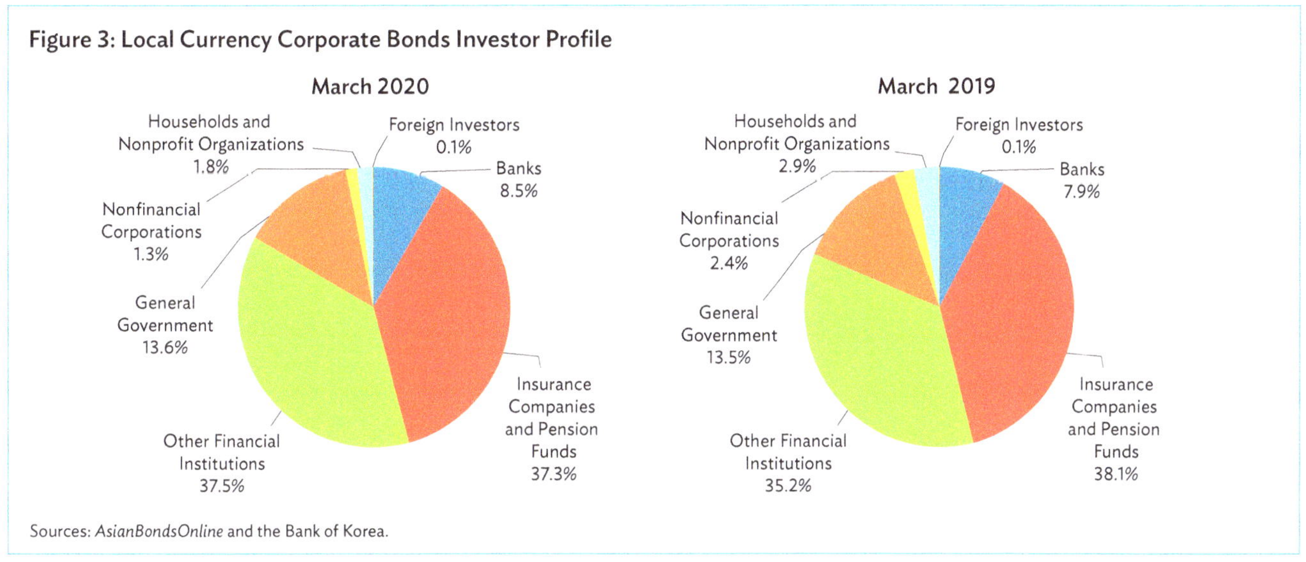

Figure 3: Local Currency Corporate Bonds Investor Profile

March 2020 / March 2019

Sources: *AsianBondsOnline* and the Bank of Korea.

35.2% in March 2019 (**Figure 3**). The share of insurance companies and pension funds declined to 37.3% from 38.1% during the same period. The share of the general government was barely changed at 13.6%, while that of banks was up to 8.5% from 7.9%. Foreign holdings of LCY corporate bonds remained negligible at 0.1%.

Strong net foreign flows into the Republic of Korea's LCY bond market continued in May, June, and July, with monthly totals reaching KRW2,821 billion, KRW3,436 billion, and KRW2,235 billion, respectively (**Figure 4**). The Republic of Korea was among the markets in the region that attracted strong foreign demand amid a surge in global liquidity, a result of the easing of central banks in response to the COVID-19 pandemic. The economy's high credit rating and robust external balances, the stable Korean won, and higher yields relative to its peers continued to be the main drivers of the strong foreign inflows.

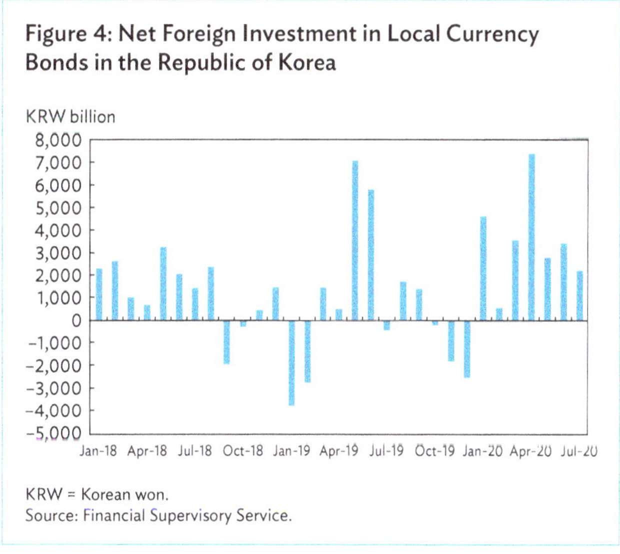

Figure 4: Net Foreign Investment in Local Currency Bonds in the Republic of Korea

KRW billion

KRW = Korean won.
Source: Financial Supervisory Service.

Policy, Institutional, and Regulatory Developments

The Republic of Korea's National Assembly Passes Third Supplementary Budget

On 3 July, the National Assembly of the Republic of Korea passed the third supplementary budget worth KRW35.1 trillion. The amount approved was lower than the proposed KRW35.3 trillion, yet it was still the largest of the three supplementary budgets passed

in 2020 in response to the economic impact of the COVID-19 pandemic, bringing the aggregate amount of supplementary budgets to KRW54.4 trillion and the total policy package to KRW277 trillion.

The Bank of Korea and the Federal Reserve Announces Extension of Currency Swap Agreement

On 29 July, the Bank of Korea and the US Federal Reserve announced the extension of the USD60 billion currency swap agreement for another 6 months until 31 March 2021. The swap agreement is expected to continue to aid in the stabilization of financial markets, including the foreign exchange market, as it will provide more dollar funding to businesses and households in the Republic of Korea.

The Government of the Republic of Korea Submits 2021 Fiscal Budget

On 3 September, the Government of the Republic of Korea submitted the 2021 fiscal budget proposal totaling KRW555.8 trillion, primarily to aid in economic recovery and support the Korean New Deal. The 2021 budget is 8.5% higher than the original 2020 budget and 1.6% higher than the final 2020 budget that included three supplementary budgets in response to the COVID-19 pandemic. Government revenues in 2021 are projected to grow 1.2% to KRW483 trillion. A fiscal deficit equal to 5.4% of GDP and aggregate government debt equal to 46.7% of GDP are expected. In addition, the government also submitted to the National Assembly its 2020–2024 fiscal management plan.

Malaysia

Yield Movements

Between 15 June and 15 August, Malaysia's local currency (LCY) government bond yields declined across all tenors (**Figure 1**). The shorter-end of the yield curve (from 1 month to 1 year) declined an average of 36 basis points (bps). Yields for longer-term tenors (from 2 years to 30 years) decreased an average of 45 bps. The yield spread between 2-year and 10-year government bonds expanded from 69 bps to 70 bps during the review period.

The movement of the yield curve in Malaysia was driven by Bank Negara Malaysia's (BNM) decision to further cut its overnight policy rate in July. The increased demand in the Malaysian debt market was also bolstered by attractive real yields amid persistent consumer price deflation. The deflationary environment and shrinking economy has led analysts to believe that BNM will reduce its policy rate by another 25 bps before the year ends.

On 7 July, BNM reduced its overnight policy rate by 25 bps to 1.75% during its monetary policy committee meeting. It was the fourth time in 2020 that BNM has reduced the policy rate, with the reductions this year totaling 125 bps. The decision came amid persistently weak domestic and global economic conditions brought about by the coronavirus disease (COVID-19) pandemic. Domestically, Malaysia's economy contracted in the second quarter (Q2) of 2020 on a year-on-year (y-o-y) basis. Consumer price inflation is also expected to remain low in 2020. The monetary policy easing aims to stimulate the economy to accelerate Malaysia's recovery.

Malaysia's economy contracted 17.1% y-o-y in Q2 2020 after increasing 0.7% y-o-y in the first quarter (Q1) of 2020, as economic activities stopped in April due to the implementation of Movement Control Order (MCO) measures. BNM expects the economy to gradually recover in the second half of 2020 given the slow resumption of economic activities beginning in May. As global economic conditions remained subdued, BNM revised its economic growth forecast for full-year 2020 to between –5.5% y-o-y and –3.5% y-o-y in August from between –2.0% y-o-y and –0.5% y-o-y in April. However,

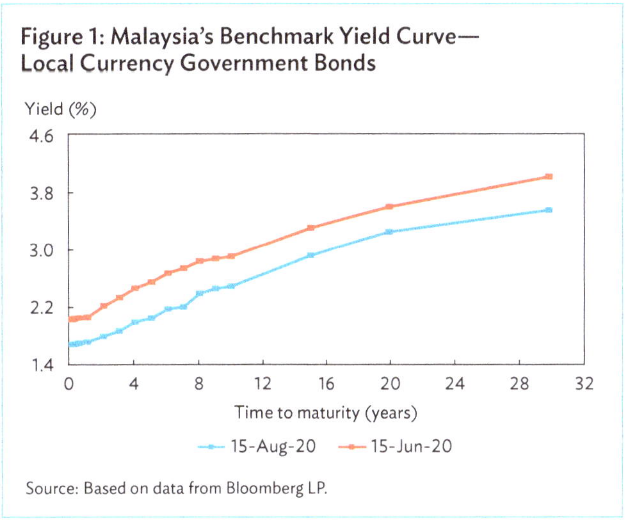

Figure 1: Malaysia's Benchmark Yield Curve— Local Currency Government Bonds

Source: Based on data from Bloomberg LP.

the central bank sees the economy rebounding in 2021, growing between 5.5% y-o-y and 8.0% y-o-y.

Prices of basic goods and services in Malaysia posted a slower decline of –1.9% y-o-y in June, driven by higher domestic fuel prices. This came after the economy recorded consumer price inflation of –2.9% y-o-y in both April and May, which was in line with BNM's expectation of negative inflation for full-year 2020 due to falling global oil and other commodity prices.

In June, the Government of Malaysia launched the Short-Term Economic Recovery Plan worth MYR35.0 billion to aid the recovery of the economy from the detrimental effects of the COVID-19 pandemic. This was on top of the MYR295.0 billion economic stimulus package launched in March and April. The recovery plan is part of the Government of Malaysia's six-staged strategy for emerging from the pandemic: resolve, resilience, restart, recover, revitalize, and reform. The first three stages have passed with the implementation of the MCO, injection of stimulus, and gradual reopening of the economy. The MCO, which started on 18 March, was a preventive measure to arrest the spread of COVID-19. On 4 May, Malaysia transitioned to conditional MCO where restrictions were loosened to allow some industries to reopen. On 10 June, Malaysia entered the recovery MCO phase wherein some interstate travel and social gatherings were allowed.

Size and Composition

Malaysia's LCY bond market expanded 1.8% quarter-on-quarter (q-o-q) in Q2 2020 to reach a size of MYR1,554.8 billion (USD362.7 billion), up from MYR1,527.8 billion at the end of Q1 2020 (**Table 1**). The growth corresponds to a 4.5% y-o-y jump from MYR1,488.1 billion at the end of Q2 2019. The growth in the LCY bond market in Q2 2020 was supported by expansions in both LCY government and corporate bonds, which accounted for 53.3% and 46.7%, respectively, of total LCY bonds outstanding at the end of June. Total outstanding *sukuk* (Islamic bonds) at the end of the review period stood at MYR976.2 billion on growth of 1.0% q-o-q from MYR966.7 billion at the end of the previous quarter, spurred by increased stocks of government and corporate *sukuk*.

Issuance of LCY bonds in Q2 2020 increased 1.7% q-o-q to MYR94.2 billion from MYR92.6 billion in Q1 2020, driven by increased government bond issuance.

Government bonds. The LCY government bond market grew 3.2% q-o-q to MYR829.0 billion in Q2 2020, up from MYR803.5 billion in the previous quarter. The growth was due to the 4.0% q-o-q increase in outstanding central government bonds, which comprised 96.2% of total outstanding LCY government bonds. This may be attributed to the government's funding needs for fiscal stimulus. Outstanding central bank bills, which comprised a 0.6% share of total LCY government bonds outstanding at the end of June, contracted 50.0% q-o-q as most bills matured and some were redeemed early amid minimal central bank bill issuance during the quarter. The outstanding stock of Sukuk Perumahan Kerajaan (3.2% of total outstanding LCY government bonds) remained unchanged from the previous quarter.

LCY government bonds issued in Q2 2020 jumped 15.4%, spurred by robust issuance of government bonds and Treasury bills. These were more than enough to offset the decline in BNM bills. Issuance of Malaysian Government Securities increased while Government Investment Issues slightly declined from the previous quarter.

Corporate bonds. LCY corporate bonds outstanding expanded 0.2% q-o-q to MYR725.8 billion in Q2 2020 from MYR724.3 billion in Q1 2020. Outstanding corporate *sukuk* rose 0.9% q-o-q to MYR582.3 billion at the end of June from MYR576.8 billion in the prior quarter.

The top 30 corporate bond issuers in Malaysia accounted for an aggregate MYR439.6 billion of corporate bonds outstanding at the end of Q2 2020, or 60.6% of the total corporate bond market (**Table 2**). Government institutions Danainfra Nasional, Prasarana, and Cagamas continued to dominate all issuers with outstanding LCY corporate bonds amounting to MYR67.6 billion (9.3% of total LCY corporate bonds outstanding), MYR34.5 billion (4.8%), and MYR33.1 billion (4.6%), respectively. By industry, finance comprised the largest share (53.6%) of

Table 1: Size and Composition of the Local Currency Bond Market in Malaysia

| | Outstanding Amount (billion) | | | | | | Growth Rate (%) | | | |
| | Q2 2019 | | Q1 2020 | | Q2 2020 | | Q2 2019 | | Q2 2020 | |
	MYR	USD	MYR	USD	MYR	USD	q-o-q	y-o-y	q-o-q	y-o-y
Total	1,488	360	1,528	354	1,555	363	3.3	8.7	1.8	4.5
Government	779	189	804	186	829	193	1.8	7.8	3.2	6.4
Central Government Bonds	742	180	767	177	797	186	3.0	9.8	4.0	7.4
of which: *Sukuk*	333	81	362	84	367	86	2.0	13.0	1.5	10.1
Central Bank Bills	9	2	10	2	5	1	(46.8)	(49.7)	(50.0)	(45.7)
of which: *Sukuk*	2	0.4	2	0.3	0	0	(71.2)	(72.7)	(100.0)	(100.0)
Sukuk Perumahan Kerajaan	28	7	27	6	27	6	0.0	(1.8)	0.0	(3.9)
Corporate	709	172	724	168	726	169	5.0	9.7	0.2	2.4
of which: *Sukuk*	555	134	577	133	582	136	6.8	13.5	0.9	5.0

( ) = negative, MYR = Malaysian ringgit, q-o-q = quarter-on-quarter, Q1 = first quarter, Q2 = second quarter, USD = United States dollar, y-o-y = year-on-year.
Notes:
1. Calculated using data from national sources.
2. Bloomberg LP end-of-period local currency–USD rates are used.
3. Growth rates are calculated from local currency base and do not include currency effects.
4. Sukuk Perumahan Kerajaan are Islamic bonds issued by the Government of Malaysia to refinance funding for housing loans to government employees and to extend new housing loans.
Sources: Bank Negara Malaysia Fully Automated System for Issuing/Tendering and Bloomberg LP.

Table 2: Top 30 Issuers of Local Currency Corporate Bonds in Malaysia

		Outstanding Amount				
	Issuers	LCY Bonds (MYR billion)	LCY Bonds (USD billion)	State-Owned	Listed Company	Type of Industry
1.	Danainfra Nasional	67.6	15.8	Yes	No	Finance
2.	Prasarana	34.5	8.0	Yes	No	Transport, Storage, and Communications
3.	Cagamas	33.1	7.7	Yes	No	Finance
4.	Project Lebuhraya Usahasama	29.4	6.9	No	No	Transport, Storage, and Communications
5.	Urusharta Jamaah	27.6	6.4	Yes	No	Finance
6.	Lembaga Pembiayaan Perumahan Sektor Awam	24.7	5.8	Yes	No	Property and Real Estate
7.	Perbadanan Tabung Pendidikan Tinggi Nasional	21.6	5.0	Yes	No	Finance
8.	Pengurusan Air	18.4	4.3	Yes	No	Energy, Gas, and Water
9.	Khazanah	14.2	3.3	Yes	No	Finance
10.	CIMB Bank	14.1	3.3	Yes	No	Finance
11.	Sarawak Energy	13.0	3.0	Yes	No	Energy, Gas, and Water
12.	Maybank Islamic	13.0	3.0	No	Yes	Banking
13.	Maybank	11.4	2.7	No	Yes	Banking
14.	CIMB Group Holdings	11.3	2.6	Yes	No	Finance
15.	Jimah East Power	9.0	2.1	Yes	No	Energy, Gas, and Water
16.	Danga Capital	8.0	1.9	Yes	No	Finance
17.	Danum Capital	8.0	1.9	No	No	Finance
18.	Public Bank	7.9	1.8	No	No	Banking
19.	GENM Capital	7.6	1.8	No	No	Finance
20.	Bank Pembangunan Malaysia	7.2	1.7	Yes	No	Banking
21.	GOVCO Holdings	7.2	1.7	Yes	No	Finance
22.	Tenaga Nasional	7.0	1.6	No	Yes	Energy, Gas, and Water
23.	Bakun Hydro Power Generation	6.3	1.5	No	No	Energy, Gas, and Water
24.	YTL Power International	6.1	1.4	No	Yes	Energy, Gas, and Water
25.	Telekom Malaysia	5.8	1.4	No	Yes	Telecommunications
26.	Rantau Abang Capital	5.5	1.3	Yes	No	Finance
27.	Turus Pesawat	5.3	1.2	Yes	No	Transport, Storage, and Communications
28.	EDRA Energy	5.1	1.2	No	Yes	Energy, Gas, and Water
29.	1Malaysia Development	5.0	1.2	Yes	No	Finance
30.	Sunway Treasury Sukuk	4.8	1.1	No	No	Finance
	Total Top 30 LCY Corporate Issuers	**439.6**	**102.6**			
	Total LCY Corporate Bonds	**725.8**	**169.3**			
	Top 30 as % of Total LCY Corporate Bonds	**60.6%**	**60.6%**			

LCY = local currency, MYR = Malaysian ringgit, USD = United States dollar.
Notes:
1. Data as of 30 June 2020.
2. State-owned firms are defined as those in which the government has more than a 50% ownership stake.
Source: *AsianBondsOnline* calculations based on Bank Negara Malaysia Fully Automated System for Issuing/Tendering data.

Table 3: Notable Local Currency Corporate Bond Issuance in the Second Quarter of 2020

Corporate Issuers	Coupon Rate (%)	Issued Amount (MYR billion)
Danainfra Nasional		
7-year Islamic MTN	2.86	0.40
10-year Islamic MTN	3.01	0.60
15-year Islamic MTN	3.27	0.60
20-year Islamic MTN	3.57	0.60
30-year Islamic MTN	3.89	0.60
Danum Capital		
5-year Islamic MTN	2.97	0.50
7-year Islamic MTN	3.14	0.50
10-year Islamic MTN	3.29	1.00
Cagamas		
1-year MTN	2.55	0.05
1-year MTN	2.65	0.03
2-year MTN	3.10	0.50
2-year MTN	2.75	0.07
2-year MTN	2.70	0.06

MTN = medium-term note, MYR = Malaysian ringgit.
Source: Bank Negara Malaysia Bond Info Hub.

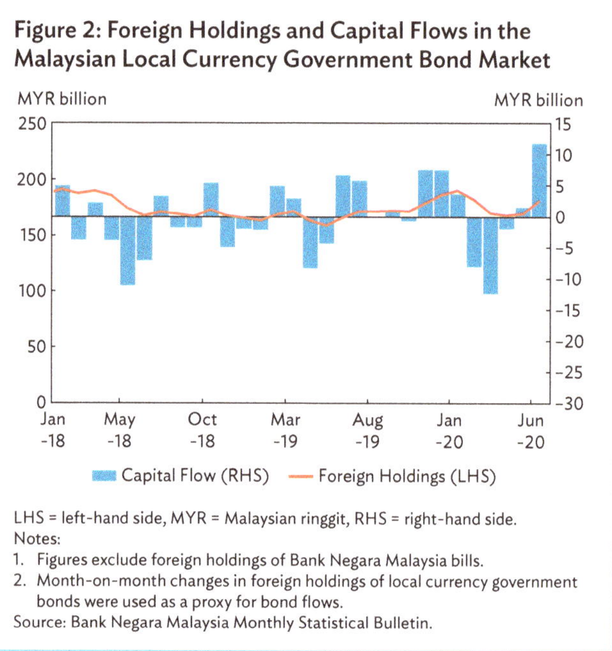

Figure 2: Foreign Holdings and Capital Flows in the Malaysian Local Currency Government Bond Market

LHS = left-hand side, MYR = Malaysian ringgit, RHS = right-hand side.
Notes:
1. Figures exclude foreign holdings of Bank Negara Malaysia bills.
2. Month-on-month changes in foreign holdings of local currency government bonds were used as a proxy for bond flows.
Source: Bank Negara Malaysia Monthly Statistical Bulletin.

the top 30 issuers with MYR235.6 billion in outstanding LCY corporate bonds at the end of June. This was followed by the transport, storage, and communications industry with MYR69.2 billion, which represented 15.7% of total LCY corporate bonds outstanding at the end Q2 2020.

Issuance of LCY corporate bonds declined 15.7% q-o-q in Q2 2020. Corporations had been cautious in their LCY bond issuances since March, with monthly issuances progressively decreasing as the Malaysian economy continued to grapple with the effects of the COVID-19 pandemic.

Danainfra Nasional issued the most tranches of Islamic medium-term notes (MTN), issuing five tranches with tenors ranging from 7 years to 30 years (**Table 3**). The 10-year to 30-year tranches were each worth MYR0.6 billion and had coupon rates of between 3.01% and 3.89%. Investment company Danum Capital issued three tranches of Islamic MTNs totaling MYR2.0 billion, with tenors ranging from 5 years to 10 years and coupon rates from 2.97% to 3.29%. Proceeds from the issuance will be used for Shariah-compliant general investments and refinancing current obligations. Cagamas, the national mortgage corporation of Malaysia, issued 1-year and 2-year MTNs. Its largest issuance was a MYR0.5 billion 2-year MTN with a 3.10% coupon rate. The financial

institution will use proceeds from the issuance for its working capital and other general corporate purposes.

Investor Profile

Foreign holdings of LCY government bonds in Q2 2020 declined to MYR518.5 billion from MYR542.2 billion in Q1 2020, albeit monthly holdings showed an increasing trend (**Figure 2**). A total of MYR11.4 billion in net capital inflows were recorded in Q2 2020, with most of the inflows coming in June. This came as yields of Malaysian Government Securities increased at the start of June amid the government's additional economic stimulus measures as part of its Short-Term Economic Recovery Plan. The inflows reversed the capital outflows of MYR16.7 billion recorded in the previous quarter amid heightened concerns over the global economic impact of the COVID-19 pandemic. As a share of LCY government bonds, foreign holdings increased to 22.7% at the end of Q2 2020 from 22.2% at the end of Q1 2020.

At the end of Q1 2020, financial institutions and social security institutions led all investors in LCY government bond holdings with 33.3% and 33.0% of the total, respectively (**Figure 3**). Financial institutions had a higher share than social security institutions at the end of March compared to the same month in 2019. Foreign holders decreased their share of total holdings to 21.8% from 23.4% during the review period. The share of insurance

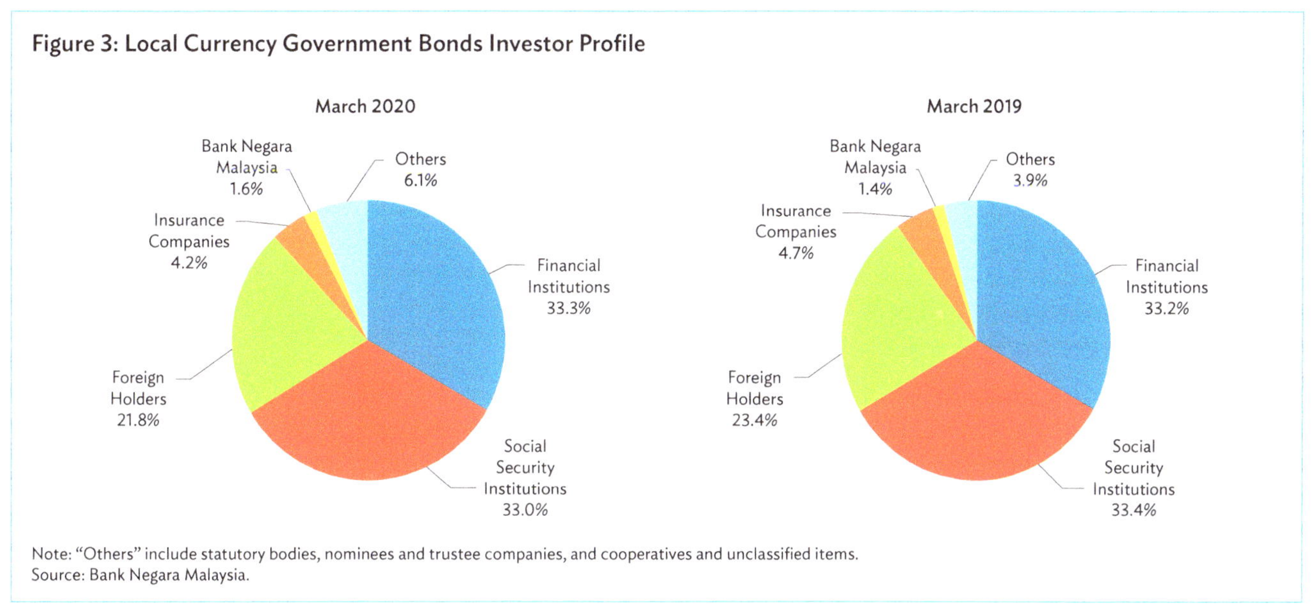

Figure 3: Local Currency Government Bonds Investor Profile

Note: "Others" include statutory bodies, nominees and trustee companies, and cooperatives and unclassified items.
Source: Bank Negara Malaysia.

companies likewise fell to 4.2% from 4.7% between Q1 2019 and Q1 2020, while the share of total holdings of BNM increased to 1.6% from 1.4%.

Ratings Update

On 26 June, S&P Global Ratings reaffirmed Malaysia's long-term issuer credit rating of A– but downgraded its outlook to negative from stable. The negative outlook implies that Malaysia is seen as susceptible to negative changes in its economic conditions but still has strong capacity to meet its debt obligations. With this outlook, the rating may be lowered over the medium term. The decision was driven by COVID-19's negative effects on the economic growth and fiscal position of Malaysia. Nevertheless, with its track record of good fiscal management, the Government of Malaysia pledged to commit to its fiscal reform agenda over the medium and long term. It also affirmed its commitment to fiscal consolidation efforts upon the recovery of the global economy.

Policy, Institutional, and Regulatory Developments

Banks to Continue Flexible Loan Repayment for Borrowers

On 29 July, BNM assured individuals and small and medium-sized enterprises affected by the COVID-19 pandemic that banks are committed to aid them as

they repay their loans. As the blanket moratorium ends on 30 September, banks stand ready to accommodate flexible loan repayment plans and other arrangements specific to a person's or company's situation. As movement controls eased and most businesses have been able to restart repaying their loans, a targeted moratorium extension and provision for flexible repayment will be provided by the banking industry to individuals who lost their jobs in 2020 and have yet to find a new one. Assistance will also be provided to employed individuals whose salary has been affected by the pandemic. Based on a person's or business' circumstances, they may be given the option to pay just the interest portion of their loan for the meantime, increase the duration of their loan, or discuss with the bank other more flexible options until they regain financial stability.

The Fintech Booster Programme Launched to Support Malaysian Companies

On 4 August, the Fintech Booster Programme of the Malaysia Digital Economy Corporation was launched. In cooperation with BNM, the program aims to help financial technology companies based in Malaysia in their capacity building. Participating companies are introduced to the following aspects of the financial technology industry: legal and compliance, business model, and technology. As a centralized hub, the program fosters collaboration between industry players—such as consultants, advisors, and solution providers—in supporting the industry's growth, development, and innovation.

Philippines

Yield Movements

The yields of local currency (LCY) government bonds in the Philippines fell for all tenors, shifting the yield curve downward, between 15 June and 15 August (**Figure 1**). Yields of bonds with shorter maturities (1-month to 1-year tenors) dropped the most, averaging a decline of 71 basis points (bps). Yields for securities with 10- to 25-year tenors dropped an average of 64 bps. Relatively smaller yield declines, averaging 37 bps, were observed for securities with 2- to 7-year maturities. The yield spread between the 2-year and 10-year tenors narrowed during the review period from 80 bps to 60 bps.

The downward bias of yield movement remains, reflecting a flight to safety amid a weak economic outlook and uncertainty posed by the coronavirus disease (COVID-19) pandemic, as well as abundant liquidity in the market as the Bangko Sentral ng Pilipinas (BSP) has been accommodative in its policy stance through rate and reserve requirement cuts to support the economy. With the pandemic ongoing, risk aversion will persist, resulting in higher buying interest for government securities and lower rates. Broader yield declines at the short-end of the curve indicate investors' preference for short-dated securities as they are on the lookout for market leads.

A deeper-than-expected contraction in the Philippines' gross domestic product (GDP) occurred in the second quarter (Q2) of 2020. The economy plunged 16.5% year-on-year (y-o-y) after declining 0.7% y-o-y in the first quarter (Q1). It was the largest quarterly drop since 1981 and put the economy into recession after nearly 3 decades of uninterrupted growth.[7] Strict lockdown measures implemented in Q2 2020 curtailed the typical growth drivers, household consumption and investment, leading to declines of 15.5% y-o-y and 53.5% y-o-y, respectively. Exports and imports also saw double-digit y-o-y declines in Q2 2020. On the other hand, government expenditure accelerated 22.1% y-o-y as a result of massive fiscal measures to keep the economy afloat.

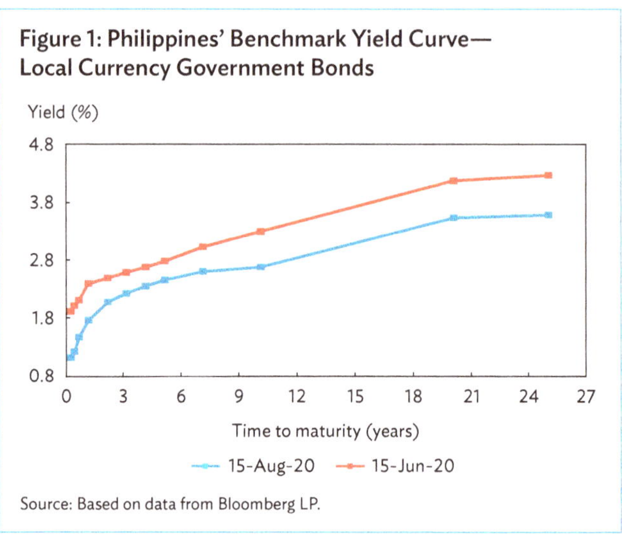

Figure 1: Philippines' Benchmark Yield Curve— Local Currency Government Bonds

Source: Based on data from Bloomberg LP.

The BSP kept its policy rate steady at 2.25% in its monetary policy meeting on 20 August as inflation remained benign and within the government's target of 2.0%–4.0%. The BSP also stated that the pause will enable the rate reductions and other monetary relief measures to fully take effect in the economy. On June 25, the central bank unexpectedly cut its overnight reverse repurchase facility rate by 50 bps. This brought down the key policy rate to a record low of 2.25% with an accumulated 175-bps cut thus far in 2020 to prop up the economy amid expectations of a protracted domestic and global recovery. The BSP also reduced the reserve requirement rates of thrift banks, and rural and cooperative banks by 100 bps each to 3.0% and 2.0%, respectively, effective 31 July. The move is expected to release PHP10 billion (USD204 million) in the system.

Consumer price inflation remained benign, which is also a factor that kept yields at bay. The inflation rate in August slowed to 2.4% y-o-y after upticks in June (2.5% y-o-y) and July (2.7% y-o-y). The decrease was largely driven by the deceleration in food prices. The year-to-date inflation rate is 2.5% y-o-y and still falls within the government target. The BSP sees inflation to tilt toward the downside amid weak domestic demand and disruptions in economic activities caused by the pandemic.

---

[7] Philippine Statistics Authority. 2020. GDP Growth Rate Drops by 16.5 Percent in the Second Quarter of 2020. 6 August. http://www.psa.gov.ph/press-releases/id/162842.

The Philippine peso has shown record strength despite the recession and rising COVID-19 cases. The peso traded at PHP48.76 against the United States (US) dollar on 15 August, marking a 3-year high. The domestic currency owed its strength to the weak demand for US dollars due to the slowdown in global economic activities. The issuance of Retail Treasury Bonds (RTBs) in July also drew in strong demand for pesos. The gradual resumption of domestic economic activities and sound financial buffers, including high gross international reserves, also contributed to the strength of the peso.

Size and Composition

The size of the LCY bond market in the Philippines continued to expand in Q2 2020, reaching PHP7,477 billion (USD150 billion) at the end of June on growth of 5.2% quarter-on-quarter (q-o-q), which was down from 6.9% q-o-q in Q1 2020 (**Table 1**). The expansion was driven by the government segment given the contraction in the corporate segment during the quarter. On an annual basis, the growth of the bond market was faster in Q2 2020 at 11.5% y-o-y compared with the preceding quarter of 7.9% y-o-y. Government bonds comprised 79.0% of the total bond market at the end of June, with corporate bonds accounting for the rest.

Government bonds. Total LCY government bonds outstanding expanded 6.8% q-o-q to PHP5,904 billion in Q2 2020, which was down from the growth in the previous quarter of 7.5% q-o-q. Treasury bills and Treasury bonds drove the increase in market size as the government boosted its borrowing to fund fiscal stimulus measures to support economic recovery amid the continuing COVID-19 pandemic. A substantial increase in outstanding Treasury bills was seen, with nearly 50% q-o-q growth on the back of higher issuance volume during the quarter. Treasury bonds grew 2.8% q-o-q, although slower compared with 6.8% q-o-q in Q1 2020, while outstanding debt from government-related entities marginally decreased due to bond maturities. On an annual basis, the government bond stock grew 11.6% y-o-y.

Total debt raised by the government in the domestic market declined 6.9% q-o-q to PHP668.6 billion in Q2 2020. The quarterly decline was due to a high base in Q1 2020 when PHP310.8 billion in RTBs were issued. Without the RTBs, bond issuance in Q2 2020 was higher than in Q1 2020 as the government increased its borrowing plan to fund efforts to cushion the economy against the negative impact of the COVID-19 pandemic. Moreover, the government wanted to take advantage of the low interest rate due to high liquidity in the domestic market. In Q2 2020, the Bureau of the Treasury's (BTr) issuances were weighted toward short-term instruments as Treasury bill issuance increased 60.9% q-o-q to PHP488.6 billion. The BTr increased the issuance of short-term securities with the addition of 35-day Treasury bills in its weekly auctions. The auctions were met with

Table 1: Size and Composition of the Local Currency Bond Market in the Philippines

| | Outstanding Amount (billion) | | | | | | Growth Rate (%) | | | |
| | Q2 2019 | | Q1 2020 | | Q2 2020 | | Q2 2019 | | Q2 2020 | |
	PHP	USD	PHP	USD	PHP	USD	q-o-q	y-o-y	q-o-q	y-o-y
Total	6,707	131	7,106	140	7,477	150	1.8	16.8	5.2	11.5
Government	5,290	103	5,526	109	5,904	119	1.7	15.2	6.8	11.6
Treasury Bills	652	13	557	11	797	16	7.4	71.2	43.1	22.1
Treasury Bonds	4,616	90	4,930	97	5,068	102	1.2	10.7	2.8	9.8
Others	22	0.4	40	0.8	40	0.8	(35.5)	(45.9)	(0.02)	83.3
Corporate	1,417	28	1,579	31	1,573	32	2.3	23.3	(0.4)	11.0

( ) = negative, PHP = Philippine peso, q-o-q = quarter-on-quarter, Q1 = first quarter, Q2 = second quarter, USD = United States dollar, y-o-y = year-on-year.
Notes:
1. Calculated using data from national sources.
2. Bloomberg end-of-period local currency–USD rates are used.
3. Growth rates are calculated from local currency base and do not include currency effects.
4. "Others" comprise bonds issued by government agencies, entities, and corporations for which repayment is guaranteed by the Government of the Philippines. This includes bonds issued by Power Sector Assets and Liabilities Management and the National Food Authority, among others.
5. Peso Global Bonds (PHP-denominated bonds payable in USD) are not included.
Sources: Bloomberg LP and Bureau of the Treasury.

strong demand, prompting the BTr to open its TAP facility to accommodate the investors. Treasury bonds issuance amounted to PHP180 billion, declining 56.6%q-o-q due to the aforementioned RTB base effect.

Corporate bonds. Debt outstanding in the corporate sector slightly declined by 0.4% q-o-q in Q2 2020 to PHP1,573 billion after registering an increase 5.0% q-o-q in Q1 2020. The decline can be attributed to the maturation of bonds accompanied by just few a corporate issuers during the quarter.

At the end of June, the banking sector remained the largest holder in the LCY corporate bond market with outstanding debt comprising 41.2% of the total corporate bond stock, up from 34.7% at the end of June 2019 (**Figure 2**). The banking sector and "other" sectors were the only sectors that saw an increase in their shares of corporate bonds compared to a year earlier. All other sectors saw lower shares at the end of June 2020 compared to June 2019, with holding firms experiencing the largest decrease from 18.2% to 14.2%.

The top 30 corporate issuers had aggregate debt outstanding of PHP1,386.2 billion at the end of June, comprising 88.1% of the total corporate bond market (**Table 2**). The banking sector led the list with outstanding bonds totaling PHP617.3 billion or 44.5% of the total LCY corporate bond market. There were 11 banks on the list, including the two top corporate issuers: Metropolitan

Bank and BDO Unibank. Holding firms were the second-largest issuers with PHP298.4 billion of bonds outstanding (21.5% share), led by SM Prime Holdings. Property firms came in third with PHP195.5 billion (14.1% share) led by Ayala Land.

Corporate bond issuance in Q2 2020 declined dramatically, falling 81.3% q-o-q and reversing the double-digit q-o-q growth in Q1 2020. Only three corporates raised funds in Q2 2020, issuing a combined PHP27.6 billion worth of bonds. The weak issuance activity from the corporate sector can be attributed to gloomy economic and business prospects due to the ongoing pandemic. Amid lingering uncertainty and halted economic activities due to the strict quarantine measures in place for the entirety of Q2 2020, firms held off expansion and issuance plans to properly assess the situation, even with low interest rates and the market awash with liquidity. **Table 3** lists all issuances in Q2 2020, which comprised short-tenor securities from the banking and property sectors.

Investor Profile

The investor landscape for LCY government bonds in June was changed from a year earlier. Contractual savings and tax-exempt institutions were the largest investors in LCY government bonds at the end of Q2 2020, with their market share rising to 39.0% from 23.2% in June 2019 (**Figure 3**). This investor group overtook banks and

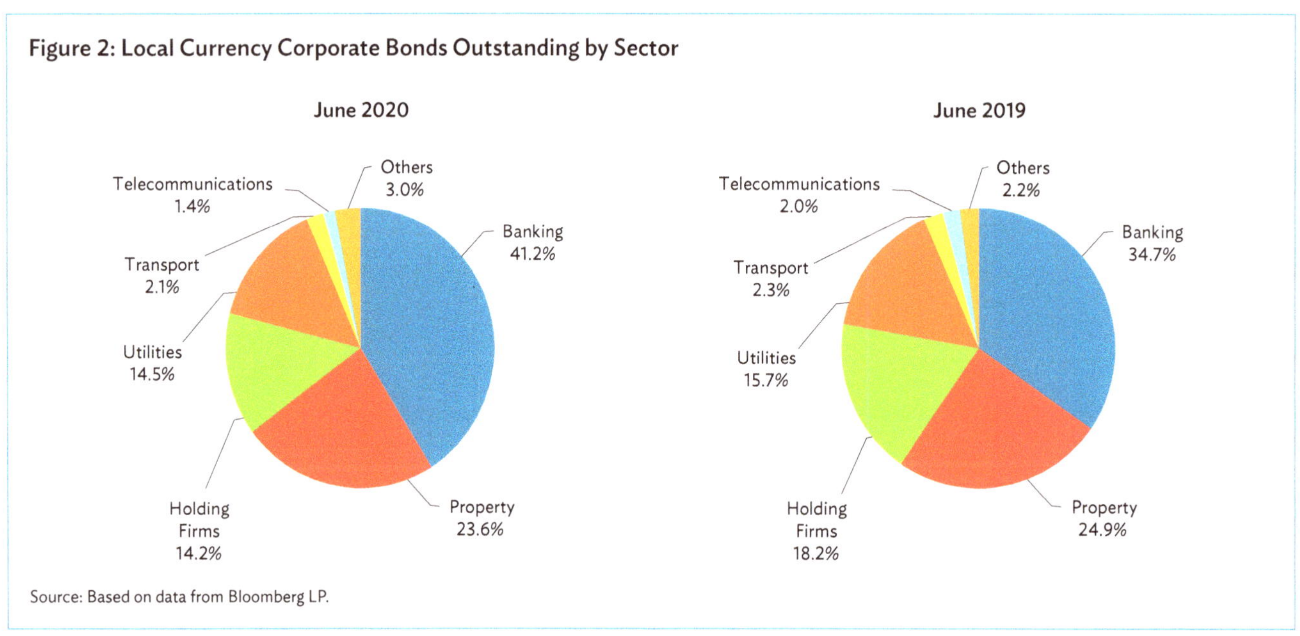

Figure 2: Local Currency Corporate Bonds Outstanding by Sector

Source: Based on data from Bloomberg LP.

Table 2: Top 30 Issuers of Local Currency Corporate Bonds in the Philippines

	Issuers	Outstanding Amount		State-Owned	Listed Company	Type of Industry
		LCY Bonds (PHP billion)	LCY Bonds (USD billion)			
1.	Metropolitan Bank	130.8	2.6	No	Yes	Banking
2.	BDO Unibank	121.4	2.4	No	Yes	Banking
3.	Ayala Land	115.0	2.3	No	Yes	Property
4.	SM Prime Holdings	103.6	2.1	No	Yes	Holding Firms
5.	SMC Global Power	80.0	1.6	No	No	Electricity, Energy, and Power
6.	Bank of the Philippine Islands	64.6	1.3	No	Yes	Banking
7.	San Miguel	60.0	1.2	No	Yes	Holding Firms
8.	China Bank	56.2	1.1	No	Yes	Banking
9.	Rizal Commercial Banking Corporation	53.6	1.1	No	Yes	Banking
10.	Security Bank	52.8	1.1	No	Yes	Banking
11.	Philippine National Bank	52.2	1.0	No	Yes	Banking
12.	Vista Land	43.6	0.9	No	Yes	Property
13.	Petron	42.9	0.9	No	Yes	Electricity, Energy, and Power
14.	SM Investments	42.7	0.9	No	Yes	Holding Firms
15.	Ayala Corporation	40.0	0.8	No	Yes	Holding Firms
16.	Aboitiz Equity Ventures	37.0	0.7	No	Yes	Holding Firms
17.	Maynilad	32.8	0.7	No	No	Water
18.	Aboitiz Power	30.5	0.6	No	Yes	Electricity, Energy, and Power
19.	Union Bank of the Philippines	26.6	0.5	No	Yes	Banking
20.	Philippine Savings Bank	25.4	0.5	No	Yes	Banking
21.	Manila Electric Company	23.0	0.5	No	Yes	Electricity, Energy, and Power
22.	Filinvest Land	22.0	0.4	No	Yes	Property
23.	San Miguel Brewery	22.0	0.4	No	No	Brewery
24.	East West Banking	17.7	0.4	No	Yes	Banking
25.	Robinsons Bank	16.0	0.3	No	No	Banking
26.	GT Capital	15.1	0.3	No	Yes	Holding Firms
27.	Doubledragon	15.0	0.3	No	Yes	Property
28.	PLDT	15.0	0.3	No	Yes	Telecommunications
29.	San Miguel Food and Beverage	15.0	0.3	No	Yes	Food and Beverage
30.	NLEX Corporation	13.9	0.3	No	No	Transport
	Total Top 30 LCY Corporate Issuers	1,386.2	27.8			
	Total LCY Corporate Bonds	1,573.4	31.6			
	Top 30 as % of Total LCY Corporate Bonds	88.1%	88.1%			

LCY = local currency, PHP = Philippine peso, USD = United States dollar.
Notes:
1. Data as of 30 June 2020.
2. State-owned firms are defined as those in which the government has more than a 50% ownership stake.
Source: *AsianBondsOnline* calculations based on Bloomberg LP data.

Table 3: Notable Local Currency Corporate Bond Issuance in the Second Quarter of 2020

Corporate Issuers	Coupon Rate (%)	Issued Amount (PHP billion)
Metropolitan Bank		
1-year bond	3.00	10.50
Ayala Land		
2-year bond	3.00	10.00
Rizal Commercial Banking Corporation		
2-year bond	4.85	7.05

PHP = Philippine peso.
Source: Bloomberg LP.

investment houses as the largest investor group, whose market share declined to 36.2% from 43.9% during the review period. Other investor group also outpaced brokers, custodians, and depositories to assume the third-largest market share by the end of Q2 2020. BTr-managed funds and government-owned or -controlled corporations and local government units maintained their respective rankings, albeit with declining holding shares. Only contractual savings and tax-exempt institutions showed an increase between June 2019 and June 2020 in both absolute government bond holdings and the share of total government bonds outstanding.

Ratings Update

On 30 May, Standard and Poor's Global (S&P) maintained the Philippines' sovereign credit rating at BBB+ with a stable outlook. The rating affirmation reflected expectations that the economy would continue to achieve above-average growth over the medium term, supported by sound external settings. S&P expects the economy to bounce back strongly in 2021 following a contraction in 2020. S&P also stated that the government's long track record of fiscal prudence would provide a buffer against the deterioration of its fiscal standing, assuming an economic recovery begins in 2021.

On 11 June, Japan Credit Rating Agency upgraded the Philippines' sovereign credit rating by a notch to A– from BBB+ but also adjusted the outlook to stable from positive. The rating agency cited the Philippines' high and sustainable economic growth performance as the basis for the upgrade. While the COVID-19 pandemic impaired the economy with the imposition of lockdown measures, Japan Credit Rating Agency views that the downturn will be limited given strong economic fundamentals, a resilient external position, and the government's massive stimulus package.

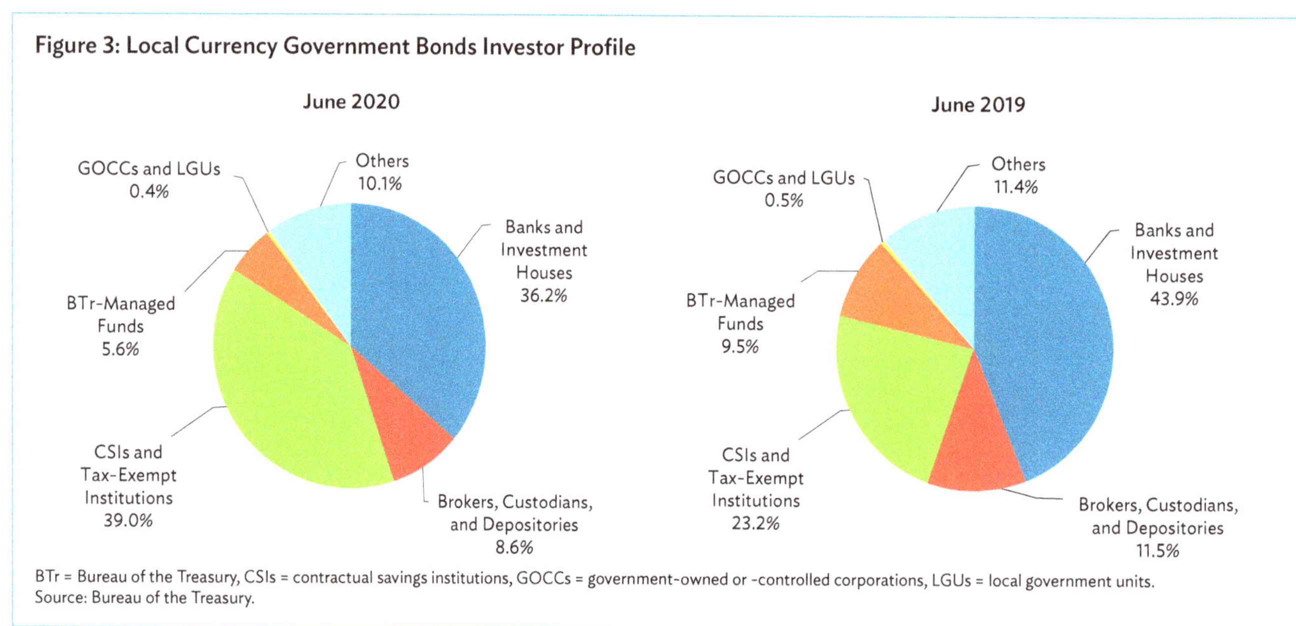

Figure 3: Local Currency Government Bonds Investor Profile

BTr = Bureau of the Treasury, CSIs = contractual savings institutions, GOCCs = government-owned or -controlled corporations, LGUs = local government units.
Source: Bureau of the Treasury.

Policy, Institutional, and Regulatory Developments

Bangko Sentral ng Pilipinas Cuts Reserve Requirements for Thrift Banks and Rural and Cooperative Banks

In July, the BSP reduced the reserve requirements for thrift banks, and rural and cooperative banks by 100 bps each to 3.0% and 2.0%, respectively. The central bank stated that the move is a part of its omnibus package of reforms to assist the banking public with their liquidity requirements during the ongoing COVID-19 pandemic and to support the transition toward a sustainable recovery after the crisis. The reserve requirement cuts are expected to increase the lending capacity of the banks and release approximately PHP10 billion in cash into the economy, which will support small businesses and rural community-based clients. The reduction is effective 31 July.

Bureau of the Treasury Launches Bonds.PH

In July, the BTr launched Bonds.PH, the first mobile application in Asia for the distribution of government bonds enabled by distributed ledger technology. The system, which utilizes blockchain technology, allows tamper-proof record keeping and can facilitate complex transactions. Such technology supports financial inclusion in the economy as it makes investing, especially to the unbanked, easier and more secure. The BTr's issuance of RTBs in July utilized this technology.

Bangko Sentral ng Pilipinas Approves the Exclusion of Debt Held by Market-Makers from Single Borrower's Limit

In July, the BSP approved a new policy that excludes debt securities acquired from market-making activities of BSP-supervised financial institutions from the single borrower's limit (SBL) as part of initiatives to develop the capital market. According to the BSP's new policy, market-making activities from 1 August 2020 to 31 July 2021 will be excluded from the SBL computation for 90 calendar days from the time of acquisition of the securities. Beginning 1 August 2021, the debt securities will only be excluded from the SBL computation for a period of up to 60 calendar days. The BSP stated that this policy will promote liquidity and transparency in the market by giving market-makers latitude to continue providing prices for debt securities in the secondary market and to make available an exit mechanism for investors to liquidate their holdings.

Singapore

Yield Movements

Between 15 June and 15 August, movements in Singapore's local currency (LCY) government bond yields were mixed (**Figure 1**). The shorter-end of the yield curve (from 3 months to 1 year) increased an average of 4 basis points (bps). Meanwhile, yields of longer-term tenors (from 2 years to 20 years) shed an average of 3 bps. The 30-year tenor recorded a much steeper decline, dropping 22 bps. The yield spread between 2-year and 10-year government bonds expanded from 62 bps to 65 bps during the review period.

Demand for short-term tenors declined as the Monetary Authority of Singapore (MAS) lowered banks' net stable funding ratio requirement in April to ensure bank liquidity and support their lending activities. This was one of the measures undertaken by MAS to support the financial sector amid economic disruptions caused by the coronavirus disease (COVID-19) pandemic. On the other hand, movement at the longer-end of the yield curve in Singapore was driven by MAS' decision in March to reduce the appreciation rate of the Singapore dollar nominal effective exchange rate policy band.

In March 2020, MAS reduced to zero the appreciation rate of the Singapore dollar nominal effective exchange rate policy band given Singapore's low rates of economic growth and consumer price inflation. The decision complemented Singapore's Resilience Budget announced in late March. As the global economic recovery remains uncertain, analysts see MAS maintaining its current exchange rate policy during the second half of 2020.

Singapore's economy contracted 13.2% year-on-year (y-o-y) in the second quarter (Q2) of 2020 after contracting 0.3% y-o-y in the first quarter (Q1) of 2020. The declining economic performance was mainly due to Circuit Breaker measures—that is, limiting movements inside the city-state to prevent the spread of COVID-19—implemented from 7 April to 1 June. In August, the Ministry of Trade and Industry downgraded its full-year 2020 economic growth forecast to between −7.0% and −5.0%. This was a narrower range from its May forecast of between −7.0% and −0.4%. The revised outlook came as Singapore experienced weaker-than-expected external demand and as international borders are expected

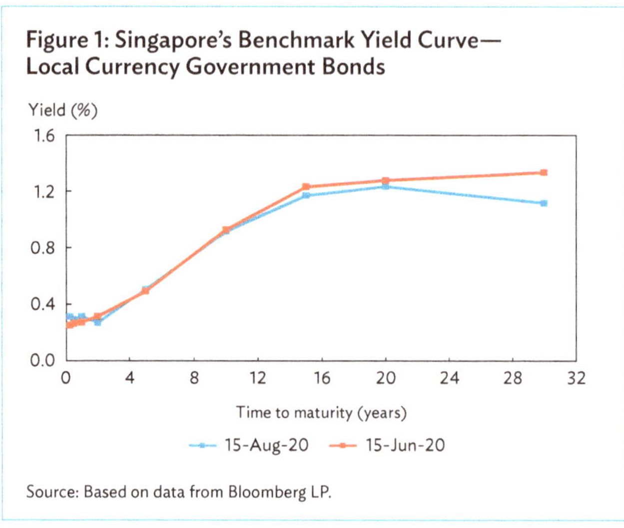

Figure 1: Singapore's Benchmark Yield Curve— Local Currency Government Bonds

Source: Based on data from Bloomberg LP.

to open more gradually than expected owing to the resurgence of COVID-19 cases in some economies.

Prices of basic goods and services in Singapore were down 0.5% y-o-y in June, compared with declines of 0.8% y-o-y and 0.7% y-o-y in consumer price inflation in May and April, respectively. The slowing rate of deflation was mainly due to a slower decline in prices of private transport. International and domestic inflationary pressures are expected to remain subdued in the short-term, prompting MAS' inflation projection for full-year 2020 to remain between −1.0% and 0.0%, the same as its forecast in March.

A bright spot in Singapore's economy is the electronics cluster, which saw its output grow 17.3% y-o-y in June. Demand for semiconductors is expected to be sustained in the second half of 2020. Singapore's Purchasing Managers' Index has also improved, reaching 50.2 in July after gradually climbing from a low of 44.7 in April. (A Purchasing Managers' Index reading above 50 indicates expansion in the manufacturing industry, while a value below 50 signifies contraction.) Economists are cautiously optimistic that this recovery can be sustained.

To support the economy amid the COVID-19 pandemic, Singapore rolled out about SGD100.0 billion in stimulus packages over four budgets. Even as the COVID-19 situation in Singapore stabilized, the protection of jobs remained one of Singapore's priorities. As its Jobs Support Scheme was set to end in August, the

Government of Singapore extended the program to March 2021, continuing its wage support to businesses to help them retain workers. This came amid Singapore's reopening after exiting the Circuit Breaker in June. Phase 1 of the reopening, called Safe Reopening, allowed essential economic activities to resume. On 19 June, Singapore entered Phase 2 (Safe Transition) where more activities were permitted as infection rates remained stable and manageable. As the situation develops, the Government of Singapore will look into moving to Phase 3 (Safe Nation), the start of the new normal where gatherings of limited size are allowed.

Size and Composition

Singapore's LCY bond market expanded 2.9% quarter-on-quarter (q-o-q) in Q2 2020 to reach SGD480.6 billion (USD344.9 billion) at the end of June, up from SGD467.2 billion at the end of March (**Table 1**). On an annual basis, growth accelerated to 13.2% y-o-y in Q2 2020 from 8.8% a year earlier. The expansion in the LCY bond market was supported by growth in both government and corporate bonds, which accounted for 63.6% and 36.4%, respectively, of total LCY bonds outstanding at the end of Q2 2020.

Issuance of LCY bonds in Q2 2020 increased 4.1% q-o-q to SGD185.0 billion from SGD177.8 billion in Q1 2020, driven by higher government and corporate bond issuances.

Government bonds. The LCY government bond market grew 4.4% q-o-q to SGD305.7 billion in Q2 2020 from SGD292.8 billion in the previous quarter. The growth was due to an increase in Singapore Government Securities (SGS) bills and bonds, and MAS bills. Outstanding SGS bills and bonds, which comprised 63.7% of total outstanding LCY government bonds, jumped 3.7% q-o-q as 6-month SGS bills have gradually replaced 24-week MAS bills since July 2019. By the end of June, outstanding MAS bills had dropped 16.5% on an annual basis.

LCY government bond issuance in Q2 2020 rose 3.0% q-o-q to SGD179.0 billion as issuance of SGS bills and bonds increased.

Corporate bonds. LCY corporate bonds outstanding increased 0.3% q-o-q in Q2 2020 to reach SGD174.9 billion at the end of June, up from SGD174.4 billion at the end of March, buoyed by the increase in outstanding corporate bonds in the real estate and transportation industry.

The top 30 LCY corporate bond issuers in Singapore accounted for combined outstanding bonds of SGD85.7 billion, or 49.0% of the total LCY corporate bond market at the end of Q2 2020 (**Table 2**). Government institutions such as the Housing & Development Board and the Land Transport Authority continued to be the largest issuers with outstanding LCY corporate bonds amounting to SGD25.2 billion (14.4% of total LCY corporate bonds outstanding) and SGD10.1 billion (5.8% of total LCY corporate bonds outstanding), respectively. By industry type, real estate companies continued to comprise the largest share (43.8%) among the top 30 issuers of LCY corporate bonds with SGD37.6 billion of aggregate LCY corporate bonds outstanding at the end of Q2 2020. The transportation industry had the second-largest share of total LCY corporate bonds outstanding at 21.9% (SGD18.8 billion).

Table 1: Size and Composition of the Local Currency Bond Market in Singapore

| | Outstanding Amount (billion) | | | | | | Growth Rate (%) | | | |
| | Q2 2019 | | Q1 2020 | | Q2 2020 | | Q2 2019 | | Q2 2020 | |
	SGD	USD	SGD	USD	SGD	USD	q-o-q	y-o-y	q-o-q	y-o-y
Total	425	314	467	329	481	345	2.3	8.8	2.9	13.2
Government	262	194	293	206	306	219	2.7	10.7	4.4	16.5
SGS Bills and Bonds	129	96	188	132	195	140	(0.2)	5.1	3.7	50.5
MAS Bills	133	98	105	74	111	80	5.6	16.7	5.7	(16.5)
Corporate	162	120	174	123	175	126	1.7	5.8	0.3	7.7

( ) = negative, MAS = Monetary Authority of Singapore, q-o-q = quarter-on-quarter, Q1 = first quarter, Q2 = second quarter, SGD = Singapore dollar, SGS = Singapore Government Securities, USD = United States dollar, y-o-y = year-on-year.
Notes:
1. Government bonds are calculated using data from national sources. Corporate bonds are based on *AsianBondsOnline* estimates.
2. SGS bills and bonds do not include the special issue of SGS held by the Singapore Central Provident Fund.
3. Bloomberg LP end-of-period local currency–USD rates are used.
4. Growth rates are calculated from local currency base and do not include currency effects.
Sources: Bloomberg LP, Monetary Authority of Singapore, and Singapore Government Securities.

Table 2: Top 30 Issuers of Local Currency Corporate Bonds in Singapore

		Outstanding Amount				
	Issuers	LCY Bonds (SGD billion)	LCY Bonds (USD billion)	State-Owned	Listed Company	Type of Industry
1.	Housing & Development Board	25.2	18.1	Yes	No	Real Estate
2.	Land Transport Authority	10.1	7.2	Yes	No	Transportation
3.	Singapore Airlines	7.9	5.7	Yes	Yes	Transportation
4.	Frasers Property	4.0	2.9	No	Yes	Real Estate
5.	United Overseas Bank	3.3	2.3	No	Yes	Banking
6.	Mapletree Treasury Services	2.7	1.9	No	No	Finance
7.	Keppel Corporation	2.7	1.9	No	Yes	Diversified
8.	Capitaland Treasury	2.7	1.9	No	No	Finance
9.	Temasek Financial	2.6	1.9	Yes	No	Finance
10.	DBS Group Holdings	2.5	1.8	No	Yes	Banking
11.	Sembcorp Financial Services	2.1	1.5	No	No	Engineering
12.	City Developments Limited	1.7	1.2	No	Yes	Real Estate
13.	Oversea-Chinese Banking Corporation	1.5	1.1	No	Yes	Banking
14.	CMT MTN	1.4	1.0	No	No	Finance
15.	Shangri-La Hotel	1.4	1.0	No	Yes	Real Estate
16.	Public Utilities Board	1.3	0.9	Yes	No	Utilities
17.	GLL IHT	1.2	0.8	No	No	Real Estate
18.	Capitaland	1.2	0.8	Yes	Yes	Real Estate
19.	Mapletree Commercial Trust	1.1	0.8	No	Yes	Real Estate
20.	Suntec REIT	1.0	0.7	No	Yes	Real Estate
21.	Singapore Press Holdings	1.0	0.7	No	Yes	Communications
22.	Hyflux	0.9	0.6	No	Yes	Utilities
23.	Ascendas	0.9	0.6	No	Yes	Finance
24.	Olam International	0.8	0.6	No	Yes	Consumer Goods
25.	DBS Bank	0.8	0.6	No	Yes	Banking
26.	SP Powerassets	0.8	0.6	No	No	Utilities
27.	Sembcorp Industries	0.8	0.6	No	Yes	Shipbuilding
28.	Singapore Technologies Telemedia	0.8	0.6	Yes	No	Utilities
29.	SMRT Capital	0.8	0.6	No	No	Transportation
30.	Wing Tai Holdings	0.8	0.6	No	Yes	Real Estate
	Total Top 30 LCY Corporate Issuers	**85.7**	**61.5**			
	Total LCY Corporate Bonds	**174.9**	**125.5**			
	Top 30 as % of Total LCY Corporate Bonds	**49.0%**	**49.0%**			

LCY = local currency, MTN = medium-term note, REIT = real estate investment trust, SGD = Singapore dollar, USD = United States dollar.
Notes:
1. Data as of 30 June 2020.
2. State-owned firms are defined as those in which the government has more than a 50% ownership stake.
Source: *AsianBondsOnline* calculations based on Bloomberg LP data.

Issuance of LCY corporate bonds soared 50.8% q-o-q to SGD6.0 billion in Q2 2020, bolstered by Singapore Airline's issuance in June.

Singapore Airlines issued the single-largest LCY corporate bond in Q2 2020, issuing a SGD3.5 billion 10-year, zero-coupon mandatory convertible bond (**Table 3**).

Proceeds from the issuance will be used to finance the airline company's capital and operational expenditure requirements. The Housing & Development Board issued a 10-year bond worth SGD800.0 million under its multicurrency medium-term note program to support development programs and finance existing borrowing. The National University of Singapore issued a green bond

Table 3: Notable Local Currency Corporate Bond Issuance in the Second Quarter of 2020

Corporate Issuers	Coupon Rate (%)	Issued Amount (SGD million)
Singapore Airlines		
10-year bond	0.00	3,496.1
Housing & Development Board		
10-year bond	1.27	800.0
National University of Singapore		
10-year bond	1.57	300.0
Tuan Sing Holdings		
2-year bond	7.75	65.0
DBS Bank		
1-year floating rate note	0.73	20.0

SGD = Singapore dollar.
Source: Bloomberg LP.

worth SGD300.0 million with a tenor of 10 years and coupon rate of 1.565%. The academic institution will use the proceeds for green projects that follow guidelines indicated in its Green Finance Network. Tuan Sing Holdings sold the bond with the highest coupon during the quarter, issuing a SGD65.0 million 2-year bond with a 7.75% coupon rate. Proceeds from the issuance will be used for property development and investment, refinancing of debt obligations, and other corporate needs. In May, DBS Bank issued the first 1-year floating-rate note, which references the Singapore Overnight Rate Average (SORA). This came amid the banking industry's transition from using the Swap Offer Rate to referencing SORA as the benchmark in Singapore's debt market. DBS Bank will utilize the proceeds for its general business needs.

Ratings Update

On 14 August, Fitch Ratings affirmed Singapore's AAA long-term foreign currency issuer default rating with a stable outlook. The affirmation reflects Singapore's strong macroeconomic fundamentals and the government's appropriate fiscal relief measures to mitigate the economic fallout from the COVID-19 pandemic. Despite Singapore's economy contracting and the deflationary environment, Fitch Ratings expects Singapore's economy to gradually bounce back during the second half of 2020 and into 2021.

Policy, Institutional, and Regulatory Developments

Monetary Authority of Singapore and United States Federal Reserve Extend Swap Arrangement

On 30 July, MAS announced that its USD60.0 billion swap facility with the United States (US) Federal Reserve, which was established in March and initially set to run for at least 6 months, had been extended up to 31 March 2021. The swap facility is intended to support banks in maintaining their liquidity position in the US dollar funding market in Singapore amid the COVID-19 pandemic. It also complements MAS' management of the Singapore dollar market. Together, these measures reinforce market confidence and stability in the Singapore financial market.

Monetary Authority of Singapore Announces Initiatives to Support Singapore Overnight Rate Average

On 5 August, MAS launched initiatives that boost the adoption of SORA as a benchmark in the Singapore financial market. On 21 August, MAS began issuing SORA-based, floating-rate notes on a monthly basis to expand money market instruments and develop the use of SORA as a floating-rate benchmark. MAS will promote transparency by publishing key statistics on various tenors utilizing SORA. To ensure compliance and robustness in the use of SORA, MAS prescribed its use as a benchmark under the Securities and Futures Act. Finally, to meet international best practices and assure market confidence, MAS issued a statement of compliance with International Organization of Securities Commissions principles. These initiatives will help Singapore's financial industry transition from the use of the Swap Offer Rate to SORA.

Thailand

Yield Movements

Between 15 June and 15 August, Thailand's local currency (LCY) government bond yields rose for most tenors, gaining an average of 4 basis points (bps) across all tenors (**Figure 1**). Yields for maturities of 1 year or below inched up 3 bps on average, while for those with maturities of 2–4 years fell an average of 5 bps. The yields for maturities of 5 years and longer rose an average of 6 bps, with the 20-year tenor showing the largest gain at 14 bps. The spread between the 2-year and 10-year tenors widened from 66 bps to 85 bps during the review period.

The rise in yields for most tenors reflected weakened appetite for Thai sovereign bonds as the spread of the coronavirus disease (COVID-19) drove the economy to its deepest contraction since the global financial crisis. Weak investor confidence over the economy's trajectory in the short-term drove up the yields at the short end of the curve. Expectations of a gradual recovery, as Thailand has recorded relatively fewer cases of COVID-19 than its neighboring economies, helped boost yields for tenors with maturities of between 2 and 4 years. The prospect of expanded government debt needed to finance economic recovery programs created upward pressure on yields for tenors with maturities of 5 years and over.

Thailand's gross domestic product (GDP) plunged 12.2% year-on-year (y-o-y) in the second quarter (Q2) of 2020 after declining 1.9% y-o-y in the first quarter (Q1) of 2020. Thailand's economy was among the hardest hit in emerging East Asia due to its heavy reliance on exports and tourism; the deeper contraction in Q2 2020 captured the effects of lockdown measures that restricted domestic travel and most business operations until May. Thailand's borders remained closed to most foreign travelers through the end of the review period.

Private consumption declined 6.6% y-o-y in Q2 2020 following a 2.7% y-o-y drop in Q1 2020. Investment contracted an even larger 8.0% y-o-y in Q2 2020 versus 6.5% y-o-y in Q1 2020. The contraction in exports quadrupled, falling 28.3% in Q2 2020 following a 7.3% y-o-y drop in Q1 2020. The plunge in imports deepened to 23.3% y-o-y in Q2 2020 from 3.1% y-o-y

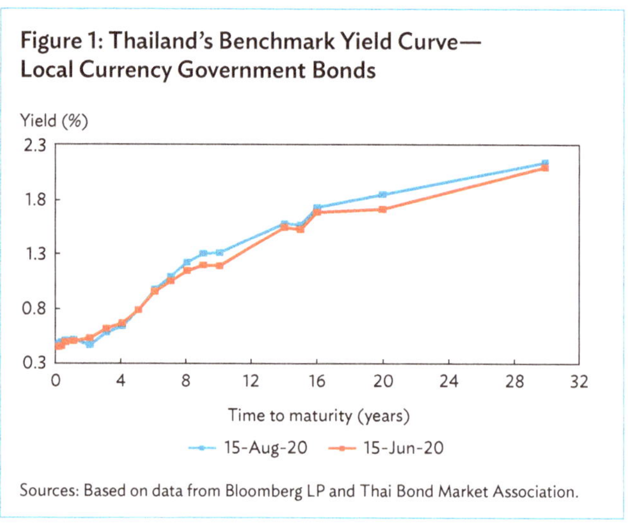

Sources: Based on data from Bloomberg LP and Thai Bond Market Association.

in the previous quarter. Due to stimulus spending, government expenditure expanded 1.4% y-o-y in Q2 2020, reversing the 2.8% y-o-y drop in Q1 2020.

In June, the Bank of Thailand (BOT) revised its full-year 2020 GDP growth forecast to –8.1% from an earlier projection of –5.3%, while raising the 2021 forecast to 5.0% from an earlier estimate of 3.0%. In August, the National Economic and Social Development Council lowered its GDP forecast to a full-year contraction of 7.3%–7.8% from an earlier estimate of a 5.0%–6.0% decline. Political risks emerged toward the end of the review period, as anti-government protests started to gain traction despite social distancing concerns. Moreover, a cabinet reshuffle after the resignation of key ministers posed a threat to the continuity of economic recovery policies.

Consumer price inflation was –0.5% y-o-y in August, remaining in negative territory for the sixth straight month. Low global energy prices and depressed demand due to COVID-19 were the key factors driving deflationary pressures. May posted the biggest drop in prices in nearly 11 years, with headline inflation at –3.4% y-o-y. Deflation has slowed since then, with readings of –1.6% y-o-y in June and –0.1% y-o-y in July, primarily due to a rise in the prices of fresh food products due to heavy rain, as well as high demand for pork due to a pig pandemic in neighboring markets. Nonetheless, headline inflation remained below the BOT's target range of 1.0%–3.0% for 2020.

Thailand's benchmark interest rate remained at a record low as the Monetary Policy Committee of the BOT decided to leave it unchanged at 0.5% in August. The BOT previously cut the policy rate by 25 bps from 0.75% in May. Since the beginning of the year, the BOT has reduced the benchmark rate by a total of 75 bps in response to COVID-19.

Among East Asian currencies, the Thai baht is among those that has depreciated the most against the United States (US) dollar thus far in 2020. Between 1 January and 15 August, the Thai baht depreciated 3.2% against the US dollar amid the negative impacts of COVID-19 on Thailand's export- and tourism-dependent economy. The BOT stressed in its latest policy statement that given the recent depreciation of the US dollar, it will closely monitor developments in the foreign exchange market as a rapid appreciation of the baht would be detrimental to economic recovery.

Size and Composition

Thailand's LCY bonds outstanding reached THB13,448.9 billion (USD435.1 billion) at the end of June on growth of 2.1% quarter-on-quarter (q-o-q) and 3.2% y-o-y (**Table 1**). The q-o-q rise in Q2 2020 reversed the 0.5% q-o-q contraction in Q1 2020, driven by strong growth in the government bond segment as the government issued debt to finance measures to combat the negative effects of COVID-19 on the economy. The annual growth of Thailand's LCY bond market weakened in Q2 2020 compared with the 4.1% y-o-y gain in Q1 2020. The Thai bond market is largely composed of government bonds, which accounted for 72.4% of the total bonds outstanding at the end June, up from 71.0% at the end of March.

Government bonds. The size of the LCY government bond market amounted to THB9,732.5 billion at the end of June, with the 4.1% q-o-q growth reversing the 1.0% q-o-q contraction in Q1 2020. Government bonds and Treasury bills, BOT bonds, and state-owned enterprise and other bonds all showed strong growth in Q2 2020 as the government issued debt to finance relief measures to alleviate the negative effects of COVID-19 on the economy. At the end of June, government bonds and Treasury bills rose 4.5% q-o-q, reaching THB5,306.4 billion, while BOT bonds amounted to THB3,633.4 on growth of 4.0% q-o-q in Q2 2020. State-owned enterprise and other bonds reached THB792.7 billion in Q2 2020, with the 1.4% q-o-q gain reversing the 1.4% q-o-q contraction in the previous quarter. On an annual basis, growth in Thailand's government bond market accelerated to 4.4% y-o-y in Q2 2020 from 2.7% y-o-y in Q1 2020.

Total issuance from the government amounted to THB2,184.7 billion in Q2 2020, as growth more than doubled to 7.5% q-o-q from 3.7% q-o-q in the previous quarter. The growth was solely driven by a sharp increase in the issuance of government bonds and Treasury bills, which rose 117.7% q-o-q in Q2 2020 as the government started issuing Treasury and debt restructuring bills. BOT bond issuance contracted 0.4% q-o-q as the central bank cut its issuance to accommodate the government's financing needs and respond to changes in investor

Table 1: Size and Composition of the Local Currency Bond Market in Thailand

| | Outstanding Amount (billion) | | | | | | Growth Rate (%) | | | |
| | Q2 2019 | | Q1 2020 | | Q2 2020 | | Q2 2019 | | Q2 2020 | |
	THB	USD	THB	USD	THB	USD	q-o-q	y-o-y	q-o-q	y-o-y
Total	13,037	425	13,169	402	13,449	435	3.1	9.4	2.1	3.2
Government	9,319	304	9,353	286	9,732	315	2.3	7.9	4.1	4.4
Government Bonds and Treasury Bills	4,754	155	5,079	155	5,306	172	(0.4)	4.9	4.5	11.6
Central Bank Bonds	3,772	123	3,492	107	3,633	118	5.4	15.4	4.0	(3.7)
State-Owned Enterprise and Other Bonds	794	26	782	24	793	26	4.7	(4.8)	1.4	(0.1)
Corporate	3,718	121	3,816	117	3,716	120	5.1	13.2	(2.6)	(0.03)

( ) = negative, q-o-q = quarter-on-quarter, Q1 = first quarter, Q2 = second quarter, THB = Thai baht, USD = United States dollar, y-o-y = year-on-year.
Notes:
1. Calculated using data from national sources.
2. Bloomberg LP end-of-period local currency–USD rates are used.
3. Growth rates are calculated from local currency base and do not include currency effects.
Source: Bank of Thailand.

sentiment amid the COVID-19 pandemic. Issuance of state-owned enterprise bonds contracted 38.5% q-o-q in Q2 2020. On a y-o-y basis, issuance of government bonds declined 5.8% y-o-y in Q2 2020 after falling 8.8% y-o-y in the previous quarter.

Corporate bonds. Outstanding corporate bonds totaled THB3,716.5 billion at the end of June, down from THB3,815.5 at the end of March. The 2.6% q-o-q contraction in Q2 2020 reversed the tepid 0.8% q-o-q growth in the previous quarter. The contraction of the corporate bond market stemmed from a continuing decline in corporate debt issuance, which fell to −23.7% q-o-q in Q2 2020 from −12.4% q-o-q in the previous quarter. Firms deferred issuance of corporate bonds as lockdown measures to contain the pandemic and ensuing economic recession dented investor confidence.

The LCY bonds outstanding of the top 30 corporate issuers amounted to THB2,142.4 billion at the end of June, accounting for 57.6% of the total corporate bond market (**Table 2**). Food and beverage firms dominated the list, with an outstanding bond stock of amounting to THB422.2 billion from five issuers. Firms in commerce and banking were the next largest issuers, with outstanding bond stocks totaling THB280.8 billion and THB260.4 billion, respectively. The majority of the top 30 issuers were listed on the Thai Stock Exchange, while only four were state-owned. Due to a large issuance during the quarter, Siam Cement overtook Thai Beverage to become the top issuer in the market at the end Q2 2020, with total outstanding bonds worth THB175.0 billion. Thai Beverage's total outstanding bonds amounted to THB173.3 billion in Q2 2020. CP ALL, Bank of Ayudhya, Berli Jucker, True Move H Universal Communication, and Charoen Pokphand Foods were the next largest issuers, each with total outstanding debt over THB100.0 billion at the end of June.

In Q2 2020, Charoen Pokphand Foods and Siam Cement were the largest issuers, with corporate debt issuance of THB25.0 billion each (**Table 3**). Charoen Pokphand Foods raised funds from six issuances of bonds with tenors ranging from 4 years to 15 years and carrying coupons ranging from 3.0% to 4.0%. Siam Cement issued a 4-year bond with a 2.8% coupon. Berli Jucker was the third-largest issuer during the quarter, with issuances amounting to THB18.0 billion from bonds with tenors ranging from 2 years to 10 years and carrying coupons

ranging from 2.1% to 3.5%. PTT Global was the next largest issuer, with multitranche issuances ranging from 7-year to 15-year bonds amounting to THB11.7 billion. Another notable issuance during the quarter was property developer Sansiri's THB3.0 billion perpetual bond with an 8.5% coupon. Proceeds from the bond sale will be used for new housing projects.

Investor Profile

Central government bonds. The profile of LCY government bonds investors was broadly stable between June 2019 and June 2020 (**Figure 2**). The combined shares of the four largest holders of government bonds in Thailand was little changed from 90.0% in June 2019 to 90.4% in June 2020. Financial corporations continued to hold the largest share of government bonds, with their share stable at 41.8% from June 2019 to June 2020. The central government's share rose from 14.1% to 17.3%, while BOT's share fell to 3.3% from 4.6% between June 2019 and June 2020. During the same period, nonresidents' share of government bonds dropped from 17.5% to 14.4% amid outflows driven by weak investor confidence as Thailand's economy suffered from the impact of COVID-19 on tourism and exports. The share of other depository corporations was little changed during the review period, inching up to 16.8% from 16.5%.

Central bank bonds. The combined shares of the top four holders of BOT bonds rose to 96.7% in June 2020 from 91.7% in June 2019 (**Figure 3**). Other depository corporations held the largest share of BOT bonds at 45.2%, up from 39.9% a year earlier. The share of financial corporations rose to 28.4% in June 2020 from 27.7% in the previous year. During the review period, BOT holdings rose to 13.2% from 10.8%, while central government holdings dropped to 10.0% from 13.3%. Nonresidents held a marginal amount of BOT bonds at the end of June 2020 at 1.2%, down from 3.5% a year earlier.

Foreign investors in Thailand's LCY bond market recorded net inflows of THB4.6 billion in Q2 2020, following net outflows of THB101.8 billion in Q1 2020 (**Figure 4**). The Thai bond market saw net foreign fund outflows amounting to THB140.3 billion from February to May amid the COVID-19 outbreak. Easing of lockdown and the government's stimulus measures provided a boost to investor confidence, resulting in net foreign inflows of THB31.8 billion in June and THB18.9 billion in July.

Table 2: Top 30 Issuers of Local Currency Corporate Bonds in Thailand

	Issuers	Outstanding Amount		State-Owned	Listed Company	Type of Industry
		LCY Bonds (THB billion)	LCY Bonds (USD billion)			
1.	Siam Cement	175.0	5.7	Yes	Yes	Construction Materials
2.	Thai Beverage	173.3	5.6	No	No	Food and Beverage
3.	CP ALL	158.9	5.1	No	Yes	Commerce
4.	Bank of Ayudhya	133.8	4.3	No	Yes	Banking
5.	Berli Jucker	121.9	3.9	No	Yes	Commerce
6.	True Move H Universal Communication	121.0	3.9	No	No	Communications
7.	Charoen Pokphand Foods	116.4	3.8	No	Yes	Food and Beverage
8.	True Corp	89.9	2.9	No	No	Communications
9.	PTT	84.7	2.7	Yes	Yes	Energy and Utilities
10.	Toyota Leasing Thailand	79.8	2.6	No	No	Finance and Securities
11.	Minor International	62.0	2.0	No	Yes	Hospitality and Leisure
12.	Indorama Ventures	61.4	2.0	No	Yes	Petrochemicals and Chemicals
13.	CPF Thailand	61.0	2.0	No	No	Food and Beverage
14.	PTT Global Chemical	51.7	1.7	No	Yes	Petrochemicals and Chemicals
15.	Banpu	48.9	1.6	No	Yes	Energy and Utilities
16.	Krungthai Card	47.2	1.5	Yes	Yes	Banking
17.	Bangkok Commercial Asset Management	44.2	1.4	No	Yes	Finance and Securities
18.	Krung Thai Bank	44.0	1.4	Yes	Yes	Banking
19.	Bangkok Expressway & Metro	41.2	1.3	No	Yes	Transportation and Logistics
20.	Global Power Synergy	40.0	1.3	No	Yes	Energy and Utilities
21.	Muangthai Capital	39.7	1.3	No	Yes	Finance and Securities
22.	TPI Polene	39.3	1.3	No	Yes	Property and Construction
23.	Bangchak Corp PCL	39.0	1.3	No	Yes	Energy and Utilities
24.	Mitr Phol Sugar	38.4	1.2	No	No	Food and Beverage
25.	Land & Houses	37.6	1.2	No	Yes	Property and Construction
26.	TMB Bank	35.4	1.1	No	Yes	Banking
27.	Sansiri	33.3	1.1	No	Yes	Property and Construction
28.	Thai Union Group	33.1	1.1	No	Yes	Food and Beverage
29.	dtac TriNet	33.0	1.1	No	Yes	Communications
30.	CH Karnchang	32.9	1.1	No	Yes	Property and Construction
	Total Top 30 LCY Corporate Issuers	**2,142.4**	**69.3**			
	Total LCY Corporate Bonds	**3,716.5**	**120.2**			
	Top 30 as % of Total LCY Corporate Bonds	**57.6%**	**57.6%**			

LCY = local currency, THB = Thai baht, USD = United States dollar.
Notes:
1. Data as of 30 June 2020.
2. State-owned firms are defined as those in which the government has more than a 50% ownership stake.
Source: *AsianBondsOnline* calculations based on Bloomberg LP data.

Table 3: Notable Local Currency Corporate Bond Issuance in the Second Quarter of 2020

Corporate Issuers	Coupon Rate (%)	Issued Amount (THB billion)
Charoen Pokphand Foods		
4-year bond	3.00	2.7
4-year bond	3.00	8.4
7-year bond	3.40	2.6
7-year bond	3.40	7.2
12-year bond	3.75	0.9
15-year bond	4.00	3.1
Siam Cement		
4-year bond	2.80	25.0
Berli Jucker		
2-year bond	2.10	1.7
4-year bond	3.00	12.3
10-year bond	3.50	4.0
PTT Global		
7-year bond	2.60	1.5
12-year bond	3.29	4.4
15-year bond	3.50	5.8
Sansiri		
Perpetual bond	8.50	3.0

THB = Thai baht.
Source: Bloomberg LP.

Policy, Institutional, and Regulatory Developments

Public Debt Management Office Launches THB1 Savings Bonds via Blockchain

On June 24, the Ministry of Finance issued THB200 million worth of savings bonds at an unprecedented face value of THB1 each through Krungthai Bank's blockchain-based e-wallet. Using the blockchain system, the Public Debt Management Office was able to lower the amount of the savings bond face value from the regular THB1,000. The small-ticket bonds were part of the government's plan to encourage low-income earners to invest in risk-free assets. The bonds were divided into 5-year and 10-year tenors, with the 5-year bond carrying a coupon of 2.4% and the 10-year bond carrying a coupon of 3.0%. The bonds were sold in under 2 minutes, prompting the Public Debt Management Office to issue a second batch worth THB5,000 million on 25 August.

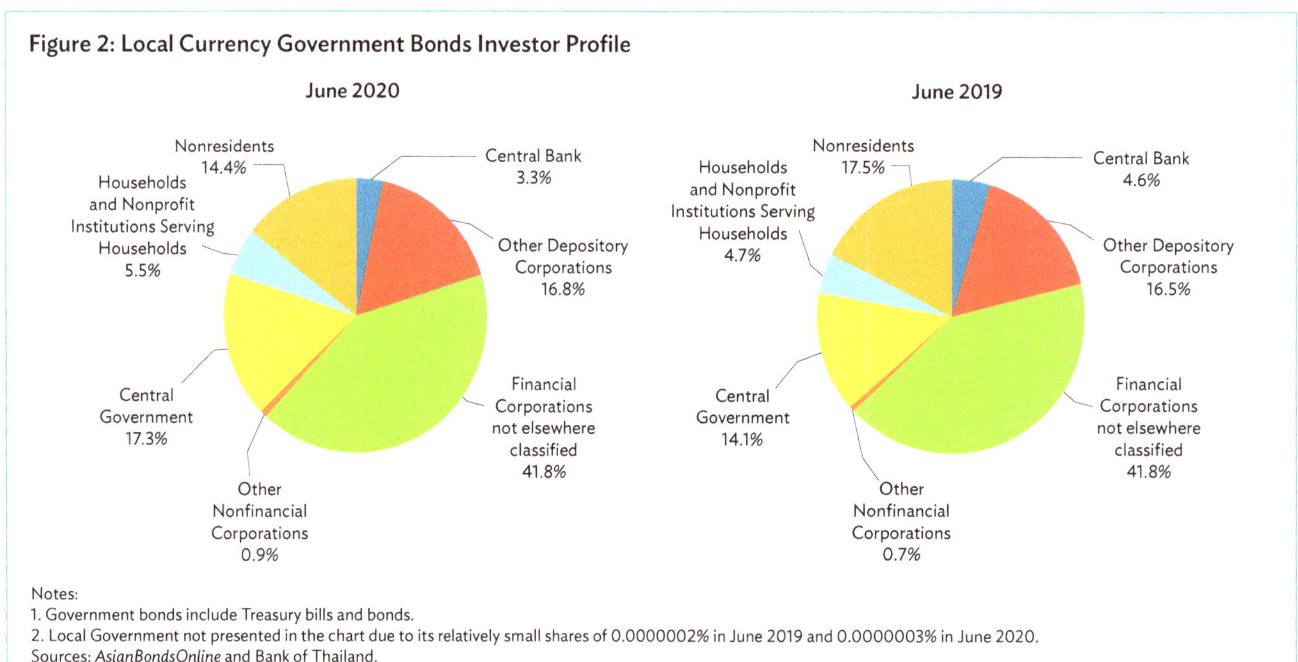

Figure 2: Local Currency Government Bonds Investor Profile

Notes:
1. Government bonds include Treasury bills and bonds.
2. Local Government not presented in the chart due to its relatively small shares of 0.0000002% in June 2019 and 0.0000003% in June 2020.
Sources: *AsianBondsOnline* and Bank of Thailand.

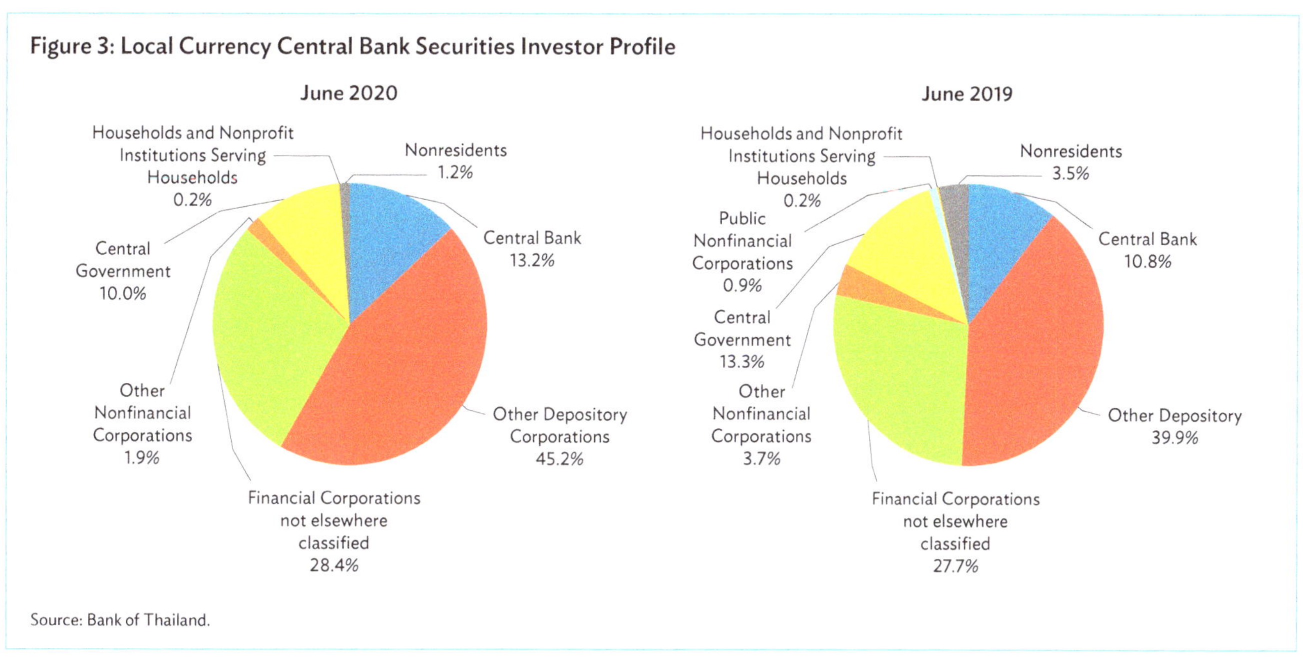

Figure 3: Local Currency Central Bank Securities Investor Profile

Source: Bank of Thailand.

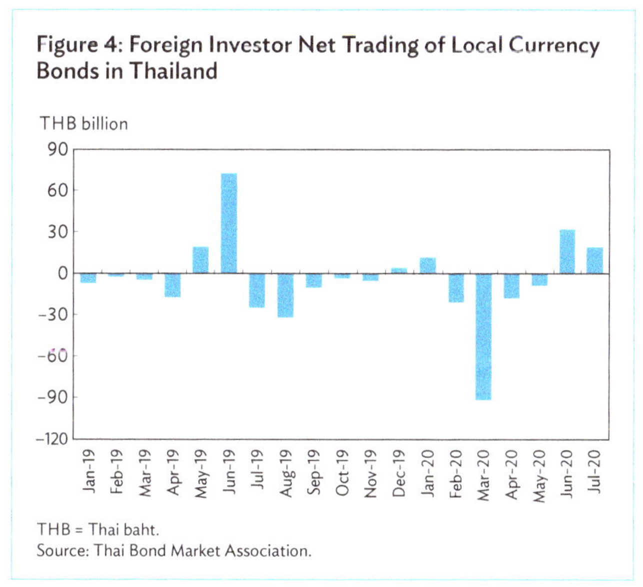

Figure 4: Foreign Investor Net Trading of Local Currency Bonds in Thailand

THB = Thai baht.
Source: Thai Bond Market Association.

Viet Nam

Yield Movements

The yields of local currency (LCY) government securities in Viet Nam fell across the board between 15 June and 15 August (**Figure 1**). Yields on bonds with maturities from 1 year to 7 years averaged declines of 37 basis points (bps), while the 3-year tenor dropped the most at 48 bps. Smaller declines were observed for bonds at the longer-end of the curve, particularly 10- and 15-year tenors, whose yields fell 14 bps and 13 bps, respectively. The yield spread between the 2-year and 10-year tenors widened from 207 bps to 237 bps during the review period.

Strong demand from investors for government securities amid abundant liquidity was the main driver of the fall in bond yields. Lower yields in short- to medium-term paper, relative to longer tenors, indicate that investors remain on the sidelines in search for market leads amid the uncertainty.

In the context of new cases of the coronavirus disease (COVID-19) reported in Viet Nam, the pandemic continues and the market remains weighed with risks. As risk aversion persists, safe-haven assets such as government securities are benefiting from strong demand, which is driving yields down.

The low-interest-rate environment, following a policy rate cut from the State Bank of Vietnam that reduced the refinancing rate to 4.5% from 5.0% on 13 May, is affecting the yield movements.

Inflationary pressures are also weak. Price increases for consumer goods in Viet Nam subsided to 0.07% month-on-month (m-o-m) in August from 0.4% m-o-m in July, marking the second month of consecutive slowdown. All commodity groups showed slight price increases except for garments; postal services and telecommunication; and culture, entertainment, and tourism where prices fell. On a year-on-year (y-o-y) basis, prices increased 3.2% in August. The inflation rate in the first 8 months of 2020 increased to 4.0% y-o-y.

The Vietnamese economy managed to grow in the second quarter (Q2) of 2020 despite the gloomy global economic forecast. Viet Nam's gross domestic product

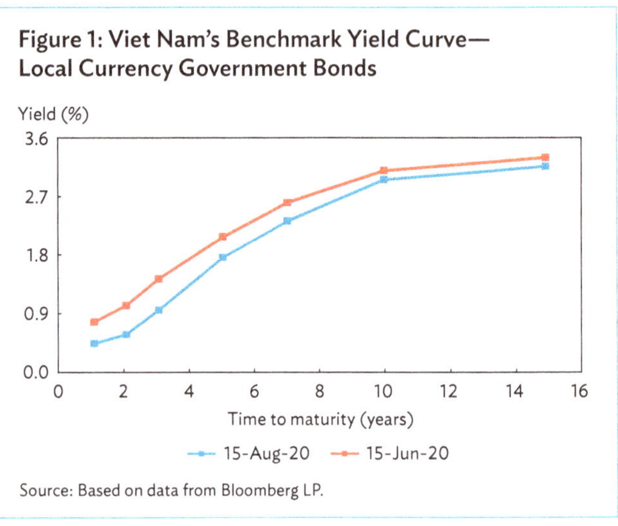

Figure 1: Viet Nam's Benchmark Yield Curve—Local Currency Government Bonds

Source: Based on data from Bloomberg LP.

posted growth of 0.4% y-o-y during the quarter, the slowest expansion in over 30 years, following growth of 3.8% y-o-y in the first quarter (Q1). The economy was hard hit in Q2 2020 by the measures put in place to contain the spread of COVID-19. The services sector dragged down Q2 2020 growth with its 1.8% q-o-q decline, while the agriculture, forestry, and fishing sector; and the industry and construction sector both expanded.

The Vietnamese dong traded at VND23,176 per USD1 on 15 August, appreciating by about 2.0% from its weakest value against the United States dollar in 2020 thus far of VND23,637 at the end of March. The strength of the dong owed to the favorable macroeconomic conditions and rising foreign exchange reserves.

Size and Composition

Viet Nam's total LCY bonds outstanding declined 1.7% q-o-q to VND1,349 trillion (USD58.2 billion) at the end of Q2 2020, reversing the previous quarter's expansion (**Table 1**). On an annual basis, the bond market expanded 9.4% y-o-y in Q2 2020, although this was slower compared to Q1 2020. The quarterly contraction in market size was due to lower outstanding debt in the government sector even as the corporate bond stock increased. Government bonds accounted for a larger share of Viet Nam's bond market at 86.2% versus corporate bonds with a 13.8% share.

Table 1: Size and Composition of the Local Currency Bond Market in Viet Nam

| | Outstanding Amount (billion) | | | | | | Growth Rate (%) | | | |
| | Q2 2019 | | Q1 2020 | | Q2 2020 | | Q2 2019 | | Q2 2020 | |
	VND	USD	VND	USD	VND	USD	q-o-q	y-o-y	q-o-q	y-o-y
Total	1,233,519	53	1,373,100	58	1,349,263	58	2.6	4.1	(1.7)	9.4
Government	1,127,565	48	1,260,477	53	1,162,754	50	3.2	2.9	(7.8)	3.1
Treasury Bonds	932,040	40	970,436	41	1,019,096	44	1.4	8.7	5.0	9.3
Central Bank Bills	32,999	1	136,986	6	0	0	573.5	(43.5)	–	–
Government-Guaranteed and Municipal Bonds	162,526	7	153,055	6	143,658	6	(3.4)	(9.8)	(6.1)	(11.6)
Corporate	105,954	5	112,623	5	186,509	8	(3.4)	18.7	65.6	76.0

– = not applicable, ( ) = negative, q-o-q = quarter-on-quarter, Q1 = first quarter, Q2 = second quarter, USD = United States dollar, VND = Vietnamese dong, y-o-y = year-on-year.
Notes:
1. Bloomberg LP end-of-period local currency–USD rates are used.
2. Growth rates are calculated from local currency base and do not include currency effects.
Sources: Bloomberg LP and Vietnam Bond Market Association.

Government bonds. Total LCY government outstanding bonds in Viet Nam decreased 7.8% q-o-q to VND1,163 trillion at the end of June. The absence of outstanding central bank bills was one of the main drivers of the decline. Outstanding central bank bills matured in Q2 2020 from VND137 trillion in the previous quarter, while there was no new issuance from the State Bank of Vietnam to support liquidity in the market.

Fewer outstanding government-guaranteed and municipal bonds at the end of Q2 2020 also drove the decline. Together, they amounted to VND144 trillion, dipping 6.1% q-o-q.

Among all types of government securities, only Treasury bonds registered positive growth in Q2 2020. Treasury bonds outstanding increased 5.0% q-o-q to VND1,019 trillion at the end of June after marginally declining in Q1 2020. While Treasury bonds generally comprise the largest share of Viet Nam's bond market, this increase did not offset the declines in other bond segments.

On an annual basis, total government debt outstanding grew 3.1% y-o-y.

The increase in Treasury bonds outstanding came on the back of a higher volume of bond offerings and issuance by the State Treasury of Viet Nam during Q2 2020 compared to the previous quarter. The Treasury issued VND54.1 trillion during the quarter, which was 61.5% q-o-q higher than the issuance in Q1 2020. The low-interest-rate environment has also been conducive for the State Treasury to accelerate fund mobilization to support the government's fiscal stimulus measures against the adverse economic impact of the COVID-19 pandemic. Despite low yields, Treasury bonds' attractiveness to investors reflects portfolio diversification to include safe-haven assets amid the pandemic and also indicates confidence in Viet Nam's economic prospects.

Corporate bonds. Corporate bonds posted growth of 65.6% q-o-q and 76.0% y-o-y in Q2 2020, bringing the total outstanding amount to VND187 trillion at the end of June. The significant increase was due to more data sources on Viet Nam's corporate bond market being used by *AsianBondsOnline*.[8] At the same time, corporates were active in mobilizing funds through bond issuance during the quarter as they reopened operations after pandemic restrictions were lifted. Also, an upcoming regulation that will raise the standards in the corporate bond market and result to stricter issuance guidelines made issuers rush to the bond market before it becomes effective on 1 September.

The aggregate bonds outstanding of the top 30 LCY corporate issuers amounted to VND147.1 trillion, or 78.9% of the total corporate bond market, at the end of June (**Table 2**). The top 30 corporate issuers were largely from the banking industry with cumulative outstanding bonds equal to VND62.7 trillion or nearly half of the top 30's outstanding debt. Firms from the property sector were

---

[8] *AsianBondsOnline* now includes corporate bond data from Vietnam Bond Market Association in addition to Bloomberg data.

Table 2: Top 30 Issuers of Local Currency Corporate Bonds in Viet Nam

	Issuers	Outstanding Amount		State-Owned	Listed Company	Type of Industry
		LCY Bonds (VND billion)	LCY Bonds (USD billion)			
1.	Vinhomes	21,390	0.92	No	Yes	Property
2.	Bank for Investment and Development of Vietnam	16,691	0.72	Yes	Yes	Banking
3.	Masan Group	9,500	0.41	No	Yes	Finance
4.	Asia Commercial Joint Stock Bank	8,300	0.36	No	Yes	Banking
5.	Vietnam Joint Stock Commercial Bank for Industry and Trade	8,250	0.36	Yes	Yes	Banking
6.	Ho Chi Minh City Development Commercial Joint Stock Bank	7,855	0.34	No	Yes	Banking
7.	Vinpearl	7,500	0.32	No	No	Hotel Operator
8.	Vingroup	7,000	0.30	No	Yes	Property
9.	Vietnam International Commercial Joint Stock Bank	4,203	0.18	No	Yes	Banking
10.	Sovico Group	4,050	0.17	No	Yes	Diversified Operations
11.	Vietnam Prosperity Joint-Stock Commercial Bank	3,900	0.17	No	Yes	Banking
12.	Sun Ha Long Co., Ltd.	3,500	0.15	No	No	Property
13.	Bac A Commercial Joint Stock Bank	3,240	0.14	No	Yes	Banking
14.	Lien Viet Post Joint Stock Commercial Bank	3,100	0.13	No	Yes	Banking
15.	Hoang Anh Gia Lai	3,000	0.13	No	Yes	Property
16.	Vietnam Technological and Commercial Joint Stock Bank	3,000	0.13	No	Yes	Banking
17.	TNL Investment and Leasing Joint Stock Company	2,926	0.13	No	No	Property
18.	Nui Phao Mining and Processing Co., Ltd.	2,920	0.13	No	No	Mining
19.	Binh Hai Golf Investment and Development Joint Stock Company	2,745	0.12	No	No	Leisure
20.	Ho Chi Minh City Infrastructure Investment	2,470	0.11	No	Yes	Infrastructure
21.	Hoan My Medical	2,330	0.10	No	No	Healthcare Services
22	Refrigeration Electrical	2,318	0.10	No	Yes	Manufacturing
23.	Vincommerce General Trading Service Joint Stock Company	2,300	0.10	No	No	Retail
24.	Ho Chi Minh City Infrastructure Investment Joint Stock Company	2,220	0.10	No	Yes	Construction
25.	Tien Phong Commercial Joint Stock Bank	2,167	0.09	No	Yes	Banking
26.	Hong Phong 1 Energy	2,150	0.09	No	No	Utility
27.	Masan Consumer Holdings	2,100	0.09	No	No	Diversified Operations
28.	Agro Nutrition International	2,000	0.09	No	No	Agriculture
29.	Joint Stock Commercial Bank for Foreign Trade of Vietnam	2,000	0.09	Yes	Yes	Banking
30.	Saigon Glory Company Limited	2,000	0.09	No	No	Property
	Total Top 30 LCY Corporate Issuers	**147,124**	**6.34**			
	Total LCY Corporate Bonds	**186,509**	**8.04**			
	Top 30 as % of Total LCY Corporate Bonds	**78.9%**	**78.9%**			

LCY = local currency, USD = United States dollar, VND = Vietnamese dong.
Notes:
1. Data as of 30 June 2020.
2. State-owned firms are defined as those in which the government has more than a 50% ownership stake.
Sources: *AsianBondsOnline* calculations based on Bloomberg LP and Vietnam Bond Market Association data.

next with VND39.8 trillion. Vinhomes held on to the top spot with VND21.4 trillion outstanding bonds in Q2 2020, almost double the amount at the end of Q1 2020.

Issuance from the corporate sector in Q2 2020 amounted to VND82.5 trillion, led by the banking sector with VND35.9 trillionin total issuances during the quarter from 65 banks. Property firms came next with VND27.9 trillion from 103 issuers. The combined issuances from the banking and property sectors comprised 77.4% of total corporate bond issuance in Q2 2020. **Table 3** lists selected bond issuances during the quarter. Vinhomes had the single-largest issuance (VND3,095 billion) followed by the Masan Group (VND3,000 billion).

Investor Profile

Pension funds and banks were the major holders of LCY government bonds at the end of June, with combined holdings of almost 90% of the total government bond stock (**Figure 2**). Pension funds holdings rose to a 45.0% share, up from 43.0% in June 2019. This increase outpaced banks whose share of government bond holdings, fell to 43.3% from 45.4% during the review period. The rankings of the remaining investor groups held steady and their shares were practically unchanged between June 2019 and June 2020. Foreign investors held only 0.6% of government securities at the end of June 2020, which is the smallest foreign holdings share among

Table 3: Notable Local Currency Corporate Bond Issuance in the Second Quarter of 2020

Corporate Issuers	Coupon Rate (%)	Issued Amount (VND billion)	Corporate Issuers	Coupon Rate (%)	Issued Amount (VND billion)
Vinhomes			Ho Chi Minh City Development Commercial Joint Stock Bank		
3-year bond	Floating	3,095	3-year bond	3.00	2,000
3-year bond	Floating	2,185	3-year bond	3.00	1,000
1.5-year bond	Floating	3,040	3-year bond	3.00	1,000
Masan Group			3-year bond	2.00	1,000
3-year bond	Floating	3,000	3-year bond	3.00	1,000
Bank for Investment and Development of Vietnam			Bac A Commercial Joint Stock Bank		
7-year bond	Floating	1,000	2-year bond	6.30	1,000
7-year bond	Floating	1,000	2-year bond	6.30	1,000
7-year bond	Floating	1,000	Sovico Group		
6-year bond	Floating	2,300	3-year bond	Floating	1,000
6-year bond	Floating	1,000			

VND = Vietnamese dong.
Source: Bloomberg LP.

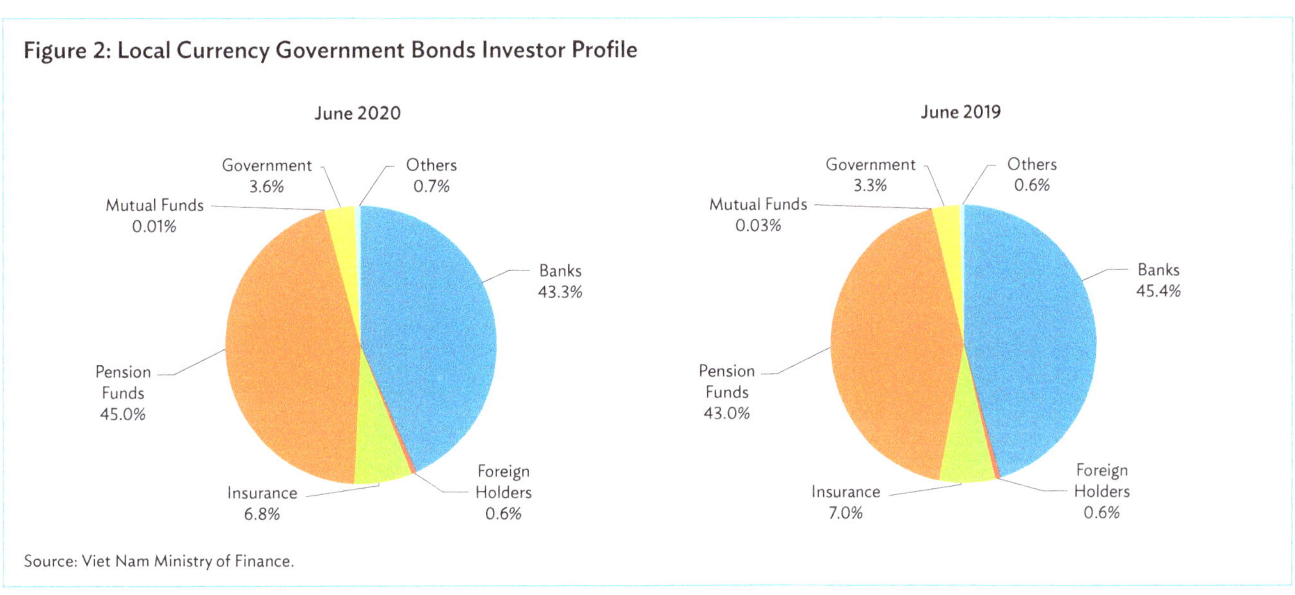

Figure 2: Local Currency Government Bonds Investor Profile

Source: Viet Nam Ministry of Finance.

all emerging East Asian economies. Mutual funds have the smallest holdings share in Viet Nam's LCY government bond market at 0.01%.

Policy, Institutional, and Regulatory Developments

Ministry of Finance Amends Decree to Tighten the Trading of Privately Placed Corporate Bonds

In July, Viet Nam's Ministry of Finance amended several points under Decree No. 163/2018/ND-CP to tighten the trading of privately placed corporate bonds in the domestic market. In the new version, depository organizations must provide information about corporate bond trading within 1 working day of the trade being completed. Regular updates about bond registration and depository must be provided to the stock exchange monthly, quarterly, and yearly. The amended decree will take effect on 1 September 2020.[9]

Viet Nam Government Issues New Decree to Raise the Standards in the Corporate Bond Market

In July, the Government of Viet Nam issued Government Decree No. 81 to raise standards in the corporate bond market and ensure information transparency. In particular, the decree will limit private issuance to minimize risks for individual investors and will impose more responsibility on underwriters when evaluating the financial capacity of issuers. The decree also states that the total bond issuance of a company cannot exceed its equity capital by five times and that the gap between two bond issuances must be at least 6 months. The issuer must also declare the purpose of the funds and provide a business plan for proper monitoring by investors. The new decree takes effect on 1 September.[10]

---

[9] Ministry of Finance, Government of Viet Nam. *New Regulations about Corporate Bond Issuance.* https://www.mof.gov.vn/webcenter/portal/vclvcstcen/r/m/page190214/ft_chitiet66?dDocName=MOFUCM179280&_afrLoop=105313418565750659#!%40%40%3F_afrLoop%3D105313418565750659%26dDocName%3DMOFUCM179280%26_adf.ctrl-state%3D1bxz51o5rj_282.

[10] Viet Nam News. *Decree Takes Effect in September to Raise Standards for Corporate Bond Market.* https://vietnamnews.vn/economy/770204/decree-takes-effect-in-september-to-raise-standards-for-corporate-bond-market.html.